THE SOMETIME CONNECTION

SUNY series,
Urban Public Policy

James Bohland and Patricia Edwards, Editors

and

SUNY series,
Public Policy

Anne Schneider and Joseph Stewart, Jr., Editors

THE SOMETIME CONNECTION

Public Opinion and Social Policy

Elaine B. Sharp

STATE UNIVERSITY OF NEW YORK PRESS

Published by
State University of New York Press, Albany

© 1999 State University of New York

For information, address State University of New York Press,
State University Plaza, Albany, N.Y. 12246

Production by Diane Ganeles
Marketing by Patrick Durocher

Library of Congress Cataloging-in-Publication Data

Sharp, Elaine B.
    The sometime connection : public opinion and social policy /
Elaine B. Sharp.
        p.   cm. — (SUNY series in urban public policy) (SUNY series
in public policy)
    Includes bibliographical references.
    ISBN 0-7914-4295-0 (alk. paper). — ISBN 0-7914-4296-9 (pbk. :
alk. paper)
    1. United States—Social policy—Public opinion. 2. Public
opinion—United States. I. Title. II. Series. III. Series: SUNY
series on urban public policy.
HN57.S49   1999
361.6'1'0973—dc21   98-53599
                                                              CIP

10 9 8 7 6 5 4 3 2 1

CONTENTS

LIST OF TABLES AND FIGURES

viii • LIST OF TABLES AND FIGURES

1

Public Policy and Public Opinion

The Elusive Connection

Introduction

Consider the following snapshots of ordinary scenes in an ordinary community in the United States on an ordinary day in the 1990s: A group of retired persons are enjoying each others' company at the corner coffee shop. All are on Social Security, and several have already made extensive use of Medicare for various hospitalizations or doctors' services. Prominent among the various topics of their conversation is the matter of a local youth who has just been arrested for a serious assault that occurred while the youth was out of prison on probation for a series of drug offenses and robberies. Not surprisingly, the conversation becomes heated as several of the coffee-drinkers rail against the failings of the criminal justice system in the country. The others listen sympathetically. They know that much of the emotional fervor comes from deep-seated fears about being a victim of crime—fears that they have sometimes felt themselves. Meanwhile, the waitress who brings their coffee is in a bit of a rush to finish her shift. Friends are caring for her child while she works the required number of hours so as to not immediately lose her welfare benefits, and the last time she was late picking up the child, there had been an argument with her friends that caused her to fear that their patience with the arrangement was wearing thin. With no family members in the area and no institutional child care that would be affordable, she isn't sure

1

what she would do if her friends refused to help. In the restaurant's kitchen, meanwhile, a newly hired assistant manager, who is an African-American, gingerly tries to negotiate a conversation with the head cook, who seems a bit belligerent. The assistant manager wonders vaguely whether the cook is yet another of the seemingly endless string of people who resentfully assume that affirmative action secured him a job that otherwise would have gone to a white person.

These hypothetical scenes illustrate how social policy touches the lives of ordinary people every day. From this perspective, governmental programs and functions ranging from Social Security to affirmative action to welfare to criminal adjudication have substantial impacts on the public. The same could be said of the regulation of abortion, sexual harassment, and pornography, school choice policies, governmental subsidies for and regulation of child care, and the numerous other items that are part of the nation's large stock of social policies. More importantly, those impacts are far from abstract. Typically, they are immediate, tangible, and intimately bound up with the fabric of people's lives. People often have very direct and personal experiences with these governmental policies; or, if they do not, they know someone who has or they have heard about someone who has.

In short, social policy has distinctly immediate and personal impacts on ordinary citizens, and they have a variety of means of coming to know in a very direct albeit anecdotal way about governmental action in this realm. For this reason, one might expect that any depiction of the American public as ill-informed and apathetic about public affairs might have to be adjusted when social policy topics are at stake. And one might even expect that changes in social policy would be driven, in substantial part if not wholly, by what the public knows about how existing programs are working and by what the public wants with respect to the problems that the programs are meant to address.

Or should we expect such a connection between what the public wants and what direction social policy takes? There are, after all, a variety of interpretations of policymaking that feature dominant roles for interest groups and governing elites and that offer very little room for the views of ordinary citizens to be significant drivers of policy change.

This book takes up the question of what role public opinion plays in social policy change. Because so many social policies have direct personal impacts and have implications for citizens' fundamental values, if we cannot find a close connection between public opinion and policy development in this realm, there is little reason to be sanguine about public knowledge and governmental responsiveness in other areas of public affairs.

To investigate the role of public opinion in social policy change, later chapters of this book will offer policy histories on social policy topics including affirmative action, abortion, welfare, incarceration, Social Security, and pornography; each policy history will be sized up against the existing evidence on trends in public opinion on those topics. But before turning to that evidence, we need to be more clear about the theoretical framework guiding the analysis.

This chapter introduces a variety of different interpretations, or models, of the nature of the relationship between public opinion and public policy. Moving from what some might view as the most cynical or least sanguine (from the viewpoint of classical democratic theory) to what others might view as the most optimistic, the chapter explores the following possibilities: (1) a "non-attitudes" interpretation suggesting that public opinion is irrelevant to public policy because public opinion, at least as evidenced in poll data, is not real or meaningful (i.e., there is nothing for policy to be responsive to); (2) a "manipulated opinion" interpretation suggesting that, to the extent that policy is consistent with opinion, it is because public opinion has been manipulated to bring it into line with policy, rather than the other way around; (3) a non-responsiveness interpretation suggesting that public policy can and often is at odds with genuine preferences of the mass public; and (4) a "responsiveness" interpretation suggesting that public policymaking is influenced by and consistent with the public's preferences.

But which of these models of the opinion-policy connection is most valid? The final section of this chapter argues that attempting to crown one of these as the definitive model is an inappropriate exercise, for two reasons. First, the utility of each interpretive model is likely to depend on key contingencies, such as the institutional venue that dominates policy decisionmaking or the structure of public opinion on the subject. Acknowledgment of a contingent perspective on these models thus points us toward the need for comparative analysis of the evidence for these interpretive models across different types of policy issues. Second, even if one focuses on a single public policy topic (e.g., welfare, affirmative action, or abortion), there may not be one model that best depicts the opinion-policy connection across all of our contemporary history. There are periods of continuity and periods of change in both public opinion and public policy over time. Tracking these continuities and changes over a relatively long period of time may very well reveal periods in which there is policy responsiveness to public opinion and periods in which there is not, periods in which the mass public reveals non-attitudes about a topic and periods in which political elites manufacture consent through the manipulation of public opinion. Furthermore, these periods may occur in interestingly different sequences for different policies. This chapter concludes with a preliminary look at several possible sequences and the implications of each.

Models of the Opinion-Policy Connection

Non-Attitudes and the Irrelevance of the Opinion-Policy Connection

While developed in response to a somewhat different set of research questions having to do with the rationality of public opinion and the capacity of the mass public to function as effective citizens, research on non-attitudes suggests that there is no such thing as meaningful public opinion. If valid, such an assessment has at least two possible implications. One is that the general public's reactions and ideas are easily manipulated by political elites—an implication that is discussed at greater length with respect to the "manipulated opinion" model (see below). A non-attitudes perspective might also be used as a foundation for arguing that public policy can be and often is inconsistent with and unresponsive to public opinion. If there is no real public opinion and if, as some of the literature suggests, popular responses to candidates and issues are instead based on gut-level, emotional reactions rather than cognitively-based reactions, then there is little need for public officials to try to create policy that is in line with public preferences. Such preferences, as registered in opinion polls, would be viewed as evanescent and an improper basis for policymaking and officials motivated by the desire for problem solving and effective governance would have no incentive to try to be consistent with it. Lemert (1992: 45), for example, suggests that policymakers don't necessarily pay attention to mass opinion as registered in polls because they are aware of the limited meaningfulness of it; and he cites studies showing that state and local policymakers "do not rely on poll-based data in forming conclusions about public opinion." For officials whose primary motivation is re-election, citizens' ignorance of public affairs and lack of firmly grounded preferences concerning policy issues provide a golden opportunity to respond to narrow, special interests or their own personal preferences, while cultivating the general public with non-substantive appeals. Non-attitudes can thus be important in interpretations of the non-responsiveness of policy to public opinion (as outlined below).

But if public opinion, at least as assessed in opinion polls, is truly meaningless, perhaps the most distinctive implication is that public opinion is by definition irrelevant to public policy. From this perspective, it is not just that public officials might choose to ignore opinion polls or manipulate citizen reactions. Both of those imply that there is at least some point in examining the consistency between opinion poll data and the state of public policy. But the most radical version of a non-attitudes model implies that there is no purpose in investigating whether poll data and public policy are consistent or inconsistent, because whatever the observed connection, it is a bogus one.

This section introduces a range of perspectives and research findings that have a bearing on the question of the reality of public opinion as measured in opinion polls. As the forgoing paragraphs suggest, some of this literature will have relevance for other models of the opinion-policy connection, most particularly the "non-responsiveness" model and the "manipulated opinion" model. This section, however, is primarily devoted to the matter of the potential "irrelevance" of opinion for policymaking.

At the most general level, the concept of non-attitudes means that public opinion, as registered in opinion polls, is not "real." Attitudes are typically defined as "relatively durable orientations toward an object" and opinions, as registered in poll responses, are ostensibly the "visible manifestation of attitudes" (Delli Carpini and Keeter, 1996: 228). "Genuine" or "real" attitudes (and the opinions through which they are manifested) are relatively durable because they are composed of a combination of cognitive elements (knowledge) and affective elements (values). One cannot have a genuine attitude toward the Earned Income Tax Credit (EITC) if one has no knowledge about what the EITC is; and if an individual knows what the EITC is, but holds no values relevant for evaluating it and therefore has no affective reaction to it, then no genuine attitude is possible (Delli Carpini and Keeter, 1996: 228–9). But the lack of a genuine attitude on a subject does not necessarily deter individuals from answering questions that are posed to them on opinion polls. Because they are unwilling to admit that they do not know anything about a topic, or that they don't care about a topic, or because they wish to be cooperative so that the interviewer will quickly finish, or for any number of reasons, respondents to opinion polls can and do offer "doorstep" opinions—i.e., meaningless responses that are disconnected from relevant facts and values. These are "non-attitudes."

At least three kinds of evidence lend weight to the argument that public opinion (under at least some circumstances) is fraught with non-attitudes: the observed instability in attitudes over time, the lack of ideological structuring or other coherent opinion patterning, and the evidence that opinion, as measured by opinion polls, can be moved or manipulated. To this might be added a line of work on the general public's lack of knowledge about and interest in public affairs.

In his seminal work on the subject, Converse (1964; 1970) reported the results of a panel study suggesting a very large proportion of apparently random changes in responses to poll items from one administration to the next, a pattern that led him to suggest that the majority of the opinions registered in opinion polls are really non-attitudes.

Still other research shows that, for much of the mass public, there is no coherent structure underlying preferences given in opinion polls. At the most general level, coherent structuring implies some sort of consistency in an individual's attitudes—i.e., that we should be able to predict their position on one issue if we know their position on another. In practice, this has translated into an investigation of the extent to which individuals' responses to various items on opinion polls are ideologically consistent.

Converse's (1964) standard-setting work in this regard shows low levels of consistency in the mass public's attitudes relative to the levels of consistency exhibited by elites. As Nie, Verba, and Petrocik (1976: 26–27) note, it is reasonably possible for an individual to have a liberal point of view on one issue and a conservative point of view on another. However, the rather extensive ideological mismatches that Converse found in Americans' issue opinions are, they argue, likely to suggest that the American public is relatively unguided by an "overarching" political ideology, that politics is so unimportant to the general public that they don't recognize the inconsistencies in their own views, and that the answers they give in opinion polls "represent superficial responses on matters to which they have given little previous thought." In their update of Converse's work, Nie, Verba, and Petrocik report increasing levels of ideological consistency in the mass public's issue preferences over time. Their index of attitude consistency (on domestic issues) increases from .24 in 1956 to a high of .51 in 1968 and 1971, an increase that they attribute in part to the increasingly ideological polarization of political rhetoric. By the same token, a gamma coefficient of .51 suggests that the average level of ideological agreement in the mass public's responses is by no means enormous. Most recently, Delli Carpini and Keeter (1996: 237) used 1988 National Election Studies (NES) data to investigate whether the general public's views on questions about the role of government in the socioeconomic sphere were organized along a single liberal-conservative dimension. Even when the study is limited in this way to questions that are most amenable to a traditional left-right structuring of political thinking, the results show very limited levels of coherent organization of the mass public's attitudes, except among the most politically knowledgeable 25% of the public.

Finally, there is evidence that "people's preferences can be moved around" (Kuklinski and Hurley, 1996: 126)—i.e., that mass opinion is noticeably affected by how issues are presented by political elites and by who takes what position on issues. This line of work on "cue giving" and related phenomena will be considered at greater length later in this chapter where it is most relevant—i.e., in the discussion of the "manipulated opinion" model. Here, however, it is important to acknowledge that this phenomenon can be used as evidence for non-attitudes. If a child indicates that he wants chocolate ice cream, but then changes to vanilla when he hears that the sister with whom he always quarrels also wants chocolate, and changes once again when he hears that his older brother is opting for chocolate, the parent might be tempted to conclude that the child has no genuine preferences of his own. Similarly, if individuals' expressed reactions to public issues shift around depending on who an issue position is attributed to, questions can be raised about whether those popular reactions have much real meaning.

A variety of scholars have offered arguments and evidence that might at least partially redeem survey-registered mass opinion from the ignominy of the non-attitudes label. One line of argument suggests that observed instability in the public's preferences on poll items reflects measurement problems that are endemic to survey research, rather than non-attitudes on the part of respondents. Achen (1975), for example, suggested that the instability in survey responses is at least in part due to ambiguity in the questions used to measure attitudes.

More recently, Zaller and Feldman (1992) have argued that response instability in surveys arises because the issues that pollsters ask about are often difficult, multifaceted ones that should be expected to generate ambiguous reactions. Complex and contentious issues can evoke a variety of different considerations, some of which might point an individual toward one conclusion, others of which might point an individual to another conclusion. Hence, we might expect that an individual's response to a survey question would change depending on which considerations are paramount in their mind at the time. The resulting inconsistencies in how individuals answer poll questions mean that they do not have "true attitudes" only if one takes true attitudes to mean fully crystallized and unambiguous reactions to complex political phenomena. But this is probably not an appropriate standard. As Zaller and Feldman (1992: 612) conclude: ". . . even when people exhibit high levels of response instability, the opinions they express may still be based on real considerations. Even when these considerations turn out to be transitory, the opinion statements they generate are not, for that reason, necessarily lacking in authenticity."

Acknowledging that public opinion can be "moved around," Kuklinski and Hurley (1996) nevertheless argue that this does not necessarily stand as evidence for non-attitudes. They refer to research by Sniderman, Tetlock, and Tyler (1993) which suggests that, if individuals *have* real attitudes, *they should be expected to change* their expressed opinions if circumstances or context change. If I initially opposed the idea of time limits on welfare benefits, but then grew to favor the idea when I learned how much they were supported by one or more politicians whose judgment I trust and whose viewpoint I usually see as similar to my own, my changing preferences do not, from this perspective, signify that my preferences are meaningless or that non-attitudes are at work. They signify, instead, that I have some rather strongly held attitudes about political leaders that help to shape my conclusions about particular issues.

And in their examination of aggregate changes in public opinion on social issues over time, Page and Shapiro (1992) note meaningful, trend-like changes, keyed to historical developments, rather than arbitrary fluctuations back and forth. They argue that collective opinion change is responsive, in an understandable way, to events and trends, such as crises, changes in income and education, and the like (1992: 321) Acknowledging that various experts and political elites surely have an influence upon mass opinion, they argue nevertheless that the selective nature of that influence suggests a rational public rather than the easy remolding of mass non-attitudes. After all, ". . . the public tends to be uninfluenced—or negatively influenced—by the statements of certain groups, namely, those whose interests are perceived to be selfish or narrow or antisocial, while it responds more favorably to groups and individuals thought to be concerned with broadly defined public interests" (Page and Shapiro, 1992: 350).

But if these various lines of argument serve to mitigate against the view that public opinion is no more than a muddle of non-attitudes, research on the public's relatively low level of information about politics keeps doubt alive about the meaningfulness of public opinion. Using a variety of measures of political knowledge, Smith (1989) concludes that the disappointing levels of political sophistication that classic voting studies found for the American public of the 1950s did not improve over the subsequent two decades, despite increases in education. Using Roper Center survey archives dating back to the 1930s and relevant items from the NES and their own survey of political knowledge, Delli Carpini and Keeter (1996) investigated the extent of the public's knowledge as evidenced by responses to over 3,700 survey items that ask factual information questions. Their results leave us with the classic dilemma of whether the glass should be depicted as half empty or half full, for indeed, majorities of the public were capable of correctly answering many of the questions. However, on balance, the results suggest substantial knowledge deficiencies. Only about two-fifths of the items generated correct responses from the majority of the public; and the items about which the public is ignorant are far from trivial. They include "important policy positions of presidential candidates or the political parties; basic social indicators and significant public policies" (Delli Carpini and Keeter, 1996: 102).

The public's relatively low level of political knowledge has many important implications. But for the purpose at hand, the key implication is the additional doubt that it sheds upon the meaningfulness of reactions given in public opinion polls. If, as a 1985 survey question revealed, only 31% of respondents knew what affirmative action was, it is more difficult to give credence to the general public's reactions when they are asked whether they favor or oppose affirmative action; and if, as a 1987 poll item reveals, only 16% of the public knew the effect of the tax law on capital gains, surely the vast majority of responses to poll questions asking people's preferences with regard to capital gains tax cuts are of suspect validity.

It might be argued that the public "knows" a great deal about affirmative action and other public affairs issues even if they can't offer the correct response when asked precise questions about such issues. Perhaps when suddenly confronted with factual questions, many individuals simply cannot quickly come up with names of political figures, definitions of political phenomena, or other information, even though they would recognize the names of such political figures and be able to make appropriate use of the language of political phenomena in their own conversations. Perhaps survey respondents, who may be distracted by other things going on while the interview is in process or otherwise unmotivated to concentrate carefully, do not reveal the level of information that they could show on a "test" that they care about or in a setting in which they get to choose the occasion for a discussion of public affairs issues.

While all of this is possible, it is also possible that the general public really does have a notably limited level of political information. And when lack of information on a particular subject is combined with a willingness to nevertheless offer a reaction to that subject on an opinion poll, we have the stuff of "non-attitudes." Here one is reminded of the various occasions on which late-night talk-show host Jay Leno has asked individuals, in informal street interviews, about their views on a completely bogus political candidate. To the hilarity of the viewing audience, some interviewees earnestly indicate that they "like" or "dislike" the non-existent candidate, or even that they have given money to his campaign. The "non-attitudes" model suggests that a substantial component of poll data on issues also includes such "non-attitudes," thus trivializing the very character of the concept of "public opinion."

Manipulated Opinion

But what if people have genuine, even passionate views on public affairs issues, but those views have been orchestrated or engineered by the propaganda of political leaders? Policy that is responsive to public opinion requires at a minimum that the content of public policy be consistent with majority sentiments in the general public. But such consistency is not sufficient grounds for finding policy responsiveness. That is because consistency between opinion and policy can result if political decisionmakers shape public opinion to bring it into line with policy rather than adopting policies that are consistent with public opinion. Such "after the fact" agreement by the public might satisfy the requirements of some versions of democratic theory; but it does not signify policy *responsiveness*. And although the shaping of public opinion by political elites might be viewed favorably, using positive terms such as "leadership," many scholars point to more alarming aspects of this model. From the most negative perspective, terms such as "demagoguery" and "propaganda" come to mind, and the manufacturing of opinion-policy congruence by opinion-shaping is no more wholesome than advertisers' orchestration of consumer demand. At a minimum, however, this model suggests that public opinion is *manipulated* by political elites, a term that allows some room for both positive and negative implications.

Perhaps the most critical analyst in this genre is Ginsberg, who argues that "the opinion that contemporary rulers heed is in many

respects an artificial phenomenon that national governments themselves helped to create and that their efforts continue to sustain"
(1986: 32). In a fashion that is reminiscent of the non-attitudes
argument, Ginsberg trivializes public opinion polls. Rather than
reflecting genuine preferences that would otherwise be exhibited in
actual political behavior such as protest activity or revealed through
the reports of activist leaders, public opinion polls have institutionalized a tame and regularized source of information that submerges
the passionately held beliefs of the most politically activated in an
undifferentiated mix of mass reactions. But Ginsberg goes beyond
this critique of the meaning of opinion polls to suggest that governments foster opinion polling because they can orchestrate its content and use the results to legitimate their activities. In short,
Ginsberg emphasizes that modern governments have become sophisticated in the use of public relations techniques, that public
opinion has been tamed and channeled through the institutionalization of opinion polls and that governments therefore can "manage, manipulate, and use public sentiment" (1986: 84).

Clearly, macropolitical institutions are organized in a way that
seems to assume the shaping of public opinion. Research on the
presidency, for example, suggests the increasing importance of a
presidential strategy of opinion leadership. Opinion leadership, or
what Kernell (1986) calls "going public," involves direct appeals to
the American public—appeals that are both self-promotional and
policy promotional for the president. And Kernell (1986: 85) acknowledges the many opportunities that the presidency offers for
such salesmanship—opportunities ranging from inaugural addresses
and State of the Union messages to more ordinary speeches to
casual comments to members of the media.

Recent research demonstrates that presidents have been able to
take advantage of these opportunities to shape public opinion, at
least to the extent of influencing what problems the American public
thinks are important. Cohen (1995), for example, finds that levels
of public concern with various problems are affected by presidential attention to those problems in State of the Union messages.
Although this influence decays quite rapidly, Cohen finds that it
holds irrespective of presidential popularity.

Other research documents the elaborate institutional arrangements that have emerged to fulfill the functions of public relations

and opinion management. Jacobs and Shapiro (1995: 192) indicate that, as early as the Kennedy administration, relatively elaborate presidential polling had begun; and they show that the "White House's institutional commitment to public opinion analysis progressively expanded" ever since. They conclude that "Presidents Kennedy, Johnson, and Nixon devoted significant institutional, financial, and personal resources to tracking public opinion and to using their public opinion analyses to make and sell the president and his policies."

In a similar vein, Maltese (1994) describes the crucial role that the White House Office of Communications has come to play in the "unending campaign" to mold public opinion in directions favorable to the president. Public opinion polling has become ever more crucial in that unending campaign. Presidential use of public opinion polls and other campaign-style tools for purposes of manipulating public opinion even after an election has been won was overtly acknowledged by officials in the Clinton White House. In 1997, for example, the newly re-elected Clinton administration was still making extensive use of the pollsters and the campaign media team of Robert Squire and Bill Knapp that had run the re-election campaign. Acknowledging this, presidential press secretary Michael D. McCurry explained "When you are responsible for governing you have to use the same [campaign] tools to advance your program, to build public support for the direction you are attempting to lead" (Mitchell, 1997: A12).

Nor is opinion management limited to the White House. While precise data on government spending for public relations purposes are not available, the annual amounts spent by individual executive branch agencies were estimated to be in the tens of millions of dollars by the early 1980s; and in their treatment of the subject, Combs and Nimmo (1993: 123) conclude that "In any event, the sums are substantial, with the total governmental outlay for federal advertising and publicity exceeding the total combined budgets of the wire services, three TV networks, and major U.S. daily newspapers."

The argument that presidents in particular and government officials more generally can shape and direct public opinion is, of course, premised on the assumption that these officials can effectively utilize the mass media for the purpose. Such an assumption would be threatened on the one hand by evidence that the mass media are autonomous and capable of resisting the manipulative efforts of public officials; it would also be threatened by evidence that the media have, in any case, minimal effects on public opinion. But contemporary research is supportive of the manipulation perspective, on both counts.

With respect to the capacity of public officials to utilize supposedly independent mass media for their own purposes, research shows how the imperatives facing the news media make them susceptible to public officials' manipulative desires. Jamieson (1992: 17), for example, acknowledges the "conventionalized journalistic norms that reward messages that are dramatic, personal, concise, visual, and take the form of narrative" and notes how these norms lead the news media to function as the vehicle for demagogic appeals, as in the domination of the 1988 campaign by the Willie Horton story. Still other research emphasizes the dependence of the mass media on government sources for timely and authoritative information. Berkowitz (1992: 81), for example, reminds us of the numerous media studies showing that "source-originated" stories dominate newspaper and television news and that "policymakers have been found to be even more influential than the overall group of news sources" (1992: 81). From this point of view, the mass media are by no means autonomous from government but instead serve as ready instruments for officials' attempts to direct what issues the public hears about and what "spin" is placed on those issues.

Kennamer (1992: 10), citing Bernard Cohen (1973: 179) suggests that ". . . the policymakers in the executive branch use the press to 'sell' policies to the Congress, or directly to the public. Congress then translates this 'public will' into judgments on the policies, often using home district newspaper articles and editorials, which have already been strongly influenced by government policymakers, as the basis of the 'public will.' Simply stated, government 'public relations activity results in press coverage, which is then interpreted as significant public opinion."

Of course, these uses of the media by political elites would be irrelevant for the actual manipulation of public opinion if, in fact, the media have a limited impact on public opinion. And, for a long time, scholarly work has been dominated by just such a "minimal effects" interpretation—an interpretation (1) suggesting that the impact of the mass media is limited to simple agenda-setting effects (i.e., influencing what topics are on people's minds) while (2) denying that the content of information in the mass media can effectively change the substantive direction of public opinion on any particular issue. But more recently, a substantial body of research has shown that media impacts are far from minimal.

Iyengar and Kinder (1987: 20–24; 30–32), for example, verify with both experimental and non-experimental analyses that television news has a strong agenda-setting effect—i.e., the importance of a problem to the mass public is a function of the extent of its coverage in the media. More importantly, their investigation of the "priming effects" of the media shows that agenda setting effects mean far more than simply pointing citizens to what topics are important without influencing what conclusions they draw about issues and candidates. Psychological theory posits that people do not make use of their entire store of information in reacting to a stimulus; instead, their reaction is based on that information which is most accessible—i.e., most likely to come to mind. Priming effects have to do with the dynamics by which certain matters are made more accessible, and hence more relevant in shaping individuals' reactions. Mass media messages such as the content of television news serve as important priming devices; and "By calling attention to some matters while ignoring others, television news influences the standards by which governments, presidents, policies, and candidates for public office are judged" (Iyengar and Kinder, 1987: 63). In particular, Iyengar and Kinder (1987: 72; 80) find that ratings of presidential character and performance are dependent on the ratings of performance on particular problems that the news media have highlighted. Even citizens' willingness to attribute responsibility for problems to the president are linked to whether or not TV news coverage connects the problem to the president (1987: 88). Thus, Iyengar and Kinder (1987: 117) argue that, rather than minimal effects, the media have powerful effects on public opinion that "rest not on persuasion but on commanding the public's attention (agenda-setting) and defining criteria underlying the public's judgments (priming)."

Similarly, Zaller's (1996) research suggests that the media can and demonstrably do have massive impacts if one looks for it in applications where there actually is variance in the content of the communication and if individual-level variation in reception of communications is appropriately measured. Zaller's work shows that there are large media effects on public opinion about public issues. And, of special importance for our consideration of the model of elite manipulation of public opinion, Zaller finds that the nature of the media effect depends on whether there are consensual or conflictual messages being conveyed by elites via the media and the balance in those messages. Media and elite consensus about a policy strengthens the role of the media in fostering mass public support for that policy. If, on the other hand, the media carries roughly balanced but opposing messages from elites, the impact of the media is to "drive liberals and conservatives into increasingly polarized opposition to one another" (1996: 54).

Research on cue-taking by the citizenry is also relevant to our discussion of the manipulation of public opinion. A considerable line of scholarship shows that, lacking comprehensive information about public affairs, citizens still make judgments about political issues using a variety of heuristics or shortcuts. One of the most important of these is cue-taking—i.e., the development of policy preferences based upon the policy preferences of leaders with whom the citizen identifies. While media representatives, organized interests, and others can serve as cue-givers, research on the importance of public officials as cue-givers is most relevant here. When they take cues from such political insiders, citizens "look to the very representatives whose decisions their opinions are supposed to guide" (Carmines and Kuklinski, 1990: 248).

Political cue-taking does not necessarily mean that citizens are developing bogus policy preferences or being dominated by the communication resources available to political elites. Acknowledging that the competitive aspect of the legislative process "ensures alternative voices and signals from which citizens can choose" and deters elected officials from deceitful cue-giving, Carmines and Kuklinski (1990: 266) choose the term "elite-driven" rather than "elite-manipulated" to characterize the phenomenon.

Nevertheless, at least some of the research on cue-taking suggests that the potential for manipulation is very much present and that some citizens, on some issues, are unduly influenced by political leaders with whom they identify. In an experimental study, Kuklinski and Hurley (1994) find that blacks' preferences with regard to the issue of black self-reliance are strongly influenced by

whether or not the statement of black self-reliance is attributed to
a black spokesperson (Jesse Jackson or Clarence Thomas) rather
than a white one (George Bush or Ted Kennedy), and that being
influenced by the messenger more than the message was especially
true to the extent that there was positive affect for the messenger.
They conclude that, "although the rationality and economy of cue-
taking are now well established, it is very possible that citizens-as-
cue-takers focus so heavily on the 'who' that the 'what' recedes to
the background" (1994: 732).

Even more direct evidence of the capacity of political elites to
shape public opinion to fit their policymaking actions comes from
research on political elites' accounts of their policy actions. That
research focuses on "justifications," which, unlike "excuses," involve
an admission of responsibility on the part of a political figure for
a particular policy decision or action; but justifications also involve
efforts to explain that the otherwise-controversial decision is not as
bad as it might seem. In short, justifications are "suited for per-
suading citizens to change their opinion about a controversial policy"
(McGraw, Best, and Timpone, 1995: 55). Using experimental methods, McGraw, Best and Timpone show that peoples' assessment of
a policy is based not only on their perceptions of the relative costs
and benefits from it, but also their acceptance of justifications of
the policy given by politicians who voted for it.

In short, there is considerable evidence to suggest that political
elites have opportunities to shape public opinion and that public
opinion is influenced by the information conveyed by political elites
through mass media channels. Whether this counts as evidence of
a manipulated public is, of course, a matter of interpretation and
definition. Page and Shapiro (1992: 356) draw a distinction between *educating* the public and *manipulating* public opinion, with
the latter defined as occurring "to the extent that the public is
given erroneous interpretations or false, misleading, or biased
information . . ." such that they "make mistaken evaluations of
policy alternatives and may express support for policies harmful
to their own interests or to values they cherish." Others have also
acknowledged that evidence of political leaders' shaping of public
opinion can be "viewed positively as the representative educating
an attentive constituency" or "negatively as the self-serving manipulation of an ill-informed public" (McGraw and Hubbard, 1996:
163).

Non-responsiveness: Public Policy that is Inconsistent with Public Opinion

In a representative democracy, it may well be expected that public policy should occasionally be inconsistent with public opinion. Elected officials are expected to take a leadership role, to balance particularistic interests against the broad public interest, and to direct government policy toward the solution of public problems even if that policy direction is not particularly popular. Even when it consists of real preferences rather than non-attitudes, popular opinion is not necessarily tempered by the many technical considerations and other constraints that must be faced in policy decisionmaking processes. Indeed, the general public sometimes demands the near impossible, as when there are simultaneous demands for more governmental services and lower taxes, beyond what efficiencies can generate (Sears and Citrin, 1982). For all these reasons, some disjunction between opinion and policy is occasionally to be expected.

Indeed, the manipulated opinion model is premised in part on the existence of these tensions, but suggests that political elites resolve them by moving public opinion toward consistency with what government is actually doing. Or, to use the language of the more positive side of the manipulated opinion model, inconsistencies between opinion and policy can be transformed into consistency if political elites appropriately educate the mass public.

But what if public opinion cannot be brought into line? Are there reasons to expect a more sustained discrepancy between opinion and policy? How could a situation of discrepancy between popular opinion and public policy be expected to obtain for long in a representative democracy? Reasonable or not, surely the public would ultimately use the devices of popular control to assert its will over governing elites. And, in anticipation of this dynamic, reelection-minded officials would presumably alter their policy stance over time to better come into line with public opinion. The non-responsiveness model consists of a potpourri of arguments and observations that suggests that, despite the existence of electoral mechanisms to call governmental officials to account, public policy may well not be responsive to the mass public.

One traditional argument focuses on differences in the salience of various issues to narrow, special interests and the mass public generally, and corresponding differences in the level of political mobilization. Gun control is the classic example in this regard. Until the 1990s, no meaningful gun control could be enacted at the federal level, despite the fact that for many years there has been consistent and quite lopsided support for gun control in the United States (Spitzer, 1995). But the general public's support for gun control was diffuse and of relatively low salience (except for brief episodes when particular incidents involving guns evoked high levels of concern) and was no match for the high levels of political mobilization of the organized gun lobby. In a situation such as this, elected officials have little motivation to be responsive to mass public opinion. In short, the re-election imperative can push policymakers to be responsive to narrow, minority interests rather than broader public opinion if the former holds re-election consequences while the latter does not.

It is sometimes argued that responsiveness to highly attentive publics and mobilized interest groups is a mechanism by which public policy is kept in line with general public opinion as well. Even Neuman (1986: 186), in the midst of an argument that is otherwise not very sanguine about governmental responsiveness to the mass public, suggests that the small segment of the American public that is attentive creates the motivation for policymaking within a broader zone of indifference. Neuman suggests that political elites are conscious of the existence of a "very small, attentive top stratum of the mass public" that can quickly mobilize broader attention to issues; that consciousness constrains political elites to "act within the constraints of an attentive public will." This attentiveness to a narrow and specialized attentive public is not, however, what an ambitious model of policy responsiveness to public opinion would envision.

The potential for sustained non-responsiveness also arises because of the low visibility and lack of electoral accountability of much public policymaking in the United States. Textbook models of officials acting in accordance with majority popular sentiment out of re-election imperatives simply do not have much bearing on public policy that is made in institutional venues where re-election imperatives are non-existent. The courts are the most obvious example in this regard, though an interesting line of research suggests other mechanisms that might lead to congruence between Court decisions and majority public sentiments (Mishler and Sheehan, 1993; Grossback,

1996). Similarly, policymaking that occurs predominantly in administrative venues cannot be expected to be driven by the same re-election imperatives that motivate legislators under the electoral accountability model. And while a variety of institutional arrangements such as presidential appointment of top-level executives, congressional oversight and involvement in administrative rule-making and the appropriations process might be expected to keep administrative agencies from too much policy autonomy, these institutional arrangements make the bureaucratic agencies at best indirectly accountable to the public. In fact, much of the value of a professional, permanent bureaucracy ostensibly lies in its capacity to bring technical expertise to bear on policy issues, in contradistinction with the popular responsiveness that is expected of Congress and the president.

Finally, public policy can remain durably out of kilter with general public opinion because, even when developed in a legislative or presidential venue, it can remain relatively invisible. The re-election imperative motivates legislators and presidents to make policy decisions in accordance with popular preferences only if the content of those policy decisions will be evident to the mass public and only if responsibility for those policy choices can be clearly traced. However, a host of decision-making arrangements have been devised to obfuscate those very matters. The use of commissions such as the U.S. Defense Base Closure and Realignment Commission to evade responsibility for painful policy choices, the cloaking of policy realities in confusing language, social constructions of target populations that disguise actual policy impacts and short-circuit citizens' capacity for critical analysis (Schneider and Ingram, 1993) and many other practices maximize "blame avoidance" while minimizing the public's capacity to grasp the character of policy that is being concocted (Weaver, 1986).

Meanwhile, Cohen (1997) offers persuasive evidence that presidents are responsive to the public primarily in the symbolic sense. In the phases of the policymaking process that are more symbolic—in particular, the problem definition phase—there is evidence of presidential responsiveness to public opinion; but "once actions become more substantively oriented, the costs of responsiveness and the benefits of policy leadership enter into the president's calculus. We then expect levels of responsiveness to decline" (Cohen,

1997: 16). Thus, for example, Cohen finds no evidence that the position that a president takes on roll call issues before Congress is consistent with public opinion on the issue. For purposes of understanding how policy could be unresponsive to public opinion in a democratic society, these findings have important implications. They suggest that elected officials can avoid the political repercussions of substantive non-responsiveness by engaging in symbolic responsiveness.

Responsiveness

Given the realities of representative government, it would be simplistic and naïve to expect that public officials would make policy decisions based solely on their perception of the general public's preferences on each issue. On some issues, there might be little popular consensus; and on many issues, technical considerations or other constraints might make it impossible or inappropriate for public policy to be crafted directly from the blueprint of public opinion. But although it might be justifiable on some grounds, public policy that is substantially and consistently at variance with popular preferences cannot be characterized as responsive to public opinion. At a minimum, policy responsiveness requires that public policy is consistent with public opinion, although that consistency might mean that policy remains within a broad zone of indifference rather than an exact correspondence between public opinion and public policy. In this sense, public opinion serves as a key constraint on governmental action, rather than a causal agent for governing outcomes. But, as the following discussion suggests, consistency between policy and opinion is grounds for concluding that policy responsiveness exists only if there is also evidence to rule out the possibility that the consistency results from political elites shaping public opinion, à la the manipulation model.

Research of several types demonstrates at a minimum that there is correspondence between policy and opinion, though it does not necessarily deal with either the possibility that opinion has been shaped by political elites or the possibility that the opinion-policy connection is a spurious one resulting from the effect of some outside influence on both opinion and policy (Page, 1994). For example, there is a considerable body of research revealing high levels

of correspondence between congressional representatives' preferences and votes on the one hand and their constituents' policy
preferences on the other. More recently, Erikson, Wright, and McIver
(1993: 95) have demonstrated through cross-sectional analysis that
policy is congruent with opinion at the state level, at least in the
general sense of a match between the overall liberalism or conservatism of public opinion in the state and the liberal or conservative
character of overall policy: "State political structures appear to do
a good job of delivering more liberal policies to more liberal states
and more conservative policies to more conservative states. Across
an impressive range of policies, public opinion counts, and not just
a little."

These cross-sectional studies of congressional representation and
policy-opinion congruence at the state level offer important evidence concerning the consistency of opinion with policy, and they
invite inferences that policy is responsive to opinion. But because
they have inherent limitations with respect to ruling out alternative causal directions, other scholars have turned to time series
analyses of the subject. The advantage of the time series approach
is that, while it cannot "kill all the demons of causal ambiguity"
(Page, 1994: 27) it at least can provide evidence of whether policy
change preceded or followed opinion change, and hence shed somewhat better light on whether opinion-policy congruence signifies
responsiveness or manipulation.

Research in this genre is also supportive of a responsiveness
model. Page and Shapiro (1983: 178–179), for example, isolated
357 instances of change in public opinion during the period 1935–
1979 and investigated the pattern of connection between these
opinion changes and various measures of public policy change, both
before and after the opinion change. Overall, and looking at policy
change one year after opinion change, they find a congruent change
in opinion and policy 43% of the time, no change in policy 33% of
the time, non-congruent change in policy 22% of the time, and
uncertain results 2% of the time. Furthermore, in the vast majority
of no-change cases, there were floor or ceiling effects or other reasons to interpret the pattern as something other than a lack of
responsiveness to opinion. And when a time lag longer than one
year is allowed, the degree of congruence between opinion change
and policy change is even greater (Page and Shapiro, 1983: 179).

Stimson, MacKuen, and Erikson (1995) also use a time series approach to investigate the opinion-policy connection and find strong evidence of policy responsiveness. Furthermore, they explore the relative importance of at least two alternative mechanisms for bringing about such responsiveness: (a) electoral turnover, leading to changes in the composition of policymaking institutions, and (b) rational anticipation, whereby existing personnel, motivated to avoid reelection defeat, change their policy position in reaction to perceived opinion shifts. They find that liberal or conservative shifts in policy direction are linked to corresponding shifts in the overall ideological predisposition of the public, and that this linkage between opinion change and policy change holds for the policy orientations of the House, the Senate, the presidency, and even the Supreme Court. While they have no method to definitively assess which mechanism accounts for policy responsiveness of the Court, they do find important differences across the other institutions. In the House it is largely a matter of rational anticipation rather than electoral turnover that brings about policy responsiveness. For the Senate and for the presidency, the more important mechanism is electoral replacement.

Yet a third type of research provides indirect support for the responsiveness interpretation. In their innovative research on the use of private polls in Kennedy's 1960 presidential campaign, Jacobs and Shapiro (1994) find that the candidate adopted policy positions in response to the contents of those private polls. This is, of course, evidence concerning responsiveness to opinion with respect to campaign issue management, which is one step removed from direct evidence of responsiveness to public opinion in policymaking processes after the election. Nevertheless, this careful historical research suggests how presidential candidates, in their efforts to manipulate the public by learning about and reflecting their concerns in the election process, can come to stake out positions that constrain and shape their presidencies toward popular responsiveness. Taking this approach one step further, Jacobs (1993) demonstrates that decisionmakers pay a great deal of attention to public opinion in the health policy domain.

Even when there is demonstrable consistency between opinion and policy, and even if shifts in opinion precede shifts in policy, the responsiveness model is still sometimes challenged on grounds that the linkage between opinion and policy is spurious. Specifically, it is sometimes argued that policy may approximate popular preferences simply because both governmental elites and the mass public happen to hold the same policy orientations, presumably because both are reacting to objective conditions or larger societal trends. Hill and Hinton-Andersson (1995: 925), for example, suggest that opinion-policy consistency can occur because of a "reciprocal influence process where elites and the mass public share policy preferences." Applying two-stage, least squares methods to analysis of policy and opinion liberalism in the 50 states, Hill and Hinton-Andersson conclude that the best explanation for opinion-policy congruence is a reciprocal influence interpretation, rather than a responsiveness or a manipulated opinion model.

In this book, an interpretation pointing to reciprocal influence will not be considered as a distinctive model of the opinion-policy connection, for several reasons. For one thing, it will generally be impossible to empirically distinguish reciprocal influence from responsiveness given the research methodology that will be used. The modeling processes used by Hill and Hinton-Andersson (1995) are viable for cross-sectional analysis of simplified indicators of state policy outcomes and state-level public opinion. But, a dynamic rather than a cross-sectional approach is ultimately most appropriate for an exploration of how public opinion relates to policy change. For such a dynamic approach, more descriptive policy histories, coupled with public opinion data that are specifically relevant to those policy histories, are preferable to highly aggregated and simplified indicators of public policy and of public opinion. The trade-off, however, is that sophisticated statistical models that might reveal reciprocal effects are not as viable.

Of course, some others have attempted to test for something like the reciprocal effects interpretation by introducing time series analyses that control for objective conditions (MacKuen and Coombs, 1981; Stimson, MacKuen, and Erikson, 1995). To some extent, it will be possible to introduce similar evidence in this volume. For example, in exploring policy and opinion with respect to imprisonment, it will be important to consider whether incarceration rates and levels of popular punitiveness are both manifestations of reaction to crime trends. But this approach also has its limits. For many social policies, it is unclear what "objective conditions" might be expected to be relevant to both opinion and policy change. In the case of affirmative action, for example, should one consider black-white differentials in earnings or objective indicators of the number of complaints of employment discrimination? The very choice of what constitutes relevant "objective conditions" is confounded in the policy debate at issue.

Finally, the reciprocal influence or shared opinion interpretation is unsatisfying on conceptual grounds. It suggests that the mass public reacts to potential problems or objective conditions without the influence of elite interpretations and that elites react to those same problems and objective conditions, unmotivated by the anticipated reactions of the general public. Given the substantial evidence undergirding both the responsiveness model and the manipulated opinion model, it is difficult to credit an interpretation that dismisses both dynamics. And, in any case, the substantive implication of the reciprocal influence model is very much like that of the responsiveness model. Ultimately, Hill and Hinton-Andersson (1995:933–34) conclude that while a model of reciprocal influences or shared preferences "does not conform to the expectation of literal mass control over public officials" it nevertheless suggests a democratic process in which "the interests of both mass and elite are still served."

A Contingent Approach to the Opinion-Policy Connection

The question of whether public opinion shapes public policy, is manipulated by elites, or is irrelevant to policy is important; but perhaps, phrased in this way, it is too simplistic. It suggests a single answer, when in fact, the linkage between policy and opinion may well depend upon several key considerations. Acknowledgment of this possibility takes us to a contingent model stipulating that the nature of the opinion-policy connection varies by type of policy.

But how should we distinguish among policy types for this purpose? What characteristics of a policy issue constitute the most important contingencies? Even an abbreviated exploration of relevant research yields a host of potentially important contingencies.

For example, the institutional venue within which policy is developed might be an important consideration. Differing venues have different biases with respect to particular policies. As Baumgartner and Jones (1993: 32) argue, this is in part because of different decisionmaking rules and norms in different venues (e.g., reciprocity norms in legislatures that do not apply in judicial settings) and in part because of constituency differences. City and state governments, for example, deal with different constituencies than do governing institutions at the national level, and hence can be expected to be "receptive to different policy images."

These differences in institutional venue have important implications for the character of policy that is developed. It is for this reason that political activists regularly engage in venue shopping—i.e., strategic efforts to have decisionmaking on an issue of concern to them situated in an institutional setting that is most congenial to their own policy predilections. For our purposes, however, the important reason to acknowledge differences in institutional venue is the possibility that there are implications for the character of the linkage, if any, between opinion and policy. For example, neither the courts nor bureaucratic agencies are structured to be responsive to public opinion in the ways that Congress and the presidency are; and the linkage between opinion and policy may also be expected to be different for state government than it is for the federal government (Page and Shapiro, 1983: 176). Hence, public policies that are developed primarily in executive branch agencies at the federal level should be less likely to exhibit a responsiveness connection to public opinion than public policies developed in state legislatures.

In addition to differences in the venues within which they are developed, inherent qualities of policy issues are often said to be important in shaping the resulting character of politics (Wilson, 1989; Lowi, 1964, 1972) and presumably therefore the character of the opinion-policy connection. For example, the straightforward distinction between foreign policy and domestic policy may be an important consideration. Page and Shapiro (1992: 373), for example, suggest that the capacity for opinion to be manipulated differs considerably between foreign and domestic policy issues: "In the domestic policy realm, sources of information are usually more diffuse and competitive, so that outright manipulation of opinion is probably much less common than in foreign policy."

Within the domestic policy realm, we can divide policy issues into those in which the stakes are primarily material benefits (e.g.,

Medicare, Medicaid, Social Security, unemployment compensation) and a set of policy issues with symbolic stakes involving morals, ethical issues, justice or civil rights (abortion, pornography, civil rights, disability rights). Policy issues do not necessarily entail one set of stakes exclusively. For example, some aspects of welfare policy in the United States (i.e., the former Aid to Families with Independent Children program and its predecessors) are very much "about" material benefits; but other aspects of welfare policy have relatively little to do with dollars and cents issues, even for a program that distributes material benefits to a targeted population. Instead, these other aspects of the welfare policy issue involve societal debates about the status of the poor and government's prerogatives in regulating the reproductive choices and personal behaviors of the poor. Similarly, affirmative action policy entails both material stakes and symbolic stakes. But, although it is not uncommon to find social policies that involve both types of stakes, any given episode of attention to a particular policy issue is typically dominated either by conflict over material stakes or conflict over symbolic stakes. And because the politics surrounding policies with material stakes might be expected to differ considerably from the politics surrounding policies with symbolic stakes, this distinction in policy type should also be viewed as a potential contingency in any discussion of the linkage between public opinion and public policy.

Other analysts distinguish "hard" from "easy" issues (Carmines and Stimson, 1989: 11) or otherwise acknowledge the fact that the politics surrounding technically complex and low salience issues are likely to differ substantially from the politics surrounding high-profile, low-complexity issues. While hard issues require substantial cognitive processing, easy issues "may be responded to, indeed even understood in a fundamental sense, at the 'gut' level" (Carmines and Stimson, 1989: 11). One of the implications of this observation is that the relevance of the non-attitudes model depends on whether the policy issue in question is a hard or an easy one. Meaningless, doorstep opinions are presumably more likely with respect to technical, complex issues that are beyond the comprehension of the mass public. Similarly, the likelihood of finding manipulated public opinion may depend upon whether the policy issue in question is a hard or easy one. The general public's capacity to react passionately to the gut-level aspects of easy issues would seem to make such issues better raw material for attempts at opinion manipulation.

In a related vein, the salience of issues to the mass public has a bearing on the likelihood of policy responsiveness. Page and Shapiro (1983: 181) for example, find that "policy congruence is higher on salient than on nonsalient issues." In a more elaborate treatment of the role of salience, Geer (1996) uses deductive models to explore the prospects for either issue followership (i.e., responsiveness) or leadership (i.e., opinion manipulation). Because elected officials are assumed to need popular approval in order to be reelected and in order to be successful in policymaking, they will ordinarily tend to respond to rather than lead public opinion; and with the advent of modern public opinion polling, political figures are much more knowledgeable about popular preferences, *at least on those issues that are salient enough to the public to provide a clear and settled picture of public opinion.* Geer concludes that efforts at leadership rather than followership of opinion are largely confined to non-salient issues, for which politicians have some perceived capacity to shape and direct an otherwise poorly-formed public opinion rather than responding to it.

Other observers have posited that elected officials are more likely to take public opinion into account on emotionally charged, moral issues than on other types of issues (Tatalovich and Daynes, 1988: 218). Mooney and Lee (1995: 615), for example, suggest that "since morality policy can be highly salient and low in technical complexity, elected officials who want to retain their positions will likely do their best to reflect general constituency opinion on it, if they are forced to take a stand." Hence, issues such as abortion and gay rights (Wald, Button, and Rienzo, 1995) are expected to be more likely to evidence policy-opinion responsiveness than would issues such as the national deficit or health care reform.

But the linkage between opinion and policy has also been said to depend upon the *distribution* of public opinion (Brain, 1991). Some issues are "bi-modal ones, involving highly divided public opinion, while public opinion on other issues is more consensual" (Strickland and Whicker, 1992). Strickland and Whicker suggest that for the types of issues that entail unimodal public opinion, there is a greater chance of responsiveness of policy to opinion because compromise positions and negotiation allow elected officials seeking the votes of the majority to come to a moderate policy position that reflects majority sentiment; in the bimodal case, however, "candidates are driven toward one of the two modes on the extremes, and public debate is more acrimonious" (Strickland and Whicker, 1992: 599); and more importantly for our purposes, this implies the difficulty of finding a policy position that is responsive to the moderate middle.

In short, a contingent approach suggests that we should not expect to find a one-size-fits-all model of the role that public opinion plays in policymaking. Rather, the nature of the connection between opinion and policy will depend on the type of public policy at issue. An analysis that takes the contingency approach theory seriously must therefore be based on an examination of a range of importantly different types of issues. This book explores the connection between public opinion and public policy in six key areas of domestic social policy: abortion, affirmative action, pornography, welfare, incarceration, and Social Security. These policy topics were chosen not only because they include many of the nation's most important social policies but also because they represent the diversity of issues that a contingency view calls for. Although the details to support this contention will be more evident in the chapters to follow, it is important to note here that this constellation of policy areas includes policies in which the dominant venue for policymaking is and has been the federal government (Social Security, pornography); topics in which the venue for policymaking has shifted back and forth between the federal and the state-local level (affirmative action, abortion, welfare, imprisonment); topics in which the courts have been a very important venue for policymaking (pornography, affirmative action); and topics in which the courts are of minimal importance compared with legislative and bureaucratic decision-making venues (welfare, Social Security). Furthermore, the set of policy topics includes one that predominantly involves material stakes (Social Security), several that predominantly involve symbolic stakes (abortion, pornography, imprisonment), and two that involve an amalgam of material and symbolic stakes (affirmative action, welfare); ones in which opinion about prevailing government policies has been relatively consensual for much of the past three decades (Social Security, imprisonment; affirmative action) and ones in which opinion has been much more divided (regulation of pornography, abortion, welfare). Finally, as the concluding chapter will show, these policy topics exhibit important variation in issue salience, and that variation is central to understanding the differences in the role of public opinion that emerge.

While the contingency approach is a step forward, however, ultimately it is too static of a representation of our topics for analysis. Policy issues that at one time are debated primarily within a framework of the distribution of material benefits are at other times redefined and become the subject of conflicts over symbolic stakes; likewise, policy that is contentious because of symbolic stakes in one era can evoke debates over the distribution of material benefits in another era. For example, the history of the disability rights movement shows how public policy toward the disabled has oscillated back and forth—at times evoking only concerns about material benefits and costs and at other times evoking concerns about rights and justice (Sharp, 1994; Shapiro, 1994). Similarly, whether the distribution of public opinion about a policy issue is bi-modal or consensual can change over time. It is this very change in policy and opinion over time that is of interest in this volume. And it is because of this dynamic focus that the chapters rely upon policy histories, matched with trends in relevant opinion data.

A dynamic, historical approach to this issue requires that we take one step beyond the insights of a contingent model. The contingency-based perspective stipulates that no single model of the opinion-policy connection may be universally applicable, and points us to important aspects of institutional venue and policy type that might help us to understand the *circumstances* under which public opinion either shapes public policy, is shaped by the policy initiatives of political elites, is inconsistent with policy, or is reduced to irrelevancy. But once we acknowledge that there are important shifts in opinion and policy issues over time, the possibility arises that a single model of the opinion-policy connection may be inadequate even to depict the dynamics within a given issue area. Affirmative action policy, for example, might be responsive to public opinion in one era but unresponsive to it in another; welfare policy might be responsive to public opinion in one era while political elites manipulate public opinion toward support of a shift in policy in another era. The various models of opinion-policy linkage may, in fact, constitute potential building-blocks for a variety of distinctive sequences. As the following section shows, a variety of conceptual developments provide support for such a notion, and help us to identify a preliminary set of theoretically and normatively important sequences.

Toward a Sequential View

The Thermostatic Sequence

One such sequence is the one captured by the thermostatic model developed by Goggin and Wlezien (1993; see also Wlezien, 1995; Wlezien, 1996).[1] In that model, the representation of public opinion in policy is dynamic. Public policy responds to public opinion and, in acknowledgment of that policy movement, public opinion reverses itself. In short, the thermostatic model stipulates that responsiveness of policy to public opinion is followed by an important feedback phase in which the public adjusts its preferences in response to policy change. Wlezien (1995: 992) finds a pattern of negative feedback of actual appropriations for defense on popular preferences for defense spending—i.e., defense appropriations have increased at times when public opinion favors higher levels of defense spending, whereupon opinion becomes less favorable to defense spending, and so forth. Similarly, Goggin and Wlezien (1993) find evidence of a thermostatic pattern (in a cross-sectional study of states rather than a longitudinal study, however) with respect to public preferences on the restrictiveness of abortion and actual state policies on abortion.

The Policy Learning Sequence

From the perspective of democratic theory, it is troubling to envision policy that is disconnected from public opinion because the latter consists only of a mass of non-attitudes. However, one hopeful sequence would involve manipulation of public opinion, in the most positive sense (i.e., leadership, educating the public), resulting in the replacement of non-attitudes by more genuine mass preferences. Such a transformation would be particularly desirable if it stemmed from information-sharing about the changing technical requirements of policy as elites themselves gradually reach more consensus on such matters. Policy might then come to be more genuinely responsive to public opinion through a dual process in which both policy and opinion are refined in the light of new knowledge.

This hopeful sequence, from non-attitudes to responsiveness via opinion manipulation, is consistent with the view of policy change and learning suggested by Paul Sabatier and Hank Jenkins-Smith (1993). In their interpretation, public policies at any point in time reflect the belief systems of advocacy coalitions—i.e., policy specialists who are inherently concerned with the attainment of policy objectives in a specialized domain. Those belief systems include "sets of value priorities, perceptions of important causal relationships, perceptions of the seriousness of the problem, and perceptions of the efficacy of various sorts of institutional relationships as means of attaining those value priorities (Sabatier and Jenkins-Smith, 1993: 35–6). Advocacy coalitions are portrayed as using knowledge instrumentally—i.e., while core values of the belief system are stable, information about the consequences of existing policies and programs do constitute a form of policy learning that is used to modify secondary aspects of the advocacy coalition's belief system. And even the core aspects of the belief system are subject to change in response to non-cognitive developments external to the policy sub-system, such as changes in socioeconomic conditions or new technological developments.

The advocacy coalition interpretation reminds us that there is much competition, debate and disagreement even among policy experts, but it points to important possibilities for policy learning at the elite level—even though such learning is a political process that is "not a disinterested search for 'truth'" (Sabatier and Jenkins-Smith, 1993: 45). For our purposes, the important point is that the politics of ideas that is fought out at the elite level may gradually seep out, first to highly attentive publics and ultimately to the public more generally. Indeed, the very politicization of the policy learning process may help to ensure that there is a transmission belt to the broader public, with transformative consequences for erstwhile non-attitudes.

The policy learning sequence emphasizes the potential for policy change and opinion change that are based upon the knowledge gained through policy experience. However, the concept of path dependency offers a very different interpretation that calls to mind a less hopeful sequence.

Path Dependence and the Downsian Sequence

From this perspective, policy change is a sequential process, with policy developments at any point in time being influenced by previous developments. But that influence may *not* consist of adaptation and constructive change, or at least not easy adaptation or immediate change in reaction to the failings or limitations of initial policy choices. Instead, as suggested by the concept of path dependency, a decision made early in an historical sequence may create circumstances in which a collective is locked into a less-than-optimal course of action because subsequent decisions reinforce the initial choice (Wilsford, 1994: 252–3).

The theory of path dependency is drawn from the literature of economic history where it has been used to account for the failure of economic systems to take optimal advantage of technological change in ways that would improve economic performance. In a classic article from this genre, Paul David (1985) describes how the QWERTY keyboard layout developed by a Milwaukee printer in the late nineteenth century has endured despite the ever-accumulating evidence that an alternative keyboard arrangement is much more efficient. The initial commitment to the QWERTY layout was reinforced by the decisions of manufacturers of typewriters, typing instructors, typists, and business managers and ultimately reinforced still further as new word-processing technologies were developed using the same keyboard layout. The resulting lock-in to a less-than-optimal technology is the essence of path dependency.

Path dependency theorists usually provide three kinds of analysis (Aminzade, 1992: 463). One kind examines significant decisions that become "decisive determinants of future opportunities"; another highlights later decision points at which alternatives to the original approach are eschewed; the third attempts to identify the reasons for continuing conformity to the original approach. A number of scholars have begun to adapt the concept of path dependency to the study of public policy change and continuity. Margaret Weir (1992: 19), for example, makes a strong argument for focusing on such policy sequences in order to understand the limitations of employment policy in the United States, arguing that "Underlying the concept of a policy sequence is the notion of 'path dependence': decisions at one point in time can restrict future possibilities by sending policy off onto particular tracks, along which ideas and interests develop and institutions and strategies adapt." Wilsford (1994) uses a path dependency framework to explain why major reform of health care systems is so unlikely. A major divergence from the path upon which health care policy is tracking requires, in Wilsford's terminology, a conjuncture of exogenous shocks capable of overcoming the institutions and processes that provide continuities to policy.[2]

Thus, while the thermostatic sequence portrays the mutually moderating effects of policy and opinion, and the policy learning sequence portrays the emergence of meaningful public opinion as an outgrowth of knowledge and policy development at the elite level, the concept of path dependency suggests that the course of policy development may become locked in; and the lock-in may over time cause policy to drift outside the zone of public acceptance. This suggests a distinctive sequence in which policy may initially be responsive to public opinion, but then quickly become mired in a relatively durable pattern of non-responsiveness. This pattern is designated the Downsian sequence because of its conceptual similarity to Baumgartner and Jones' (1993: 88) discussion of agenda setting in the form of a "Downsian mobilization." In their analysis, a Downsian mobilization involves an initial period of popular concern about a problem and enthusiasm for the governmental initiative that is put forth to solve the problem. However, the governmental initiative that is responsive to popular concern creates an institutional sub-system in the form of bureaucratic agencies and programs, Congressional subcommittee turf, and interest group networks which endure long after the public's attention to the initial problem has faded. And eventually, that institutional sub-system can come to be viewed as the problem rather than the solution.[3]

The Broken Thermostat

If policy lock-in can lead to a Downsian sequence of responsiveness followed by an extended period of non-responsiveness, it may also be the central dynamic in another undesirable sequence. In this scenario, policy initially changes in response to public opinion. But, in contrast with the thermostatic sequence, opinion does *not* moderate in recognition of the change in policy. The public's call for more spending on X, tougher sanctions for Y, or a less permissive regulatory stance on Z yields corresponding increases in spending, tougher sanctions, or less permissive regulations; but public opinion still registers a demand for more spending, tougher sanctions, and so forth. Over an extended period of time, such a scenario yields policy that appears to be locked into a never-ending spiral, trending in a direction responsive to a public that appears itself to be locked into a set of preferences that do not acknowledge major policy commitments.

To focus on the exploration of these distinctive sequences is not to deny the importance of issue characteristics and institutional venues as important contingencies for understanding the link between opinion and policy. In fact, these contingencies may be crucial elements in the development of these sequences. In his investigations of the thermostatic sequence, for example, Wlezien (1995: 983) suggests that there are likely to be systematic differences across policy domains due to the differences in the availability of good policy information for the public in different policy domains. Our task therefore is twofold. First, we should identify the sequence that best depicts the opinion-policy connection for each policy topic. Second, we need to compare and contrast the findings across the various policy topics, with an eye toward learning how the differences in policy issue characteristics and in institutional venue shape the evolution of the sequences that we observe. Chapters 2 through 7 take up these tasks for six different policy topics: imprisonment, affirmative action, welfare, abortion, Social Security, and pornography. Chapter 8 presents a synthesis of the comparative findings and a discussion of their theoretical and normative implications.

2

Imprisonment and Public Opinion
The Broken Thermostat

Overview

There is perhaps no more weighty manifestation of the consequences of public policy than that which deals with the use of governmental authority to deprive individuals of their liberty, nor can one imagine an area of public policy in which the legitimacy of governmental action is more critical. For this reason, the linkage between public policy and public opinion is especially important with respect to the nation's approach to incarceration of its citizens. This chapter examines the substantial growth in this country's use of the imprisonment option since 1973 and considers the linkage between that trend and changes in public sentiments on crime and punishment.

The extent of imprisonment in the United States is, therefore, treated as a key policy manifestation in this chapter. Obviously, imprisonment is but one element of a large and complex criminal justice system, and a host of different public policies might be expected to affect this element. Absent any change in sentencing policies, for example, more aggressive law enforcement efforts which yield larger numbers of arrestees might be expected to increase the numbers being sent to prison. In short, while the criminal justice system is often criticized for being a chaotic "non-system," policy decisions in one portion of the criminal justice system clearly can have implications for the other portions. However, this chapter focuses on policymaking with respect to the elements of the criminal justice system that are most proximate to the incarceration deci-sion—i.e., to legislatively enacted changes in sentencing policy that have affected the behavior of both judges (on the input side) and parole boards (on the release side). While judges and parole boards might be less likely to feel pressure from the public, elected officials might be expected to be highly sensitive to public preferences as they make policy concerning the punishment of criminals.

As this chapter shows, a bundle of closely related and very impor-tant policy developments at both the federal and state level have transformed this end of the criminal justice system in ways that have made imprisonment much more widespread. But has this trans-formation been responsive to public opinion? As the chapter will show, the move toward dramatic increases in prison population oc-curred after public opinion had been trending in a much more pu-nitive direction on criminal justice issues, suggesting policy-opinion responsiveness. However, despite that dramatic policy response and the implications that it has had for prison overcrowding, the need for new prison construction, and consequent impacts on public budgets, public opinion still exhibits a very high level of concern about crime and punishment that suggests the desire for still more punitive measures. Unlike the thermostatic model envisioned by Wlezien and Goggin (Goggin and Wlezien, 1993; Wlezien, 1995), public opinion has not moderated in acknowledgment of a major shift of policy. Instead, in the face of sustained popular pressure for harsher treat-ment of criminals, public officials have continued to pursue policies that yield ever-larger rates of imprisonment, while adopting coping strategies such as the privatization of the incarceration function as a way of dealing with the increasing strains on the over-burdened correctional system. This chapter therefore documents an opinion-policy linkage that might be designated the "broken thermostat." In such a model, there is correspondence between public opinion and policy, but the linkage is ultimately pathological.

Imprisonment in America: A Policy History

Trends in Imprisonment

Any investigation of this topic must begin with recognition of the tremendous increase in the use of imprisonment in this country over the past two decades. Since 1973, the number of prisoners has increased at a rate that is "by far the most dramatic" in U.S. history, such that by the early 1990s the size of the prison population was triple what it had been in 1973 (Selke, 1993: 1). Donziger (1996: 15) uses even more dramatic language to describe the increase: "Since 1980, the United States has undertaken one of the largest and most rapid expansions of a prison population in the history of the Western world. Between 1980 and 1994, the prison population tripled from 500,000 to 1.5 million."

The conventional wisdom is that this escalation in imprisonment was a response to substantial increases in crime beginning in the 1960s. And, indeed, crime rates in the United States have increased in the past three decades, if one uses the FBI's Uniform Crime Reports (UCR) as the measure of crime. However, the validity of this data and the reality of the increasing crime that it reports have been challenged on several grounds. For one thing, computerization and other improvements in law enforcement record keeping and reporting may mean that apparent increases in crime are actually an artifact of these improvements. Furthermore, because some police departments count crimes based on arrestees rather than victims, multiple perpetrator incidents create artificially inflated crime numbers. This, coupled with the fact that the allocation of some federal monies according to crime rates give police departments incentives to inflate crime numbers, give important reasons for doubt about the UCR (Donziger, 1996: 4)

The weaknesses of the UCR led to the institutionalization of an alternative method for measuring the extent of crime in the United States—the national sample crime victimization survey that has been conducted annually by the Census Bureau since 1973. That survey asks respondents whether they have been victims of any of the following seven crimes: rape, robbery, assault, personal theft, household theft, burglary, and motor vehicle theft (Donziger, 1996: 5).

The two alternative indicators of crime give sharply different portraits of trends in crime in the U.S. since 1973. Figure 2-1, incorporating all forms of crime and victimization, shows this dramatically. Since 1973, UCR-reported crime has increased sharply, with occasional and temporary downward corrections. In the same period, data from the National Crime Victimization Survey suggest that overall crime was first stable throughout the 1970s, slowly declined through the 1980s and showed an upward shift in the

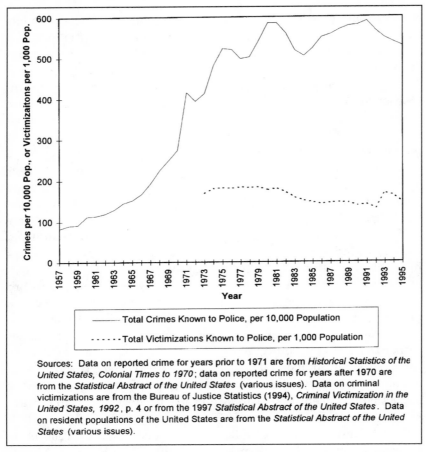

Figure 2-1. Trends in Rates of Total Reported Crime and Total Crime Victimizations, 1957–1995

early 1990s. If we focus on violent crimes rather than total crime (data not shown), a very similar pattern is revealed.

These discrepancies in official statistics about crime trends in the nation make it difficult to interpret whether or not increases in imprisonment are simply the result of crime increases and the functioning of existing criminal justice policies in dealing with them, or the result of policy changes directed toward the increased use of imprisonment as a policy option. Stated another way, the discrepancies complicate our ability to objectively assess trends in the imprisonment phenomenon itself. Trends in the raw numbers of prisoners, like the dramatic figures on prison populations cited at the outset of this chapter, are often reported by the media or in publications intended for popular consumption. They should, however, be standardized. As Figure 2-2 shows, it matters a great deal whether the figures on imprisonment are standardized by overall population, by UCR-based crime data, or by crime data from the national victimization survey. While all three versions show a trend toward increased imprisonment in the United States, the growth in imprisonment relative to the number of reported victimizations is more substantial than the growth in imprisonment relative to the

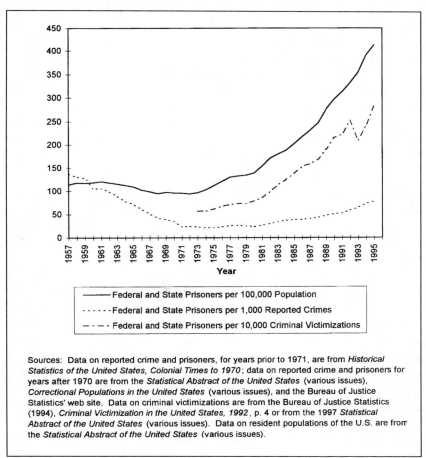

Sources: Data on reported crime and prisoners, for years prior to 1971, are from *Historical Statistics of the United States, Colonial Times to 1970*; data on reported crime and prisoners for years after 1970 are from the *Statistical Abstract of the United States* (various issues), *Correctional Populations in the United States* (various issues), and the Bureau of Justice Statistics' web site. Data on criminal victimizations are from the Bureau of Justice Statistics (1994), *Criminal Victimization in the United States, 1992*, p. 4 or from the 1997 *Statistical Abstract of the United States* (various issues). Data on resident populations of the U.S. are from the *Statistical Abstract of the United States* (various issues).

Figure 2-2. Trends in Imprisonment, 1957–1995, Adjusted for Total Population, for Reported Crime, and for Criminal Victimizations

overall population of the United States; and the growth in imprisonment relative to the dramatically growing number of UCR-reported crimes is least impressive of all.

Despite the differences in magnitude, however, all three standardizations underscore that a veritable sea change in public policy concerning crime and punishment occurred, beginning in the 1970s. While rates of incarceration were stable (if standardized by population) or declining (if standardized by UCR-reported crimes) in the 1960s, that pattern was altered in the early 1970s as rates of imprisonment in this country began an expansionary turn. And the trend toward greater use of incarceration escalated in the 1980s. As a result, even relative to UCR-reported crime, which provides the most conservative standardization, imprisonment has increased 155% between 1973 and 1993.

Clearly, there is more going on than the swelling of the nation's jails as a mechanical response to increasing crime. As Figure 2-2 clearly shows, imprisonment is increasing faster than crime. This is consistent with a considerable body of research which suggests that the link between crime and imprisonment is more limited than might be imagined because factors other than crime play such an important role in determining rates of imprisonment. For example, some research on the impact of various demographic variables on imprisonment rates suggests that states with larger black populations have higher rates of imprisonment, above and beyond differences in violent crime rates—a finding that can be interpreting as showing the impact of institutional racism on imprisonment (Selke, 1993: 3–4). Similarly, McGarrell's (1991) comparative state policy analysis shows that state political culture is a significant determinant of juvenile incarceration rates. He interprets the fact that states with individualistic political cultures were more likely to show increases in juvenile incarceration as showing "the responsiveness to politicized party demands for punitive crime control measures within the individualistic political culture . . ." (McGarrell, 1991: 274). More generally, an investigation of changes in both correctional philosophy and specific policy decisions involving matters such as mandatory sentencing, parole, habitual offender laws, and the like show clearly how governmental policy has major relevance for prison populations. The following sections provide a closer look at the history of criminal justice policy relevant to imprisonment, highlighting the specific policy developments that constitute the sea change in public policy and that are driving the continuing escalation in prison populations in the United States.

Developments in Sentencing Policy

It has often been suggested that criminal justice policy has both a conservative and a liberal variant and that there has been an ebb and flow of dominance of these views in policy over time, with a law and order approach in the 1920s and 1930s, a resurgence of liberalism in the 1950s through the 1960s and conservatism regaining the dominant position in the 1970s (Marion, 1994: 12–13). While such interpretations, based on traditional left-right ideological characterizations, fit the policy history to be outlined here, it may be useful to introduce additional terminology that is much more focused upon the phenomenon of imprisonment.

A discussion of criminal justice policies relating to corrections must acknowledge four differing purposes of imprisonment. On the one hand, sending a criminal to prison may serve a *rehabilitative* purpose. That is, it may be assumed that activities and programs imposed on criminals during their period of confinement may serve to transform them into productive, law-abiding citizens ready to take their place in society once again. On the other hand, imprisonment may be viewed primarily as serving an *incapacitative* purpose—i.e., preventing the offender from committing another crime for the duration of his or her confinement. The incapacitative goal of corrections does not presume that the offender will be transformed during confinement and safe for release to society. Indeed, the goal of incapacitation seems premised upon the notion that, since offenders cannot be assumed to be "cured" by their imprisonment, the best way to protect society from them is to maximize the time that they are separated from society. Imprisonment can be viewed as having a *deterrent* purpose—i.e., preventing future criminal behavior by providing a demonstrable threat, either to the individual offender who is experiencing the punishment (specific deterrence) or to others who, observing the punishment, take the threat of it into account in decisions about their own behavior. Finally, imprisonment can be viewed as having the goal of *retribution*—i.e., the purpose of realizing justice by meting out punishment for an offense, regardless of whether the punishment serves any crime control purposes through deterrence, rehabilitation, or incapacitation (Griset, 1991: 32).

While these contrasting and somewhat contradictory perspectives on corrections can co-exist uneasily at any point in time, considerable evidence suggests that the rehabilitative ideal was dominant in the period prior to 1973, embedded in systems of indeterminate sentencing at both the state and the federal level. But the dominance of the rehabilitative ideal collapsed in the early to mid-1970s, with the policy manifestation of the collapse being the introduction of determinate sentencing (Zimring and Hawkins, 1995; Rothman, 1995; Griset, 1991).

Indeterminate sentencing involves judicial imposition of relatively open-ended sentences, which provide substantial discretion to correctional authorities and parole boards for the determination of when a prisoner is ready for release. The practice of indeterminate sentencing is intimately intertwined with the rehabilitation paradigm. Indeterminate sentencing is based on the principle that different offenders require different lengths of confinement because, even if they have committed the same crime, they may differ with regard to what it will take for remediation. An offender's time in prison should, under this model, include a set of "treatments" tailored to the individual, as in the manner of a medical model. And, just as it may not be possible in advance to know how long a course of medical treatment may take before a patient is cured, so also is it inappropriate for judges to lay out in advance a specific sentence. Instead, parole boards, basing their decision on the input of correctional authorities who have worked directly with the prisoner, are in the best position to decide when a prisoner is reformed and ready for release.

Indeterminate sentencing, and the rehabilitation model that it epitomized, came under sustained attack in the late 1960s and early 1970s on a variety of grounds. On the one hand, critics charged that the state was not capable of providing effective "treatment" to offenders, in the manner of the medical model. Skepticism about the effectiveness of prisoner rehabilitation abounded in the light of evidence of recidivism and an outpouring of studies showing no rehabilitative impact (Blumstein, 1983: 232; Griset, 1991: 28–9). But there were also concerns that indeterminate sentencing provided the legal mechanism for discrimination. At a minimum, indeterminate sentencing was inevitably linked to disparities in sentencing, and disparities came to be viewed as inequities. Finally, in an era in which the legitimacy of state authority generally was under heavy attack, indeterminate sentencing was criticized for giving the state open-ended control over offenders and for introducing bogus "treatment" arguments as grounds for restricting individuals' liberty longer than was necessary (Griset, 1991: 30–31).

But if these critiques, emanating largely from liberals, were in the vanguard of the challenge to indeterminate sentencing, the call for a transition to determinate sentencing was quickly taken up by conservatives who were equally skeptical of the effectiveness of prison as a place for rehabilitation and who saw the discretion of indeterminate sentencing as undercutting proper attention to the certainty of punishment. In fact, the most common interpretation of the wave of sentencing reforms that occurred after 1973 is that conservative forces hijacked the reform movement, transforming it to one that emphasized an increasingly punitive approach. Liberal critics of indeterminate sentencing, such as the National Council on Crime and Delinquency, were interested in replacing the existing system with an approach that would reserve imprisonment only for a very small number of dangerous offenders. However, it was unclear that suitable criteria could be developed for distinguishing which offenders constituted the few who should be imprisoned. And, having conceded that the rehabilitative goal of prisons was problematic, liberals left the field wide open for conservatives who had no qualms about the propriety of a more expansive use of incarceration. The "expansionist notion of general incapacitation was an easy winner" because, in the wake of the elite consensus about the problems of indeterminate sentencing, the "liberal prison reductionists could provide no convincing limiting principle to serve as a barrier to expansionist domination" (Zimring and Hawkins, 1995: 11–12).

While there is widespread agreement that the dominance of the rehabilitation model came to an end in the early to mid-1970s, there is some disagreement about the philosophy that has replaced it. Summarizing the transition to determinate sentencing, Zimring and Hawkins (1995) argue that incapacitation became, by default, the paradigmatic goal. Griset (1991: 32) argues instead that "the determinate ideal elevated retribution as the primary purpose of sentencing" and suggests that the crime control orientation inherent in each of the other goals (deterrence, rehabilitation, and incapacitation) was being eschewed. Similarly, Blumstein (1983: 233) suggests that the rehabilitation ideal was giving way "to a new emphasis on punitiveness, reflecting a pressure for greater retribution and an increased desire for crime control."

The story is further complicated by the proliferation of sentencing approaches that have replaced indeterminate sentencing. A number of quite different reforms, each bearing the label of determinate sentencing, were introduced beginning in the 1970s, and modifications to these reforms have further complicated the picture (Griset, 1991: 39–40). And in recent years a number of policies have been introduced that are quite consistent with the move toward determinate sentencing, even though they do not bear that label. As the following review shows, these varied sentencing policies and reforms have become packaged together in an increasingly punitive approach to crime and punishment and are all implicated in the upsurge in prison populations.

Determinate Sentencing. One important move away from the rehabilitative ideal is determinate sentencing. It is designed to remove the discretion that parole boards traditionally exercised in determining the length of a prisoner's stay by either abolishing or sharply curtailing parole and requiring that judges set a specific term of sentence rather than a range of years. The specific term of sentence imposed by the judge can be adjusted only for limited and specified credits, such as detention time served while awaiting trial and "good time" served after sentencing. There are, however, several versions of determinate sentencing. In a legislative model of determinate sentencing, state legislatures attempt to exert control over judicial discretion by stipulating what prison terms will be. In a sentencing commission model, the legislature creates a special commission which is to create sentencing guidelines that judges are to follow (Griset, 1991: 40–47).

Given the varied forms that it takes, there has inevitably been disagreement in reports about the number of states adopting it, though it is clear that the period for adoption of this innovation began in 1975 and reached a crescendo in 1984 when the federal government adopted determinate sentencing through the Sentencing Reform Act. According to Marvell and Moody (1996: 108), ten states adopted determinate sentencing laws in the 1976–1984 period. Griset (1991: 210) notes that in one 1983 report, the Bureau of Justice Statistics identified 25 states as having determinate sentencing while in another report the same year, it identified nine states in that category.

Other states made at least partial moves in the direction of determinate sentencing. Pennsylvania, for example, replaced its indeterminate sentencing system in 1982 with a "quasi-indeterminate" system in which a sentencing commission sets guidelines, there is no earned time credit, inmates can't be paroled until they have served at least the minimum portion of the sentence (which can be no more than half of the statutory maximum), and the parole board determines, after this, when the inmate will be released (Benekos, 1992: 6) By 1991, legislators in Pennsylvania were pushing for an even more determinate model of sentencing that would more explicitly establish the length of sentence and release date at the time of sentencing and largely remove the parole board from the process (Benekos, 1992: 6).

There is some dispute about whether determinate sentencing is, in fact, implicated in the growth of prison populations. While a number of analysts argue that it is (Zimring and Hawkins, 1991; Rothman, 1995: 34), some research suggests a more complex picture. Based on a multiple time series analysis of the ten states with determinate sentencing, Marvell and Moody (1996: 119–20) find that only for Indiana is there evidence that a determinate sentencing law is linked to expansion of the prison population; in Minnesota and Washington, determinate sentencing laws appear to have reduced prison populations, and in other states determinate sentencing either shows no impact on prison population or shows mixed, non-robust results depending on the time lag used.

One reason for these complicated findings is that determinate sentencing laws in the states have been motivated by conflicting impulses, just as the intellectual challenge to the rehabilitative ideal and elite arguments about determinate sentencing have come from opposing quarters. In some states, determinate sentencing reflects a punitive reaction to the alleged leniency of parole boards, and carries expectations that the specific sentences in the determinate sentencing scheme will be lengthier than those imposed in an indeterminate sentencing regime; in other states, determinate sentencing has been motivated more by concerns about sentencing disparities in indeterminate sentencing systems—concerns that focus on inequitably long sentences for some offenders (Marvell and Moody, 1996: 110).

Yet another reason for the ongoing debate about the impact of determinate sentencing on prison populations is the problem of classification. A number of state sentencing laws are described as determinate sentencing systems by some authors but not others. For example, while Marvell and Moody (1996: 109) categorize only 10 states as having adopted determinate sentencing, Griset (1996: 129) argues that "about one-third of the states enacted determinate sentencing laws and abolished parole release . . ." This is in part due to differing interpretations of what elements of a sentencing law are required in order for it to be defined as a determinate sentencing system; it is also due to the fact that states adopting determinate sentencing schemes have tended to tinker with them, adding or subtracting features in ways that make categorization difficult. For example, some states, such as Colorado, adopted determinate sentencing and subsequently re-instituted parole.

Meanwhile, determinate sentencing has also been instituted at the federal level. The U.S. Sentencing Commission's guidelines took effect in November 1987 and are "the most controversial and disliked sentencing reform initiative in United States history" (Tonry, 1993: 131). Criminal justice practitioners dislike them on grounds that they take away too much judicial discretion while giving prosecutors more discretion, that they are overly complex, that they are inequitable because they take into consideration only characteristics of the offense and prior convictions, and that they are too punitive, leading to much larger proportions of convicts getting sent to prison (Tonry, 1993: 131–2). At the time of this article, there were "well-known and well-regarded guidelines systems in Minnesota, Washington, and Oregon" that are less complex (Tonry, 1993: 136).

Mandatory Minimums. Mandatory minimum sentences are legislatively prescribed sentences that stipulate fixed minimum sentences for particular crimes, thus removing judicial discretion on the lower end of the sentence range. While they are conceptually distinct from the sentencing guidelines that characterize determinate sentencing schemes, they are based upon the same hostility to indeterminate sentencing; and, as Rothman (1995: 34) argues, the determinate sentencing movement more generally has facilitated the emergence of mandatory minimum sentences as well: "Once the levying of punishment became more mechanical (consult the chart) than individual (tell me your life story), mandatory minimums assumed a surface logic." Wallace (1993: 9) argues that the wave of attention to determinate sentencing has been accompanied by waves of new mandatory minimum sentences, and that, while the former has involved long-term, rational deliberation, the latter is the result of angry, impulsive action. While some mandatory sentences have existed for a long time, broad-ranging ones really date from 1950s vintage legislation prescribing mandatory penalties for drug trafficking—an approach which was copied by a number of the states. Within a decade and a half, however, Congress had repealed most of these mandatory minimums for drug offenses on grounds that they were inappropriately severe and too rigid. But, at about the same time (1971) the push for sentencing guidelines began—an intellectual and political movement that was realized in 1984 when the Sentencing Reform Act was passed. But in that same legislation, there were new mandatory minimum sentences as well, such as the five-year one for possession of a gun while committing a crime of violence and a mandatory fifteen-year sentence for gun possession by anyone with three prior convictions for burglary or robbery (Wallace 1993: 9–10).

And there were more to come. Beginning in 1984, additional mandatory minimums came to be enacted regularly, and on a two-year pattern geared to the election cycle (Tonry, 1993: 141). For example, the 1986 Anti-Drug Abuse Act contained numerous drug-related mandatory minimums and the 1988 anti-drug legislation added many more, "including 20 years for 'continuing criminal enterprise' drug offenses or using a weapon during a violent or drug-related crime, and mandatory life for use of a machine gun or silencer or for any drug offender with three prior state or federal drug felony convictions . . . A few more mandatory minimums were approved in the 1990 crime bill, including 10 years for the Crime du Jour—being a savings-and-loan 'kingpin' " (Wallace, 1993: 10).

Quoting a count by Stephen Schulhofer from 1993, Rothman (1995: 34) indicates that there are "over one hundred such provisions in the federal code." And Rothman (1995: 42) notes that the 1994 federal crime bill added still more mandatory minimum sentences.

Truth in Sentencing. In addition to determinate sentencing schemes and mandatory minimums, the trend toward increased use of imprisonment includes "truth in sentencing" laws that require an offender to serve all or virtually all of the sentence, hence removing all or most of the possibility for early release on parole (Donziger,1996: 19–26) The federal government has thrown its support behind truth in sentencing laws by making the availability of most of the grant-in-aid money for prison construction that was authorized in 1994 legislation contingent upon states' adoption of such truth in sentencing laws. Under this mandate, "participating states must adopt a 'truth in sentencing' formula under which offenders must serve no less than 85% of sentences that are five years or longer; the states must also have in place a 'binding sentencing guidelines system in which the sentencing judges' discretion is limited to ensure greater uniformity in sentencing'" (Rothman, 1995: 42).

"Three Strikes" Laws. Finally, the move toward harsher and more deterministic sentences is epitomized by so-called three strikes laws which require the imposition of a life sentence for those convicted of a third felony, though states' "three strikes" laws vary in the type of felony that gets counted as a strike. California, which has one of the most extensive "three strikes" laws, includes nonviolent, less serious felonies in the strike count; and, in 1994, 70% of second- and third-strike cases handled in the state were in this category, leading some critics to complain that such laws "cast a very wide net, and most of the people caught in it do not require the kind of punishment the proposals mandate" (Donziger, 1996: 20).

As of 1994, roughly a third of the states had imposed some form of "three strike" law (Eckl, 1994: 17). And state legislatures are bracing for the expected fiscal impact of the laws. In Georgia, budget analysts have predicted that the fiscal impact of that state's "three strikes" law will be $2.5 million in fiscal year 1999 when the law is first implemented and $98.6 million by the year 2008 (Eckle, 1994: 17). More recent evidence suggests, however, that both the fiscal and the criminal justice impact of "three strikes" laws may be more limited, because many states that have adopted such statutes are not actually putting them to use. A study commissioned by the National Institute of Justice reported in 1996 that only nine federal offenders had been processed through to sentencing under the federal version of "three strikes," that in six states with such laws no one had received a "three strikes" conviction and that, in another five states, less than four such "three strikes" convictions had been rendered. The states that have adopted dramatic "three strikes" statutes already had persistent offender statutes on the books— statutes which provided judges with *discretionary* authority to give substantially increased penalties to repeat offenders. Prosecutors and judges are pursuing cases under this rubric, rather than the more dramatic, but less discretionary "three strikes" statutes (Butterfield, 1996: A1).

Public Opinion

The preceding section suggests that public policy with regard to imprisonment shifted dramatically in the United States beginning in the early 1970s. Rejecting the rehabilitative ideal and declining rates of imprisonment that characterized the decades prior to 1973, criminal justice policy took a more punitive turn, embracing the incapacitation ideal and a series of sentencing policies that have steadily increased the size of the prison population. But is this sea change in public policy in synch with public opinion?

As it turns out, there is considerable disagreement about this issue. Some have characterized the American public as having an insatiable appetite for punishment for criminals, while others have argued that the public is actually less punitive than policymakers believe (Selke, 1993: 1–3). As is so often the case, the contrasting conclusions arise in part from the fact that there are no consistently-asked public opinion poll questions to provide completely satisfying evidence about the public's wishes for more, less, or about the same levels of imprisonment, let alone the specific contingencies under which more incarceration is preferred. Analysts and commentators have had to make do with varied forms of second-best evidence to assess public opinion on this topic.

Figure 2-3 shows trends on three criminal justice-related polling questions from the National Opinion Research Center's General

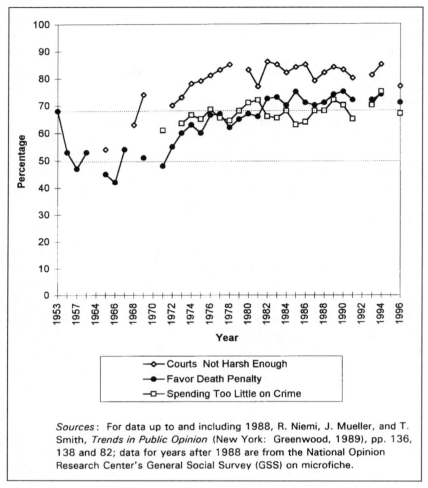

Figure 2-3. Public Opinion on Three Criminal Justice Issues

Social Survey that often serve as barometers for public opinion about crime and punishment: whether we are spending too much, too little, or about the right amount on crime; whether the courts are too harsh or not harsh enough, and whether the individual favors the death penalty. Of these three, the item on whether the courts are harsh enough comes closest to this chapter's concern with sentencing policies and incarceration rates. However, a look at all three items is useful. While there is no consistently-asked poll item on the public's preferences for spending on prisons specifically, the "spending on crime" item provides a global criminal justice spending preference item that parallels the spending preference items used in other chapters of this volume. And the three items, taken as a set, provide better triangulation than a single item on the question of whether or not public opinion has moved in a more punitive direction regarding criminals.

While there are some differences, responses to the three items generally track closely together. Figure 2-3 suggests that, since the mid-1960s, there really have been only two phases of public opinion about crime and punishment: an initial phase (1966 to approximately 1980) of sharply increasing concern and punitiveness, and a second phase (1980–1993) in which the high-water mark of public concern from the first phase is sustained, relatively unchanged. The death penalty series, which is available for a longer period of time, suggests that what is being characterized here as an "initial" phase may actually be a return to a quite punitive posture in the mid-1950s. But clearly, the 1966–1980 phase represents a tidal shift in public opinion away from a low-point in popular punitiveness that was registered in the mid-1960s. With respect to this initial phase, for example, support for the death penalty grew from 45% in 1965 to 67% in 1980, the percentage responding that we were spending too little on crime increased from 61% in 1971 to 72% in 1981 and the percentage believing that the courts are not harsh enough escalated from 54% in 1965 to 83% in 1980.

In the second phase, there is some instability from year to year, but by and large little evidence that the public is ready to back away from the thresholds of concern and punitiveness that were established by 1980. The high point of support for the death penalty, for example, was 75% (in 1985 and 1990) and the level of support for the death penalty stood at 74% in 1994 and 71% in 1996—hardly a dramatic change. The high point of concern that the courts are not harsh enough was 86% (in 1982) and the percentage registering this concern still stood at 85% in 1994. Only in 1996 is there a noticeable drop in the percentage responding this way. Even so, the vast majority (77%) of respondents still indicate a belief that the courts are not harsh enough. Only on the matter of spending on crime has public opinion occasionally slipped back below the two-thirds threshold of substantial majority support. But for most of the second phase, more than two-thirds of those polled wanted more spending.

When compared with the policy trends that have already been outlined (see Figure 2-2), this data on public opinion suggests an interesting sequence. In the 1960s and early 1970s, when the public was already quite concerned that courts were not harsh enough and public opinion with respect to criminal justice issues generally was trending in a more punitive direction, rates of imprisonment were stable or declining relative to crime (depending upon which indicator of crime is used). Clearly, in this period, policy was *unresponsive* to opinion. By the mid- to latter-1970s, however, policy had begun a dramatic shift in the direction of public opinion. Imprisonment rates moved noticeably upward, hand in hand with ever-increasing majorities responding that the courts were not harsh enough and that too little was being done about crime.

It is important to acknowledge this phase of apparent responsiveness, because some research conducted in the 1970s and early 1980s suggested a quite different conclusion. Based upon single-state data or a limited number of states, that research has suggested that policymakers and the general public at the time both held relatively liberal, rehabilitation-oriented attitudes, but that policymakers mistakenly perceived the public to be more punitive (Riley and Rose, 1980; Gottfredson and Taylor, 1987). These studies, occurring during the transformative period when the rehabilitative ideal was de-legitimized and public policy shifted accordingly, would seem to suggest a great irony—that policymakers, in an effort to be responsive to a mistaken perception of popular impatience with rehabilitation and growing punitiveness, unnecessarily moved correctional policy in a punitive direction. However, the evidence here from national sample data covering a more encompassing time period suggests that policymakers were far from mistaken in their perceptions of the growing punitiveness of public opinion.[1]

Admittedly, there is not universal agreement that the poll data used here properly measure punitiveness of attitudes toward crime and punishment. Innes (1993: 225–6), for example, argues that it is problematic to view the "courts not harsh enough" question as an indicator of a punitive public. He notes that: ". . . in several analyses, the relationship of the question on the harshness of the courts

to any of these measures—liberalism on civil liberties, racial attitudes, fear of crime, or importance of crime as a national problem—has been consistently very weak or nonexistent." Instead, Innes suggests that the question may be a better indicator of critique of the courts as an institution. But it is hard to imagine what kind of mass public critique of the courts could be suggested by these poll results other than the notion that too many offenders are getting off too easily, and that is precisely the sentiment that would seem to make the trend toward more incarceration consistent with public opinion on the matter. The fact that the "courts not harsh enough" question tracks so closely with support for the death penalty provides further grounds for taking the public's response to the item as reflecting a punitive trend. And the fact that individuals' responses on the "courts not harsh enough" question are only weakly related to their responses on liberalism or racial attitude measures hardly seems to constitute an indictment of the validity of the courts question as an indicator of punitiveness. Indeed, the overwhelming majorities that for over a decade have favored the death penalty and harsher courts would seem to suggest that, on the matter of the need for punitive policy for criminals, there is more of a national consensus than an ideological divide. In short, this critique of the extent to which these poll items reflect punitiveness is simply unsatisfying.

A more interesting body of evidence comes from experimental studies which suggest a discrepancy between some elements of the "get tough" turn in sentencing policy and public opinion. In contrast with the move to harsher, mandatory minimum sentencing and "three strikes"-style approaches, some experimental evidence shows that ordinary citizens would give sentences proportional to the severity of the repeat offender's prior crimes rather than giving recidivists a mandatory life prison sentence (Finkel, Maloney, Valbuena, and Groscup, 1996: 481). Such experimental results are in stark contrast with the widespread support for "three strikes" policies that were uncovered in a 1994 poll. That poll, asking whether the respondent was in favor of giving a sentence of life imprisonment to those convicted of a serious crime for the third time, netted almost 80% in favor (Roberts, 1996: 489).

Still other research has been offered to discount the validity of standard poll items such as the one used here to assess support for the death penalty. Some of that research shows that when respondents are given an alternative to the death penalty, such as a sentence of life without the possibility of parole, only about a quarter of the respondents in a late 1980s poll preferred the death penalty. Similarly, 1991–1992 poll data from another study shows that the public preferred life without prison and prison work programs to death sentences (McGarrell and Sandys, 1996: 502; 507). Results such as these have fueled the bonfire of criticism of traditionally used indicators (such as the "courts not harsh enough" item). Julian Roberts (1996: 491), for example, concludes that such indicators "misrepresent the true tenor of public reaction. When respondents are given a more fully articulated question, or additional information about specific cases, social reaction to sentence severity is rather different . . ." In domino-like fashion, the conclusion that recent criminal justice policy trends and incarceration rates are responsive to public opinion would fall if these criticisms of key indicators really undermine a punitive characterization of public opinion.

In a related vein, there has been debate about whether the general public shared policy elites' reworking of correctional philosophy away from the rehabilitative ideal. There is evidence from a series of Harris polls for Zimring and Hawkins' (1995: 9) argument that the credibility of the rehabilitative role of prisons had eroded substantially in this country by the late 1970s. When given the choice between "rehabilitation," "protection," or "punishment," as the proper main emphasis for prisons, 73% chose rehabilitation in 1970; but by 1978, that figure was 48% and by 1982 it was 44% (Mayer, 1992: 360). The conventional wisdom is that this, like the trends in poll data on the courts not being harsh enough, constitutes evidence of a punitive public.

However, a strong case has been made that this substantial decline in support for the priority of rehabilitation should not be construed as evidence that the public wants a punitive approach toward prisoners or rejects rehabilitation ideal (Innes, 1993: 228–9). Although there has been a dramatic decline in the percentage saying that "rehabilitation" should be the main emphasis of prisons, "rehabilitation" was still, even in the early 1980s, a more frequent choice than any of the other response categories (44% compared with 32% for "protection" and 19% for "punishment").

And there is other evidence of popular support for rehabilitation, in scattered poll items asked in years after the Harris item was discontinued. For example, a Gallup question asking whether it is more important for prisons to punish men for their crimes or "get them started 'on the right road'" had 59% of respondents choosing the latter, rehabilitation-oriented response in 1982 and 48% in 1989. Even higher support for rehabilitative approaches is found when the actual term rehabilitation is not used. For example, overwhelming majorities favor requirements that prisoners learn a skill or learn to read and write and favor educational and vocational training programs for prisons. Reviewing all this evidence, Innes (1993: 230) concludes that while the general public may exhibit punitive reactions to "criminals," they are not necessarily oriented primarily toward punishment for "prisoners" but instead want prisons to deal constructively and humanely with inmates.

These observations serve as an important refinement on the debate about "the punitive public." They might, for example, suggest that policies such as the re-institution of chain gangs are not necessarily consistent with public opinion nationally. While the rehabilitative ideal may have suffered relative to the goals of incapacitation, deterrence and retribution, there is still considerable support for reformative programs in prisons. They also suggest that public opinion on crime and prisons is more nuanced than global indicators such as the "courts not harsh enough" item can show. Under certain conditions, for certain kinds of offenders, mass public preferences may not fit the simplistic stereotype of "lock 'em up and throw away the key."

But to acknowledge all of this does not necessarily mean that the punitive turn evidenced in global indicators should be dismissed as bogus. One can be punitive in the sense of supporting expanded use of incarceration without totally rejecting the potential for prisons to rehabilitate. Indeed, while many citizens may want longer prison sentences simply for incapacitation or retribution, others may support the nation's skyrocketing trends in imprisonment because they believe that prisons are the place for rehabilitation of offenders. And to acknowledge that the public is not necessarily willing to impose the same, harsh sanctions on all offenders, regardless of circumstances, does not take away the fact that, when asked to generalize, the public's bottom line conclusion is that sentences need to be stiffer.

Hence, there does *seem* to be a mandate for the policy initiatives and resulting prison population growth that we have observed, i.e., a correspondence between opinion and policy in the period since 1973 that altered an earlier period in which there was a lack of correspondence between opinion and policy.[2]

Non-attitudes, or Ineffective Policies

Of course, there are other possibilities. For one, even if one agrees that the survey data taken as a whole does suggest a punitive public, that constellation of punitive public opinion results might be dismissed as a classic manifestation of non-attitudes. And if the expressed preferences for stiffer sentences are not real attitudes, then any correspondence between them and actual policy trends constitutes a coincidental or a meaningless linkage.

The "non-attitudes" perspective, based upon classic work by Converse (1964; 1970), rests upon several kinds of evidence. Instability of individuals' responses to political poll questions over time is one; a lack of logical coherence or ideological consistency among the opinions expressed by individuals is another. More recently, experimental evidence that people's preferences can be "moved around" in response to relatively minor changes in message content or context has contributed to the arsenal of evidence that the mass public has superficially held and relatively meaningless preferences rather than meaningful attitudes on political issues (Kuklinski and Hurley, 1996: 126).

Some of the research on public opinion on criminal offenders seems to fit comfortably into the "non-attitudes" tradition. For example, findings of a relatively weak link between political ideology and preferences for more or less stringent court sentences (Innes, 1993: 225–6) might be construed as the kind of ideologically unstructured thinking that is at the heart of the non-attitudes argument. There is also evidence that individuals' opinions about proper punishment for criminals can be readily "moved around." Irwin and Austin (1994), for example, note that the public image of criminal offenders is out of touch with the reality in that the crimes of those sent to prison are not as serious as the popular wisdom would suggest, nor are prisons populated primarily with hard-core career criminals. They also report that "when respondents are given scenarios that are closer to the actual crimes of most people sent to prison, the majority recommend some punishment other than imprisonment. A national poll taken by the Wirthlin Group in 1991 found that four out of five Americans favored a non-prison sentence for offenders who are not dangerous . . . In Alabama and Delaware, focus group analysis conducted by the Public Agenda Foundation found that when citizens were given detailed data about the crimes committed and the relative costs of various sanctions available to the courts, the public strongly supported non-prison sentences for inmates convicted of nonviolent crimes (who represent the vast majority of prisoners)" (Irwin and Austin, 1994: 61). But, of course, that is the kind of information that they suggest the public does not normally have at its disposal, nor is it the kind of information that political leaders use in their rhetoric about crime and punishment. Absent that kind of information, the mass public's response to poll questions about crime and incarceration presumably exemplifies non-attitudes—i.e., punitive but superficial reactions that would all-too-easily change if questions were framed differently or if fuller context were provided.

Because the analysis in this chapter rests largely upon examination of trends in aggregate public opinion rather than analyses of individual-level opinion change, a detailed assessment of arguments like those above will not be attempted. It is worth noting, however, that the equation of individual opinion change with non-attitudes is being questioned. Zaller and Feldman (1992) emphasize the complex array of "considerations" that can influence individuals' responses to poll questions on important public issues and acknowledge that high levels of instability in individual responses might reflect the fact that individuals have authentic but very multifaceted, nuanced attitudes. Other scholars have gone even further, suggesting that change in expressed preferences might result from the holding of real attitudes (Sniderman, Tetlock, and Tyler, 1993; see also Kuklinski and Hurley, 1996) that direct individuals to attend carefully to changes in circumstance or context.

Although analysts of opinion change at the individual level have only recently begun to rethink whether such change signals "nonattitudes," scholarship on public opinion in the aggregate is firmly grounded in interpretations of the rationality of opinion change in response to particular events or long-term social trends.

In their influential work, for example, Page and Shapiro (1992: 353–4) acknowledge that there are very large changes in public opinion on social issues, but interpret these changes in the collective policy preferences as meaningful if they can be shown to be sensibly and logically linked to social and economic trends or major public events, all of which can influence public opinion either directly or as mediated by "interpretations of experts, commentators and public officials, as reported in the mass media." From this point of view, then, public opinion should not necessarily be construed as an inauthentic collection of "non-attitudes" simply because it can be moved around by events and the persuasive efforts of elites.

When approached from this perspective, collective public opinion about crime and punishment in what this chapter has identified as an initial phase (early 1960s to late 1970s) would seem to escape the "non-attitudes" label. As we have seen, public opinion in that phase was trending in a noticeably more punitive direction, exhibiting substantial increases in the percentages of those wanting more crime spending, seeing the courts as not harsh enough, and favoring the death penalty. This is an understandable pattern at a time when crime rates were on the upswing—crime rates that were being reported in the media at a time when victimization surveys were not yet available to challenge the Uniform Crime Reports evidence.

Nor was the increasing crime rate the only relevant development. In the 1960s, demonstrations, protest, and civil disobedience stemming from the civil rights and anti-war movements were creating a climate that to some citizens appeared as a breakdown of law and order (Rosch, 1985: 27). A series of controversial Supreme Court decisions on the rights of the accused added fuel to the fire by appearing to limit the effectiveness of the criminal justice system. These developments, coupled with rising crime rates, suggest that in this early period attitudes about crime and punishment were grounded in the realities of convulsive historical events and disturbing social trends. There is not much room in this picture for a non-attitudes interpretation of collective public opinion.

This is not to argue, of course, that the public's views were necessarily "correct," nor that they were uninfluenced by the mobilizing efforts of political figures and other elites. In fact, the 1960s witnessed important efforts to mobilize public opinion on issues of

crime and punishment. Sensing the discontents that were generated by crime, civil disorder, and Court actions, the Republican
Party under the leadership of Barry Goldwater chose to pursue
"law and order" themes in the 1964 presidential election (Cronin,
Cronin, and Milakovich, 1981: 12–19). The Goldwater-Johnson show-
down in 1964 led to a particularly clear exposition of competing
views on issues of crime and punishment, with Goldwater pushing
for "get tough" policies and a less permissive court system while
Johnson emphasized the need for anti-poverty and education programs to fight the social problems that he defined as the root of
crime (Cronin, Cronin, and Milakovich, 1981: 24). Goldwater lost
the election, on issues unrelated to crime and punishment, and the
Johnson administration pursued a liberal approach to criminal
justice issues that, in retrospect, was substantially at odds with
public opinion.[3] But the highly politicized debate about crime and
punishment was far from over. Four years later, Republican candidate Richard Nixon would re-visit the debate, making "law and
order" the centerpiece of his successful Presidential campaign.[4] In
the course of these two campaigns, issues of crime and punishment
were elevated to the status of a visible, national debate. As Mayer
(1992: 19) notes, the conventional wisdom about the consequences
is quite correct: ". . . liberals got the worst of this debate, and . . . public opinion became increasingly outraged by horror stories about
brutal criminals set free on technicalities or through the ministra-
tions of misguided social workers" (Mayer, 1992: 19).

There are, in short, very good reasons for rejecting the notion
that public opinion about crime and punishment was a simple
manifestation of non-attitudes in the 1960s and much of the 1970s.
Fears may have been overblown, but attitudes rooted in deep-seated
fears are very real. And opinions may have been heavily influenced
by the rhetoric of two super-heated presidential campaigns. But
this in itself does not constitute grounds for a non-attitudes conclusion. In short, the movement of public opinion in a more punitive
direction during this period is fully consistent with important events,
trends, and mobilizing episodes.

But what of public opinion in the 1980s and 1990s? In this
phase, events and trends relevant to criminal justice issues had
changed considerably. Even the Uniform Crime Reports were showing a leveling in overall crime rate (and a noticeable dip in crime

from 1980–84), and victimization surveys were providing fuel for elites inclined to argue that crime rates were actually declining. The massive protests and social disorders of the 1960s and 1970s were a fading memory. Most important, public policy had moved dramatically toward "get tough" policies that were yielding very large prison populations.

If public opinion had reversed itself after several years of this change in direction we would have a perfect example of Goggin and Wlezien's (1993; Wlezien, 1995) thermostatic model of public opinion. But this is not the case. Even after nearly two decades in which the growth of imprisonment outpaced both population growth and crime, there is near consensus among the mass public that the courts are not harsh enough, and the other indicators of public opinion on criminal justice matters show negligible signs of moderating from a punitive stance. Public opinion polls, in this case, are showing no sign that the public recognizes the major escalation in incarceration that has been occurring nor any evidence that the public is ready for government to scale back on that escalation. "Although we have become more punitive than at any other time in our history, the public still believes that America is soft on crime and wants legislators and the courts to 'get tougher' on crime, especially in the face of what they believe are rising crime rates and a declining standard of living" (Irwin and Austin, 1994: 11). Rather than the thermostatic model of Wlezien, the sequence depicted here suggests a *broken thermostat*.

An alternative interpretation would hold that this is not a case of a broken thermostat so much as a thermostat with a very long lag cycle. Specifically, it might be argued that public opinion is taking a long time to moderate because changes in policy (here, incarceration) have not yielded the outcomes to which the public would actually respond (i.e., crime reduction). From this point of view, the thermostat is not broken; instead policy action has failed to significantly change the temperature.[5]

Such an interpretation applies a version of the thermostatic model to this policy domain that would not necessarily be applied in other domains—i.e., demonstrable evidence of policy impact or progress in ameliorating a problem before opinion is expected to adjust. This stronger version of the thermostatic model looks not just for a connection between policy *outputs* and opinion but for a connection between policy *impacts* and opinion. Perhaps in policy domains involving problems about which the public has more direct experience (or at least believes it has direct experience) this stronger version of the thermostatic model makes sense, while in other policy domains, such as defense spending, the public is necessarily more beholden to the interpretations of policymakers. That is, because citizens might not expect to be able to assess whether an increment in defense spending actually influences national security, public opinion in that domain responds to changes in defense spending but not national security.[6]

Although this alternative interpretation is intriguing, this chapter will remain with the original version of the broken thermostat. Shifting the grounds upon which public opinion should be expected to adjust introduces a host of new problems. For example, should we expect public opinion to react to *actual* crime rates or *perceptions* of crime? In addition to being strikingly insensitive to the dramatic movement in policy output (i.e., increased incarceration) that has been documented in this chapter, a comparison of Figures 2-1 and 2-3 suggests that the public has also been insensitive to downward movements in objective crime rates. Data from the victimization survey suggest a modest but long-term decline in crime rate; and the UCR data show a notable albeit temporary drop from 1980–1984. But there is no evidence of preference adjustment in response to either of these. To sustain the possibility that the thermostatic model is nevertheless at work here requires that we move away from objective measures of policy problem-solving to perceptions.

Indeed, the existence of official statistics showing a leveling or decline in crime rates does not necessarily translate into reassurance if high profile criminal activity, such as drug-related drive-by shootings and car-jacking, are galvanizing public attention. In general, statistical data on crime trends may not be as relevant as other evidence in shaping the public's responses to crime. This has been demonstrated in MacKuen and Coombe's (1981) research investigating the comparative impact of the media and of "objective conditions" such as crime rates on public opinion. That research shows that, in contrast with economic issues, on crime the public's agenda is "more sensitive to the symbolic representation of public life than to any measure of the world they were actually experiencing." (MacKuen and Coombs, 1981: 88). In the decade or more since, a considerable body of research has developed showing that the mass media are implicated in the public's fear of crime, although the relationship is mediated by a number of factors (Heath and Gilbert, 1996). Local television news coverage, which tends to emphasize more serious crimes, may be an especially important vehicle for enhancing popular conceptions of the seriousness of the crime problem (Gebotys, Roberts, and DasGupta, 1988) and framing the crime issue in ways that enhance punitiveness toward individual offenders while insulating government officials from accountability (Iyengar, 1996). Finally, crime stories simply get far more coverage in the United States than stories on sentencing policy and the status of the nation's prison population.

If the criterion for the thermostatic model then becomes adjustment of public opinion in response to *perceptions of policy impact*, then comparable diagnoses of the other policy issues covered in this volume would require both clear definitions of the relevant impacts to be expected and information about the public's perceptions of those impacts. For example, it would be necessary to determine whether the "problem" that welfare policy is trying to solve is poverty, lack of work motivation and skills, or the inappropriate personal choices of poor people; and it would be necessary to track changing perceptions of the poverty level, work efforts, or out-of-wedlock pregnancies by poor women. As the welfare example illustrates, neither agreement on the key goal of public policy nor data on the public's perceptions of the status of progress toward that goal are likely to be readily available across the policy topics examined in this volume.

Given these complications, the more straightforward version of the thermostatic model is applied here—i.e., policy is expected to change in response to changes in popular preferences, and popular preferences are expected to subsequently change in reaction to changes in policy. When, instead, preferences fail to adjust despite a substantial shift in policy, the interpretation is one of a broken thermostat. But the alternative interpretation that has just been explored reminds us that, at a minimum, there are a number of reasons why public opinion would fail to adjust. Failure of policy to have discernible impacts is one possible reason. Yet another possible reason is the continued mobilization of popular concern about the initial problem—i.e., news coverage and political rhetoric that sustains a heightened sense of the problem, regardless of either policy efforts or objective indicators of improvements in the problem condition. In the domain of crime and corrections, there is ample evidence that in addition to the media's role in sustaining the anxieties that fuel a punitive public mood about criminal justice issues, public officials have continued to stoke the issue. Richard Nixon's success in defining "law and order" as a national-level campaign issue provided a model that has been adopted repeatedly by presidential candidates in the 1980s and 1990s. This is evident in Figure 2-4, which shows the number of dates on which presidents and, in presidential election years, opposition party nominees for the presidency, mentioned crime or the closely related issue of drugs. During the mid- to latter-1970s, when criminal justice policies were beginning the dramatic turn toward determinate sentencing policies and heavier use of imprisonment that was documented earlier in this chapter, there is no evidence of election year cycling of crime and drug issues. Neither in presidential elections, nor in off-year elections in which presidents can serve as the most visible, national leader for their party do presidents or their opponents raise these issues more frequently than in the preceding, non-election year. But by the mid-1980s, an election year cycling of this issue is very apparent. In four of the six election years from 1984 to 1994, crime and drug issues are raised more frequently, and sometimes much more frequently, than they are in the immediately preceding year.

And the data in Figure 2-4 is only a glimpse at a phenomenon that is presumably replicated for elected officials more generally. It would not be surprising if one were to find a similar election year cycling of this issue in Congressional races, gubernatorial campaigns, contests for state legislative seats, and many other venues. It is as though there is a rhetorical arms race from which politicians do not believe they can stand down. Nor is the substantive content of the remarks made when crime and drug issues are raised dominated by softer, liberal themes of social programming for crime prevention. In the contemporary era, politicians of both parties appear to assume that a "get tough" approach to crime is a prerequisite for a successful campaign. This is epitomized by President Clinton's successful appropriation of the crime issue in the 1996 election. Clinton's support for expanding the death penalty and for

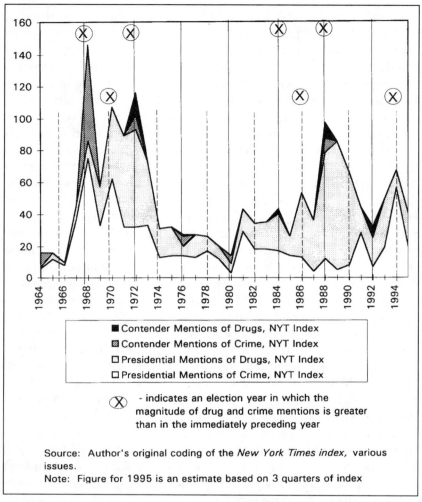

Figure 2-4. Crime and Drug Issue Mobilization—The President and Presidential Contenders

major new spending programs for both prison construction and federal aid for localities to hire new police officers translated into a partisan draw on the crime issue in 1996 (Johnston and Weiner, 1996).

It is important to note that this political arms race may even enhance the impact of media coverage on public opinion. Zaller (1996: 54) argues that, in contrast with the conventional wisdom that the media have "minimal effects" on public opinion, massive media effects can be expected if there is media and elite consensus about a policy. There may not be full consensus among all elites. Indeed, the academic literature on crime and punishment issues is replete with strident debate on the matter. But the political arms race provides something like a consensus of political elites that may serve to enhance the impact of the media in conveying messages about the pervasiveness of crime and the need for strong measures against criminals.

Thus, in the period when the thermostatic model would have required public opinion to adjust downward from its punitive high-water mark, it has instead been sustained at that level by a barrage of crime stories in the media and repeated mobilization by elected officials of both parties. This is no more a non-attitudes scenario than was the case in the first phase of public opinion. Very real concerns underlie the policy preferences exhibited by the public, even if, as some critics would argue, those concerns are over-blown, pushed by the fear-mongering of politicians, and insensitive to the massive changes in prison population that have already occurred. Popular attitudes about crime and punishment might be unfounded, but this is not the same as saying that they are non-attitudes. In the light of all this, we can diagnose the policy history of crime and corrections in the U.S. as constituting a broken thermostat sequence, while at the same time appreciating the powerful reasons for the continuing, punitive stance of public opinion.

On the Possibility of Coincidental Responsiveness

This chapter has argued that, after a period of non-responsiveness to public opinion about crime and punishment issues in the 1960s, public policy turned toward a variety of criminal justice policies, particularly involving sentencing, that are much more consistent with the highly punitive tenor of public opinion. Furthermore, although this policy shift has generated huge consequences in terms of exploding prison populations and costs, public opinion has not noticeably moderated from its punitive stance. Despite the budgetary consequences and other strains presented by this situation, elected officials have continued to fan the flames of popular concern with mobilizing efforts keyed to the election cycle. In the contemporary period, government is locked into a pattern of continued

ensuing adjustments in public opinion, policy has been locked into an incarceration-oriented mode. The special status of crime as an election issue, along with the media's role in keeping the public concerned about crime and criminals, help to ensure that public opinion does not moderate from the highly punitive consensus where it has stood for a decade and a half. And officials' responsiveness to that opinion is reinforced by interest group pressures from a corrections-commercial complex. In short, opinion and policy on crime and punishment exemplifies a broken thermostat rather than the thermostatic model suggested by Goggin and Wlezien (1993; and see Wlezien, 1995).

This broken thermostat situation is troubling. It means that the consequences of policy action are ignored. The public and its representatives can adopt a "lock 'em up and throw away the key" approach without immediately having to deal with the consequences. For example, only when overcrowding got really bad did a number of states attempt to deal with it by introducing policy that would prevent the addition of new mandatory minimums or new prison terms without a linkage back to capacity or cost issues (see Gottfredson and McConville, 1987). Instead, the criminal justice system, with its many interlocking parts, adapts as best it can. Meanwhile, the public's capacity to share in any meaningful "policy learning" is short-circuited.

3

Affirmative Action

A Downsian Sequence

Introduction

Chapter One documented the possibility that the development of public policy might be subject to a variety of path dependencies whereby decisions at a critical point in history send policy off onto a relatively durable track, even if that track is in some sense sub-optimal. Of particular concern for this analysis is the possibility that public policy may become locked into a track that takes it beyond the limits that are acceptable to mass preferences. In this regard, Baumgartner and Jones (1993) have used Anthony Downs's (1972) ideas of issue attention cycles to describe a "Downsian mobilization" in which an initial period of popular concern about an issue is followed by a dramatic fall-off in public interest in the problem. Extending this idea, we might expect cycles of policy development that begin with substantial responsiveness to public opinion (during the phase of frenzied popular concern with a problem), only to be replaced by a sustained period of discrepancy between public opinion and policy as the institutional sub-system responsible for policy implementation makes key decisions that move policy away from the initial consensus. In this volume, such a sequence of initial policy responsiveness followed by a sustained period of non-responsiveness is referred to as a Downsian sequence. The contention of this chapter is that affirmative action constitutes an example of just such a Downsian sequence. The most recent developments in this policy history, however, suggest that, while it is sustained, a Downsian sequence is not necessarily permanent. The conjunction of exogenous shocks to the policy sub-system can overcome the institutional inertia that yielded the sustained period of policy non-responsiveness. There are hints in recent developments that such a major divergence from the Downsian sequence into which affirmative action has been locked may be afoot.

Demonstrating a Downsian sequence for affirmative action requires that we define affirmative action in a way that includes a host of formal and informal policies that provide compensatory preferences to racial minorities in the workplace and in college placement. If there is evidence of stable, long-standing opposition to such preferences on the part of large majorities of the American public,[1] the non-responsiveness phase that is featured in the Downsian sequence can be demonstrated. This chapter will provide evidence of such long-standing public opposition to preferences and offer a policy history that reveals the emergence and surprising longevity of a national policy commitment to affirmative action in the sense of preferences.

Whether an opinion-policy discrepancy of this kind is warranted in light of the nation's racial history, its continuing problems of unequal racial opportunity, and the unwillingness of the majority to accept extraordinary efforts to overcome these problems, or whether the opinion-policy discrepancy constitutes a failure of democracy are core questions in contemporary debates on this issue. They are not, however, the core questions for this chapter. Rather, the purpose of this chapter is to empirically explore the political dynamics of this important case. How did policy come to be unhinged from opinion? And how has non-responsiveness been sustained, through very different presidential administrations and other important political changes? Does this case exemplify arguments about the likelihood of opinion-policy disjunction when policy is developed largely in institutional venues such as the courts and administrative agencies? The importance of the Equal Employment Opportunity Commission (EEOC) and the Supreme Court in shaping affirmative action policy would seem to suggest this. But, as this chapter will show, there is much more to the story than this. The nature of business accommodation to affirmative action policy, the special moral power of the civil rights lobby, and the political utility of affirmative action as a "wedge issue" are part of the story as well.

Affirmative action encompasses women and the disabled as well as racial minorities. However, this chapter will focus on the racial dimensions of the policy history and on public reaction to affirmative action with regard to racial minorities. This is because crucial moments of policy-making concerning affirmative action involved the dynamics of racial politics, not gender issues. In fact, women and minority groups other than African-Americans have, in many ways, been "conspicuously absent in the affirmative action debate" (Skrentny, 1996: 15). Likewise, the chapter focuses primarily upon affirmative action in the workplace, although affirmative action programs in university admissions have at times moved to the forefront of the debate. The roots of affirmative action, however, lie in the quest for equal employment opportunity. And while policy developments concerning education and even voting rights have sometimes had implications for affirmative action in the workplace, these various spheres of action represent distinctive contexts with different policy histories.

The ferocity of contemporary debates suggests that an explosive new episode in the history of affirmative action in the workplace is upon us. Empirical inquiry can easily be lost in the thunder of this ongoing controversy. In documenting the reasons for long-term discrepancy between opinion and policy,[2] however, such an inquiry may provide the best basis for interpreting the potential for change.

Public Opinion on Affirmative Action and Discrimination

The anchor for this chapter's interpretation of affirmative action policy and opinion is evidence of sustained popular opposition to racial preferences. Affirmative action policy is, of course, rooted in a longer, broader history of the development of civil rights protections. For this reason, most treatments of the topic acknowledge the virtual sea change that has occurred from the 1940s to the 1960s in general attitudes toward racial discrimination, culminating in near-unanimity by 1972 that racial discrimination in employment is wrong. These results come from National Opinion Research Center polls asking "Do you think that Negroes/blacks should have as good a chance as white people to get any kind of job, or do you think white people should have the first chance at any kind of job?" In 1944, 52% of respondents thought whites should have the first chance at jobs; by 1972, only 3% espoused this position (Mayer, 1992: 22 and 366).

Paul Burstein (1985: 51) has noted not only this and other evidence of a major shift in public opinion towards racial tolerance and egalitarianism in the pre-1965 period, but also a strong statistical connection between this opinion change and growing Congressional support for equal employment opportunity (EEO) legislation. Ultimately, he concludes that both the initial passage of equal employment opportunity legislation in the Civil Rights Act of 1964, and the strengthening of equal employment opportunity law in 1972 amendments were direct, albeit somewhat delayed responses to the sea change in public opinion: "It would thus be fair to say that Congress responded strongly, perhaps primarily, to the public's preferences when it considered EEO legislation . . . as soon as it was clear that the public favored EEO, was increasingly favorable to legislation on the subject, and felt strongly about it, Congress adopted legislation that was a breakthrough in the struggle for equality of opportunity" (Burstein, 1985: 67).

Affirmative action thus grew out of a significant episode of *policy responsiveness concerning employment discrimination*. For several reasons, however, an analysis of "affirmative action" policy *per se* must focus primarily on policy and public opinion in the post-1964 period. First, as later sections of this chapter will show, affirmative action in the contemporary sense of preferences for women and minorities did not emerge as a distinctive policy until several years after the passage of the Civil Rights Act of 1964. In fact, because that legislation was enacted amidst explicit discussion about quotas and preferential treatment and included an explicit provision that the act *not* be interpreted as requiring preferential treatment on account of racial imbalance, it would not be reasonable to interpret its passage as legislative endorsement of a policy of special preferences for women and minorities.

Second, there is no systematic, national polling data to tell us what public opinion was concerning affirmative action in the pre-1960s period, nor even in the 1960s. While questions about equality and job discrimination were asked, as noted above, questions about preferential treatment of minorities to compensate for discrimination were only rarely and sporadically asked, despite controversy over the subject of quotas and preferences in the development of the Civil Rights Act of 1964 (Belz, 1991: 24). Presumably this was because the meaning of affirmative action as it would later be implemented by EEOC was not yet widely evident. Isolated instances in which poll questions on affirmative action were asked in the 1960s suggest that, even in this early period, the general public was highly opposed to preferential treatment. For example, in a June 1966 Harris Poll survey, respondents were asked: "Some people suggested that Negroes, who are 10 percent of the population, should be guaranteed 10 percent of the jobs that are available. Would you favor or oppose such a quota system?" Only 15.1% of white respondents favored the quota system.

For these reasons, this chapter takes issue with interpretations which stress the popularity of affirmative action in its earliest years. Williams (1996: 249), for example, suggests that affirmative action was a popular policy throughout the Johnson and Nixon years, and that it became controversial and divisive only with the souring of the economy in the latter 1970s and later with the Reagan and Bush administrations' efforts to capitalize on the natural inclination of the working classes to "turn against each other on racial grounds rather than turn against capital." While economic undercurrents and the activities of Republican administrations may have fanned the fires of controversy over affirmative action, claims about the popularity of affirmative action in the Johnson and Nixon administrations are meaningful only if "affirmative action" is conflated with the much broader concepts of "civil rights" or "equal opportunity" for minorities.[2] There are no available poll data to support the contention that affirmative action in the sense of special preferences for minorities enjoyed such popularity.

By contrast, John David Skrentny (1996) offers a compelling case (based upon evidence other than poll data) that a color-blind model of racial justice rather than a preference-based model defined the limits of acceptable action and rhetoric during this initial period. A color-blind approach, which defined active discrimination based on race as the problem and the elimination of all racial considerations as the solution, was consistent with the abstract individualism and equal opportunity principles of American political culture. And while those principles have occasionally been supplanted by competing principles, such as the consensus surrounding outright preferences for veterans, the American cultural experience with race has ruled out the legitimacy of racial preferences not so much because they involve preferences but because they would give racial minorities a morally deserving status that is not consistent with prevailing cultural values. At least for the white majority in America, a preference-based approach to remedying the problems of inequality of job opportunity for racial minorities is not a legitimate option. Acknowledging this political reality, black civil rights leaders almost universally adopted the rhetoric of a color-blind approach and astutely avoided the language of racially targeted preferences.

But, as the following policy history will show, developments in the early 1970s nevertheless moved equal employment opportunity policy away from a color-blind approach and institutionalized affirmative action around a preference-based approach, giving affirmative action a controversial status that propelled it into public opinion polls. From its first appearance there until the present, that public opinion data show overwhelming and sustained opposition to special preferences as a remedy for problems of racial discrimination.

The earliest available repeated national polling data that asks specifically about affirmative action in the sense of racial preferences is from the latter 1970s. The Gallup Poll has periodically since 1977 asked the following question: "Some people say that to make up for past discrimination, women and members of minority groups should be given preferential treatment in getting jobs and places in college. Others say that ability, as determined by test scores, should be the main consideration. Which point of view comes closest to how you feel on this matter?" Only 10 or 11% of respondents chose "preferential treatment" as their point of view when the question was asked in 1977, 1980, 1984, 1989, and 1991. In May of 1976, Harris repeated the poll question (cited earlier) concerning a quota system guaranteeing 10% of jobs for Negroes. Of whites responding, 20.4% were in favor; 50.5% of black respondents were in favor. In 1991 and 1992, NBC asked a question similar to Gallup's repeated question on "special preferences" to "make up for past discrimination" but focused only on "blacks and other minorities" without mentioning women. Only 18% of 1991 respondents and 15% of 1992 respondents indicated that blacks and other minorities should receive special preference in hiring to make up for past inequalities. In a 1994 Associated Press poll, 12% of whites and 46% of blacks expressed support for such hiring preferences in a virtually identically worded question.

It is generally known that tradeoff questions produce different responses than non-choice, Likert-type question. Hence, it is not surprising that other, Likert-type poll questions that have been used to tap respondents' reactions to affirmative action have elicited levels of support that are higher than those elicited by the Gallup item's "stark contrast between preferences and ability." Nevertheless, levels of support are still quite low. A National Election Studies item, for example, asks how strongly the respondent agrees or disagrees with the following statement: "Irish, Italians, Jewish and many other minorities overcame prejudice and worked their way up. Blacks should do the same without any special favors." In the five years between 1986 and 1994 in which this question was asked, the percentage giving a pro-affirmative action response (i.e., "disagree somewhat" or "disagree strongly") has never exceeded 24% and usually was less than 20% (Steeh and Krysan, 1996: 130–131). Even when the poll question avoids any potentially unfavorable comparisons with other ethnic groups *and* asks about the giving of preferences in hiring and promotion "where there has been job discrimination against blacks in the past," substantially less than a majority of respondents favor the giving of preferences to blacks. On six out of the 11 occasions on which the CBS/*New York Times* poll asked this question (July 1987, 1990, 1991, 1993, February 1995, and April 1995) no more than one-third of respondents favored preferences, and on all but two of the occasions no more than 38% favored preferences (Steeh and Krysan, 1996 145).[3]

Responses to yet another type of survey question suggest that negligible support for "hiring preferences" for minorities is partly rooted in perceptions that such preferences amount to quotas. For example, the Harris Poll has repeatedly asked: "Do you favor or oppose affirmative action for women and minorities in employment, *provided there are no rigid quotas*" [author's emphasis]. From 67 to 69% of respondents favored affirmative action four of the five times this question was asked between 1978 and 1984 (61% favored in

1983). Clearly, strong opposition to quotas is the key to the difference between these results and those outlined above. The reassuring language about quotas in the Harris Poll item generates much more favorable responses while the "racial preferences" language in the other poll questions elicits very widespread opposition to affirmative action.

The evidence suggests that, whether one agrees or disagrees with the majority public's distaste for preference-based affirmative action, that distaste cannot be dismissed as a manifestation of non-attitudes. For one thing, there have been neither erratic changes in aggregate opinion on the matter over time, nor glaring instances in which aggregate opinion failed to change in response to obviously relevant events. Once affirmative action, in the sense of race-conscious, preference-based remedies was set in place as the policy direction for equal employment opportunity (as documented in the policy history below), readings of public opinion registered opposition; and that opposition has been sustained just as the policy direction has been sustained.

Individual-level research also supports the conclusion that public opinion on affirmative action is not a matter of non-attitudes. In their study of responses to a variety of racial issues, Sniderman and Piazza (1993) explicitly consider the matter of non-attitudes and acknowledge that surprising numbers of individuals do change their positions on some racial issues when they are presented with counter-arguments. As we noted in Chapter One, such change does not necessarily reveal non-attitudes. But as further evidence for a non-attitudes interpretation of this change, Sniderman and Piazza (1993: 155) show that those who switched positions on racial issues "tended to be people who hadn't acted on a relevant reason for taking it in the first place"—i.e., switchers' initial view on racial issues was not linked to ideological orientation or feelings about blacks. But, the important thing for our purposes is how different affirmative action is from the other racial issues examined in the study (such as government spending to help blacks). Sniderman and Piazza (1993: 145) find that "The positions white Americans take on affirmative action are markedly firmer, less malleable than the positions they take on more traditional forms of government assistance for the disadvantaged." Unfortunately for our purposes, the affirmative action question that respondents were asked in the

Sniderman and Piazza experiment refer to college admissions rather than employment.[4] But their findings are at least suggestive that people's responses with respect to race-conscious employment policies are far from non-attitudes—that instead the "question of quotas and preferential treatment engages people's fundamental beliefs about fairness" (Sniderman and Piazza, 1993: 148–149).

Still other research supports the interpretation that the majority's negative reaction to affirmative action is not simply a matter of non-attitudes. In addition to instability in responses, a non-attitudes interpretation suggests that individuals are taking a position on affirmative action even though they do not have a "consistent reason for taking the position" (Sniderman and Piazza, 1993: 155–156). But Kluegel and Smith (1986) have found that whites in America are opposed to affirmative action (in the sense of job preferences for minorities) because they are not convinced that racial minorities now face real obstacles to economic opportunity. Kluegel and Smith (1986: 185) take note of the fact that "declining traditional racial prejudice has not been accompanied by increasing recognition of structural limits to blacks' opportunity. To the contrary . . . the white American public in general believes that opportunity for blacks is less restricted now than it has been in the past." In an attempt to explain the determinants of whites' attitudes toward affirmative action, their analysis of 1980 survey data (1986: 209) concludes that "beliefs about how the American stratification order does work significantly affect whites' support for these programs net of the influence of economic self-interest and racial affect . . . Opposition to all programs in part rests in the tendency of most Americans to deny the importance of structural causes of poverty." Similarly, in their work on the topic, Sniderman and Carmines (1997) find a variety of reasons for white opposition to affirmative action—reasons ranging from blatant racial intolerance to beliefs that affirmative action is not justified by mere under-representation of minorities. While these beliefs may be neither accurate nor laudable, they nevertheless entail the kind of consistency that means a non-attitudes interpretation is inappropriate for this policy topic.

In sum, there seems to be a long-standing consensus in the United States that job discrimination is wrong. But there is also a long-standing hostility to explicit racial preferences and quotas to remedy job discrimination. Unless survey questions provide strong reassurances that affirmative action does not mean such racial preferences and quotas, there are very high levels of opposition to affirmative action—opposition that is firmly rooted and *not* a manifestation of non-attitudes. And these high levels of opposition are sustained across the entirety of the nation's experience with affirmative action.

The Development of Affirmative Action Policy

Phase #1: The Foundation Period (1940s–1964)

As public opinion moved from the 1940s to the 1960s in the direction of greater support for governmental action to remedy the effects of racial discrimination in the workplace, public policy followed suit—first in quite limited ways, and then in landmark legislation. In the 1940s and 1950s, limited action came at the state level in the form of state fair employment practice commissions that made it illegal to discriminate on the basis of race, color, religion, or national origin. These commissions, established in 26 states, investigated complaints of discrimination and used conciliation, public hearings, cease and desist orders, and reinstatement orders as remedies when claims of discrimination were founded. The difficulty of proving discrimination to the satisfaction of such commissions, coupled with their general orientation toward prevention rather than punishment, relegated these state commissions to marginal status in the unfolding civil rights era (Belz, 1991: 14–15; Skrentny, 1996: 29 and 118–19).

A more proactive approach to the problem of job discrimination and the first use of the term "affirmative action" emerged from the White House in the Kennedy administration. In 1961, Kennedy issued Executive Order #10925 which called for "affirmative action" on the part of federal contractors to insure that individuals are treated without regard to race, creed, color, or national origin. As implemented by the Presidents' Committee on Equal Employment Opportunity, this policy relied heavily on the use of statistical evidence of minority under-representation in the workforce as the basis for obtaining voluntary agreements from private contractors to remedy the under-representation. Looming over those voluntary agreements, of course, was the implied threat of contract cancellation or ineligibility for contracts (Belz, 1991: 19). While this executive order was narrow and limited in the sense that it was directed only at action that could be controlled through the federal contract compliance process, it set a significant precedent.

But although the seeds of a more forceful, proactive approach to affirmative action were planted in the implementation of this executive order, this foundation period for affirmative action policy actually culminated in major legislation that ostensibly put the full weight of federal policy behind a more conventional approach. As Burstein (1985: 128) has argued, Title VII of the Civil Rights Act of 1964 was conservative and traditional in important ways: "Title 7 created enforcement procedures closely modeled on those of other statutes, oriented toward protecting the rights of the accused, voluntary conciliation, case-by-case resolution, and heavy reliance on prosecution by individual victims of discrimination." This conventional approach is not surprising, given the way in which equal employment opportunity legislation was developed. In a fashion that perfectly epitomizes Polsby's (1984) conceptualization of "incubated" policy innovation, equal employment opportunity gestated in Congress for over 25 years, gradually accumulating support around proposals modeled on an EEO bill drafted in the mid-1940s and on principles and ideas already embodied in the National Labor Relations Act and New York State's evolving equal employment opportunity law (Burstein, 1985: 37).

The result was legislation that was path-breaking in the sense of establishing the federal government's presence in the private labor market as an anti-discrimination regulator. But the tools for achieving the purpose were not radically new (Burstein, 1985: 37). As enacted in 1964, Title VII of the Civil Rights Act made it unlawful for an employer or labor union (above the size of 25 employees or members) to discriminate in the terms and conditions of employment against an individual because of his or her race, color, religion, sex, or national origin. Enforcement of the act was placed in the hands of a newly created Equal Employment Opportunity Commission (EEOC), which was empowered to investigate individuals' complaints of discrimination and, if reasonable grounds for the complaint were found, to use informal methods of conciliation to try to change the discriminatory practice. The EEOC was not empowered to take the employer or union to court if conciliation failed; instead, the legislation left this to the individual complainant. However, the act stipulated that a court finding an employer or union guilty of discrimination could issue a cease and desist order directed at the discriminatory practice and could demand appropriate remedies, including reinstatement on the job or as a union member, or the hiring of the complainant, either with or without back pay. While litigation was thus generally left to the individual complainant, Title VII did empower the Attorney General to initiate civil suits against employers or unions "engaged in a pattern or practice of denying rights secured by the act" (Belz, 1991: 26).

The passage of the Civil Rights Act of 1964 may be viewed as the culmination of a long foundation period in U.S. policy history concerning job discrimination and equal employment opportunity. During that period, the seeds of the controversy over a race-conscious, preference-based approach to employment opportunity were planted, in part through the approach to affirmative action that was being pursued in the federal contract compliance venue and in part through the debate surrounding passage of the Civil Rights Act of 1964. But in order to get support for passage of that legislation, Title VII was crafted in a way that specifically directs policy away from race-based, preferential treatment and toward a color-blind model of policy for equal employment opportunity. (Belz, 1991: 26). This is specified in section 703 (j) of the Civil Rights Act of 1964, which stipulates:

Nothing contained in this title shall be interpreted to require any employer . . . to grant preferential treatment to any individual or group on account of an imbalance which may exist with respect to the total number or percentage of persons of any race . . . employed by any employer . . . in comparison with the total number or percentage of persons of such race . . . in any community . . . or in the available workforce in any community (as quoted in Skrentny, 1996: 121).

The language of section 703 (j) appears to clearly proscribe the sorts of statistically-based, racial group-oriented, preferential hiring strategies that would eventually be promulgated as affirmative action policy-making unfolded. But at least in 1964, public policy formally institutionalized a color-blind approach.

The foundation period for affirmative action policy was thus responsive to public opinion in the sense of reflecting the growing national consensus about equal employment opportunity. Only the less-visible policy surrounding Executive Order #10925 moved in a proactive direction that laid the groundwork for a preference-based approach that later polls would show to be well outside the mainstream of popular sentiment.

Phase #2: The Institutionalization of Non-Responsive Policy (1965–1980)

In the 1965–1980 period, Congress was not completely silent on the matter of equal employment opportunity policy. It did amend Title VII of the 1964 Civil Rights Act with its passage of the Equal Employment Opportunity Act of 1972—legislation that strengthened the EEOC by giving it the power to file suit against offending employers. And in the passage of that legislation, Congress rejected further anti-quota amendments. But apart from this fine-tuning activity, Congress was relatively disengaged from affirmative action policy developments in this period. Instead, decisions in three other institutional venues moved affirmative action in a new and more controversial policy direction. In the bureaucratic venue, the Office of Federal Contract Compliance, the Equal Employment Opportunity Commission and the Civil Service Commission moved toward reliance upon statistical evidence and group preference-based remedies, including mandatory goals and timetables. In the White House, President Johnson's Executive Order #11246 and the Nixon administration's reaffirmation of the Philadelphia Plan for affirmative action in the construction industry also moved policy in the race-conscious, preference-based direction. In the judicial venue, the Supreme Court's 1971 decision in *Griggs v. Duke Power* legitimated a disparate impact theory of discrimination that provided important support for the new approach to affirmative action.

In the area of affirmative action for federal contractors, President Johnson issued Executive Order #11246 in 1965. That executive order renewed the call for federal contractors to "take affirmative action to ensure equality of employment opportunity without regard to race, religion and national origin" and created, within the Labor Department, an Office of Federal Contract Compliance (OFCC) to administer the mandate (White House, 1995a). The OFCC required would-be contractors to submit an affirmative action plan to be reviewed prior to the awarding of a contract. Such plans had to provide numerical information about minority representation in the contractor's workforce, and if under-utilization were evident, had to include specific "goals and timetables" for achieving equal employment opportunity.

By 1967, the OFCC was focusing specifically upon the construction industry where there had been longstanding evidence of job discrimination and union resistance to equal employment opportunity. In this battle with the construction trades, the OFCC made use of even more overtly quota-like policy tools. Federal contractors in Cleveland and Philadelphia were subjected to requirements that they submit affirmative action plans incorporating manning tables that specified how many minority employees would be hired in each area of employment; and, in contrast with an approach to affirmative action that emphasizes outreach and effort toward equal opportunity, this "Philadelphia Plan," as it came to be known, demanded results in the form of numerical evidence of minority representation (Belz, 1991: 32).

Given the controversy that these quota-like arrangements evoked, one might have thought that the Republicans would exploit the issue and that a redirection in policy would follow with Nixon's assumption of the White House in 1969. But Nixon won office in 1968 on a low-key, centrist campaign that deliberately avoided taking a strong stand on civil rights (Graham, 1990: 302–4). More generally, Nixon adopted an approach to affirmative action that was geared toward short-term, tactical political advantage (Graham, 1990: 302) and based on the same group-oriented premises that had moved the OFCC toward group preferences. In the blunt language of contemporary politics, Nixon saw the possibilities of using racial hiring targets in the construction industry as a wedge issue that could work to his advantage. By making a controversial gesture in support of minority hiring in the construction trades unions, Nixon could foment "discontent and factional rivalry in two of the liberal establishment's major supporters. The Democratic leadership, formerly committed to a color-blind approach, would thus have to put one group over the other on a controversial issue" (Skrentny, 1996: 182). And so, in 1969, Nixon "suddenly revived the moribund Philadelphia Plan" and, in the face of efforts by conservative Republicans and southern Democrats to remove its racial job quotas, "the Nixon administration hurled the full force of its lobbying muscle against them" (Graham, 1990: 321).

Meanwhile, implementation of equal employment opportunity policy with respect to federal government employment had been placed in the hands of the Civil Service Commission in 1965. In contrast with the proactive, statistics-based approach that the EEOC was developing in dealing with the private sector, critics claimed that the Civil Service Commission (CSC) was not aggressive enough and by the late 1960s some proponents were pushing to have responsibility moved into the hands of the EEOC. By 1970, criticism of the CSC had built to the point that legislation transferring its federal equal employment opportunity policy to the EEOC was introduced in Congress (Kellough, 1989: 20).

But in 1971, in a memorandum from the chair of the Civil Service Commission, federal agencies were empowered to use numerical goals and timetables as a tool for affirmative action in federal employment. This administrative policy move, which was sustained throughout the next two decades, propelled affirmative action into the more obvious and aggressive stance that makes it controversial. Proponents argued, however, that it was necessary because simple nondiscrimination approaches would not rapidly remove the consequences of prior discrimination, because the federal government needed to serve as a model employer in this regard, and because the federal government's workforce needed to be representative of those it served (Kellough, 1989: 3–4). In Rosenbloom's analysis (1977), CSC's adoption of "goals and timetables" was a way of showing its aggressiveness and preventing its loss of jurisdiction over the program to the EEOC. Nevertheless, perceptions that the CSC was not aggressive enough in its pursuit of affirmative action caused it to lose its responsibility for the EEO program in federal government employment to the EEOC, as part of a major reorganization in 1979. The EEOC then mandated that the EEO plans of federal agencies incorporate numerical goals and timetables whenever statistical analysis of workforce data showed that there was under-representation of minorities (Kellough, 1989: 21).

In addition to these important developments in bureaucratic agencies and the White House, this period included a significant Supreme Court ruling on employment discrimination. In *Griggs v. Duke Power Co.*, black employees at Duke Power Company had claimed that the company's reliance upon qualifications such as a high school diploma and a passing grade on an objective test were discriminatory because they were not essential standards for business performance, yet systematically screened blacks out of hiring and promotions. The Court, ruling unanimously in favor of the plaintiffs, stipulated that employers were restricted to bona fide occupational qualifications—that is, to tests or other requirements that were genuinely necessary and demonstrably linked to successful job performance. The ruling thus made it illegal for a company to use employment criteria that happened to systematically work to the detriment of minorities if that employment criteria could not be shown to be a true business necessity.

In his interpretation of this ruling, Belz (1991: 51) argues that the Court was adopting a disparate impact theory of job discrimination that "shifted civil rights policy to a group-rights, equality-of-result rationale that made the social consequences of employment practices, rather than their purposes, intent, or motivation, the decisive consideration in determining their lawfulness." Others might argue, of course, that an employment requirement that did not genuinely relate to job performance but which systematically disadvantaged minorities reveals an intent or motivation to screen out minorities. The key point here is that businesses now had the burden of showing that their hiring and promotion qualifications were bona fide and necessary; and since they could be found guilty of discrimination even without a showing of the intent to discriminate, they were more at risk. The result of this was that employers were propelled into more aggressive affirmative action policies as a proactive form of defense. "If the threat of liability was a possible incentive to quota hiring under the disparate treatment concept of discrimination, minority preference was practically required in order to protect against charges of disparate impact discrimination. The logical premise of disparate impact theory was group rights and equality of result" (Belz, 1991: 550).

There were other court decisions during this period that were specifically related to employment discrimination. Unlike the fundamental doctrinal statement that the *Griggs* case represents, however, such cases largely dealt with narrower technical matters, and most particularly with the issue of whether and how statistics could be used to make a case of discrimination under Title VII (Skrentny, 1996: 163).

Of greater significance was the *Bakke* case, though it dealt with affirmative action in university admissions rather than in employment. However, the *Bakke* case galvanized attention because it focused quite directly on affirmative action of the sort that was, in common parlance, already being referred to as "reverse discrimination." Hence, the potential implications for the overall controversy over affirmative action were considerable. In *Regents of the University of California v. Bakke (1978)* the court ruled that the university's policy of reserving specific medical school admission slots for minorities was a form of reverse discrimination. However, it declared such an approach unacceptable primarily on grounds that it had been fashioned as a proactive, diversity-enhancing measure rather than a remedy for a specific finding of discrimination. A majority of the justices in the *Bakke* case endorsed race-conscious approaches if used for remedial purposes.

With the policy developments of the 1965–1979 period in place, affirmative action had come of age. Interpretations of the meaning of affirmative action by the courts and by executive branch agencies made clear that something more than a lack of overt discrimination in the workplace was expected; indeed, affirmative action policy had gone beyond expectations of special promotional or outreach efforts meant to insure equal awareness of employment opportunities. The policy grounds had shifted toward statistically quantifiable equality of results and the preference-based employment methods that are required to achieve such results. The self-defensive actions of employers responding to these policy interpretations shifted the ground even further in the direction of quota-like practices.

Before continuing with the policy history of affirmative action in the post-1980 period, it is important to consider why and how public policy in this case moved so dramatically away from public opinion. If racially conscious, preference-based programs to insure equal employment opportunity were inconsistent with mass sentiments, as the opening section of this chapter suggests, what accounts for the relatively rapid embrace of such programs and principles in the wake of legislation that ostensibly enshrined a color-blind model of employment policy? One possibility that can always be explored when policy is inconsistent with mass opinion is that a set of powerful, special interests lobbied successfully for outcomes important to them. But that possibility can be relatively quickly dismissed here. Civil rights groups did not initially dare to press for a race-conscious policy of special preferences for fear that such a campaign would be totally damaging to their legitimacy (Skrentny, 1996: 30–33).

Perhaps the most obvious explanation for the development of a policy-mass opinion disjunction has to do with the venue for policy-making. The courts and administrative agencies were the key locales for the development of affirmative action policy, and these institutional venues are neither designed for direct responsiveness to mass preferences nor expected to act in consort with public opinion.

However, there are two problems with an explanation that relies on simplistic notions of institutional venue for affirmative action policy-making. For one thing, recent research raises questions about the conventional view of the court's insulation from public opinion. Mishler and Sheehan (1993), for example, find that at least in the period from 1956 to 1980 the Supreme Court did *not* function as a counter-majoritarian institution. The ideological direction of its decisions was consistent with long-term trends in aggregate public opinion. Second, even if one concedes the relative insulation of the courts and the bureaucracy from public opinion, that acknowledgment only stipulates that policy-making in those venues is less institutionally constrained by public opinion—i.e., why policy emanating from these settings might not necessarily be responsive to mass opinion. Such a recognition does not explain what prompted policy-makers in these venues to embrace the race-conscious, preference-based approach that they did. Perhaps the best explanation for this is provided by Skrentny (1996), who weaves together a number of key factors: the crisis conditions presented by the race riots in American cities in the mid-1960s, the limitations of a color-blind approach and the appeal of a race-conscious approach given the demands of administrative pragmatism, and the Court's evolving role as the last bastion for the protection for racial minorities.

In Skrentny's interpretation, racial violence created crisis conditions that heightened the validity of race-conscious benefit programs generally as a means for reestablishing order and control. Extending this interpretation, which has also been offered by others (Jencks, 1992: 58), Skrentny argues that the alternative solution, which would have emphasized repressive actions, was constrained by an historical context which placed the morality of American domestic responses on view for a global audience that was already critical of U.S. forces pitted against a nonwhite population in Vietnam (1996: 108).

Affirmative action thus became a more legitimate idea, at least among policy elites, because of its potential for crisis management. That legitimation process was furthered in the courts because of the special, institutional logic of the courts. In the courts, the disparate impact principle which legitimated a race-conscious approach to affirmative action was promulgated in ways that emphasized tradition and precedent, thus obscuring the major policy change that was involved in the *Griggs* case. The traditions and precedents involved drew from the court's developing role as a protector of last resort for racial minorities in cases involving schooling and voting, even though employment situation was arguably different (Skrentny, 1996: 166–173).

Perhaps the most compelling piece of Skrentny's argument, however, has to do with the imperatives facing bureaucratic agencies in general and the Equal Employment Opportunity Commission (EEOC) in particular. This argument is based upon the premise of "administrative pragmatism"—i.e., the notion that the leadership of any bureaucratic agency is driven toward workable strategies and the avoidance of demonstrable agency failure. A color-blind, anti-discrimination approach to enforcement of the Civil Rights Act was simply unsuitable in this regard, because it required proof of discriminatory intent on a case-by-case basis—something that is difficult under the best of circumstances. As a presidential review of affirmative action thirty years later would acknowledge: "The difficulty was that formal litigation-related strategies are inevitably resource-intensive and often dependent upon clear 'smoking gun' evidence of overt bias or bigotry, whereas prejudice can take on myriad subtle, yet effective, forms. Thus, private and public institutions alike too often seemed impervious to the winds of change, remaining all-white or all-male long after court decisions or statutes formally ended discrimination" (White House, 1995a). The EEOC was further hobbled in its initial years by weak leadership, limited resources, staff turnover, and a deluge of discrimination complaints that led to an immediate backlog. In this context, an affirmative action approach became a compelling tool for the EEOC to free itself from the constraints of fighting employment discrimination through the difficult and self-limiting methods of case-by-case adjudication of discrimination complaints. Once the EEOC (in 1966) began to require all employers to report on the racial composition of their workforce, it could look for statistical disparities in employment by race across entire industry sectors and initiate investigations or hearings on behalf of racial minorities as a group in industries with suspect numbers (Skrentny, 1996: 111–133). In this fashion, the EEOC's need to make visible progress with its mission pushed it in the direction of a statistics-based, group conscious approach that is one of the hallmarks of affirmative action.

Phase #3: Continuity Amidst Controversy (1980–1992)

Given what we have already shown about the long-standing hostility of the public to group preferences and quotas, it is not surprising that a sharp shift in the salience of affirmative action policy occurred in the wake of the developments in the institutionalizing phase of affirmative action. By the latter 1970s, the topic of affirmative action had gone from virtual nonexistence to frequent coverage (see Figure 3-1). Just as the pollsters were not asking the public about affirmative action during much of the crucial period in which it was being developed, the national media, as represented by *New York Times Index* listings, ran only a handful of stories on "affirmative action" during all the years from 1964 to 1976. But from 1977 onwards, the *New York Times* ran at least 50 stories on affirmative action in most years.

Interestingly enough, the ebb and flow of media coverage of "affirmative action" does *not* show a pattern geared to the electoral

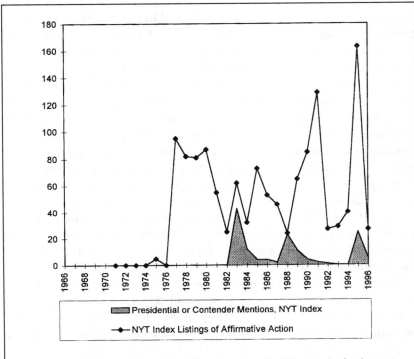

Figure 3.1. Agenda Status of Affirmative Action: Attentive Publics, Presidents and Presidential Contenders

cycle. If anything, stories on affirmative action have been noticeably *less* plentiful in most of the election years after 1980—and especially in the presidential election years—than they have been in non-election years. This does not necessarily mean that affirmative action has not been a wedge issue on the political scene. Indeed, the special value of affirmative action as a wedge issue may be illustrated by the pattern in Figure 3-1. Affirmative action has become very controversial, and attentive publics have been quite attuned to the topic from ongoing developments both nationally and locally, whether or not an election year was in progress. Rather than having to create a flurry of attention to the issue in election years, political leaders who are so inclined can capitalize on the wellspring of controversy that chronically attends this explosive issue. As Figure 3-1 shows, presidents and the presidential nominee from the other major party have relatively rarely mentioned the affirmative action issue. But even a limited number of references to this explosive issue may be all that is needed for a Republican candidate to create divisions and strategic problems within the Democratic party. Furthermore, politicians other than the president may be counted upon to carry the ball on this issue, thus providing the rhetoric needed to make use of it as a wedge issue while deflecting criticism from the president. As the following section will show, William Bradford Reynolds arguably played this role of presidential "lightning rod" (Ellis, 1994) during the Reagan administration.

Despite the fact that affirmative action has been controversial enough to serve as a wedge issue, and despite the emergence of conservative Republican leadership in the White House during the Reagan and Bush administrations, the course of affirmative action policy was not dramatically altered in the period from 1973 to 1992. There were some new policy developments, some of which qualified or toned down a racially-conscious, preference-based approach. But a much more major reversal of policy would have been required to bring policy back into consistency with the mass public's objections to quotas and racially preferential policies. The policy change that occurred during this period does not constitute that sort of major reversal. Hence, this must be characterized as a period of continuing policy non-responsiveness.

There is by no means consensus about this interpretation of policy continuity. Some writers are more inclined to characterize the Reagan administration as ushering in a stand-down in affirmative action. Jencks (1992: 24–5), for example, notes that in the Reagan administration ". . . federal pressure on private employers to hire more blacks was reduced." More specifically, Jencks (1992: 50) notes that the Reagan administration "exempted some firms from affirmative action requirements, loosened the standards a firm had to meet for its program to be acceptable, and quietly reduced the threat of sanctions if firms failed to make good on their promises. Budgets were cut at both EEOC and the Office of Federal Contract Compliance Program . . ." Similarly, Kellough (1989: 21) points to a substantial policy shift on affirmative action during the Reagan administration: "Under new guidelines for federal EEO, issued by the EEOC in 1987, federal agencies were in fact no longer required to develop numerical goals and timetables to address the under-representation of minorities and women, but they were permitted to do so at their discretion." And Williams (1996: 251–2) likewise emphasizes what she views as an assault on affirmative action in the 1980s, an assault manifested in Labor Department proposals in 1981 and 1982 to weaken OFCCP regulations; Department of Justice accusations that the OFCCP was approving agreements that contained quotas; the FCC's 1986 decision to discontinue preferences for women and minorities in the competition for TV and radio licenses; Reagan administration opposition to back pay awards and the associated decrease in such awards from $9.2 million in 1980 to $1.9 million in 1986; the doubling in the share of EEOC cases in which the commission issued a finding of no cause; and the sharp drop in class action settlements.

Other interpretations acknowledge some change but emphasize policy continuity during this period. For example, Belz (1991: 196) suggests that the administration's policy was one of a high profile but largely symbolic anti-quota campaign with the Justice Department in the lead, combined with a lower-key but more substantive set of minor adjustments that helped to sustain the status quo in affirmative action policy in ways that mattered: "Instead of consistently opposing race-conscious affirmative action throughout the government, the administration tried to limits its excesses and make it more politically and administratively palatable" (Belz, 1991: 183). As specific evidence for these claims, he notes that, although Assistant Attorney General for Civil Rights William Bradford Reynolds publicly denounced the use of quotas as a remedy for discrimination (and entered amicus briefs in court cases to this effect) he publicly ascribed to the *Griggs* disparate impact concept, to the use of statistical evidence in discrimination cases, and the use of back pay, promotional priorities, retroactive seniority, reinstatement and hiring as remedies for specific cases of discrimination" (Belz, 1991: 185). And, despite his emphasis upon affirmative action policy change in this period, Jencks nevertheless (1992: 50) acknowledges policy continuity as well: "Nonetheless, many of the rules put in place during the 1970s remained in force, and both EEOC and OFCCP remained more active than they had been in the 1960s."

A look at quantitative evidence of the EEOC's activities also suggests that affirmative action efforts were sustained, despite some temporary reversals (see Figure 3-2). It is true that the period of sustained growth in EEOC staffing came to a halt in this era; but there were not dramatic cuts in staff size during the 1980s. And while there at first appears to be a sharp drop in the number of

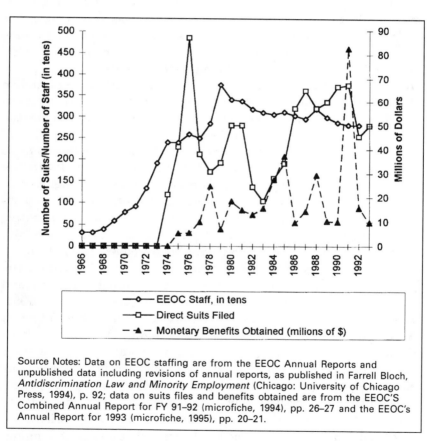

Source Notes: Data on EEOC staffing are from the EEOC Annual Reports and unpublished data including revisions of annual reports, as published in Farrell Bloch, *Antidiscrimination Law and Minority Employment* (Chicago: University of Chicago Press, 1994), p. 92; data on suits files and benefits obtained are from the EEOC'S Combined Annual Report for FY 91–92 (microfiche, 1994), pp. 26–27 and the EEOC's Annual Report for 1993 (microfiche, 1995), pp. 20–21.

Figure 3-2. Affirmative Action Efforts: EEOC Budget and Performance

direct suits filed by the EEOC in the early 1980s, it is important to note that this is a sharp drop only if compared to a single year, 1976, in which an unusually large number of direct suits had been filed. When compared to the other years in the Ford and Carter administrations, the EEOC's output of direct suits filed is not very different. Indeed, the number of direct suits filed increased noticeably in Reagan's second term so that, by 1988, the EEOC's output was at the highest level in its history with the exception of 1976.

There are at least two good reasons for the divergence in interpretations of the extent of affirmative action policy change during the Reagan administration. One reason is that the intention to make dramatic policy changes and the administration's capacity to do so are two different things. Wood and Waterman (1991: 806–7) suggest that there was a substantial effort early in the Reagan administration to reduce the aggressiveness of affirmative action policy but that this was very short-lived and quickly reversed. The effort was based on the use of the appointment power. Specifically, Reagan appointed Michael Connolly as head of the EEOC Office of General Counsel in 1981—a controversial appointment because Connolly had a history of representing large companies fighting discrimination charges. Symbolically, Connolly appeared to represent the forces of reaction against affirmative action, and though he was successfully confirmed, his appointment was strongly challenged by civil rights groups. "The Connolly appointment produced an immediate decline of 4.57 litigations per month followed by a continued movement to a level 18.28 litigations per month below" the mean litigation level prior to the appointment (Wood and Waterman, 1991: 807). However, Connolly resigned in January 1983 and was replaced by David Slate, an individual much more acceptable to civil rights groups and proponents of affirmative action in Congress. And in the wake of the Slate appointment, litigations increased noticeably and remained on the increase through the 1987 time frame studied by Wood and Waterman. This episode shows the rapid disengagement of the Reagan administration from what initially seemed to be strong efforts to de-claw affirmative action policy.

The second reason for conflicting interpretations of affirmative action in the Reagan era is that different aspects of affirmative action policy may be the focus for interpretation. Some aspects of affirmative action policy are quite visible and formal, such as the issuance of executive orders and the appointment of key personnel whose background or stated orientation have both symbolic and substantive implications; others are much less visible and more informal, such as the issuance of internal memoranda and other policy directives within the bureaucracy. The Reagan administration opened with affirmative action policy initiatives that were quite visible and formal, giving the appearance of major change, and perhaps leading some to over-interpret the extent of change. But before any dramatic change could be effective, the administration scaled back its ambitions for affirmative action reform and pursued incremental change through less visible and less formal means. The EEOC, in a low key way, moved away from quotas in Reagan's second term, under the chairmanship of Clarence Thomas, who "*informally* told the general counsel not to approve agreements with goals and timetables in them" (Skrentny, 1996: 226, emphasis in original). Likewise, the EEOC under Thomas quietly moved to de-emphasize the bringing of charges of systemic discrimination based on statistics, placing more emphasis on litigating individual cases of alleged discrimination (Belz, 1991: 189).

Meanwhile, the OFCC proposed regulatory revisions to ease up on affirmative action, but was met by Congressional opposition. Instead, the policy change was quietly effected through "informal policymaking. Through internal directives, orders, and notices that were considered consistent with existing regulations, it modified the executive order program" (Belz, 1991: 194). Goals and time-tables were maintained, but contractors' goals for minority hiring were eased, some corporations were allowed to adopt standardized affirmative action plans, and voluntary self-monitoring and compliance was introduced. (Belz, 1991: 193–4).

For proponents of affirmative action, the personnel appointments and rhetoric of the Reagan administrative surely seemed quite threatening. And it might also be argued that the policy changes that were informally and quietly implemented through administrative actions during this period were meaningful and important. However, none really constituted a wholesale stand-down from a race-conscious, preference-based approach to affirmative action. In this sense, the period constitutes a curious continuity in a policy that has remained controversial and unpopular.

A reversal in affirmative action policy during this period might also have been expected to result from Reagan's appointments to the Supreme Court. In the late 1980s, two cases, in particular, appeared to signal a judicially-directed shift in affirmative action policy. In *Wards Cove v. Atonio* (1989), the court ruled that employees in job discrimination cases had to not only show statistical disparities in employment, but also to identify the specific employment practice or practices that created the disparity. This decision, which would make it more difficult for minority employees to successfully show job discrimination, presumably eased the pressure which motivated employers to undertake aggressive programs of affirmative action. And in *Richmond v. J.A. Croson Company* (1989), the court struck down a minority set-aside plan under which the city of Richmond, Virginia had required contractors to award 30% of all contract work to minority firms in order to eliminate the effects of past discrimination. Speaking directly to the issue of racial preferences, the court held that racial classifications could not be used in state and local government contracting programs except as narrowly tailored and temporary remedies when prior discrimination had been established (LaNoue, 1992). These cases were widely viewed as taking the pressure off of employers and thereby undermining affirmative action programs (Wilson, 1992), even though the *Wards Cove* case in particular has also been acknowledged to amount to no more than a return to the standards placed upon employers in the *Griggs* case (Casey and Montgomery, 1992).

But the rulings evoked Congressional action that was designed to move policy back in the direction of strong grounds for plaintiffs in job discrimination cases. The Civil Rights Act of 1991, for example, was an explicit attempt to counter the court's decision in *Wards Cove* ("The Civil Rights Act of 1991...", 1993) and to shift the burden of proof about employment practices with disparate impacts on minorities and women back to employers. In addition, the legislation provided for punitive and compensatory damages in cases of job discrimination based upon sex, religion, and disability (Ross, 1992).

Affirmative action policy has thus been supported and sustained by Congressional action in ways that at least partially short-circuit Court rulings that threatened its foundation. At the same time, congressional action shows how symbolic attacks on quotas—the most volatile aspect of affirmative action—can coexist with legislative measures that reinforce the essential disparate impact principle of affirmative action. While its provisions explicitly renewed the pressure on employers in disparate impact cases, the Civil Rights Act of 1991 also included explicit anti-quota language, stipulating that nothing in the act be interpreted to "require, encourage, or permit an employer to adopt hiring or promotion quotas on the basis of race, color, religion, sex or national origin, and the use of such quotas shall be deemed to be an unlawful employment practice" ("Compromise Civil Rights Bill Passed," 1992: 255). It is doubtful whether this language can be more potent than the anti-quota language in the Civil Rights Act of 1964, especially since the 1991 legislation defines a quota rather narrowly as "a fixed number or percentage of persons of a particular race, color, religion, sex or national origin which must be attained, or which cannot be exceeded, regardless of whether such persons meet necessary qualifications to perform the job" ("Compromise Civil Rights Bill Passed," 1992: 255).

Phase #4: The Reversal of a Non-Responsive Policy? (1993–Present)

Despite its controversial character, affirmative action policy remained largely intact even through the Reagan and Bush years; and, in the wake of Supreme Court cases that limited affirmative action in some ways, congressional action reaffirmed the disparate impact principle that is a centerpiece of affirmative action. With the election of a centrist Democrat as president in 1992 and a Republican Congress in 1994, the issuance of a notable series of Supreme Court decisions in 1995 and 1996, and the politicization of the issue both at the state level and in the 1996 presidential campaign, affirmative action policy has since then been subject to substantial challenge. So far, there has been no definitive reversal of affirmative action policy at the national level; but there have been important developments suggesting a retrenchment from the most overtly preference-based approach to affirmative action.

In the case of *Adarand Constructors v. Pena* (1995), the Supreme Court ruled, in a case involving a federal highway contracting project with special set-asides for minority businesses, that race-conscious remedies are presumed unconstitutional unless they can survive the test of strict scrutiny—i.e., be shown to be narrowly tailored to accomplish a compelling governmental interest. The decision thus subjected the federal government to the same requirements in its affirmative action programs that the court had imposed on state and local programs in *Richmond v. Croson* in 1989. In her written opinion, Justice Sandra Day O'Connor pointedly offered support for the concept of affirmative action, however, suggesting that "strict scrutiny" is not an unattainable standard and holding the door open for race conscious affirmative action programs to survive that test. However, two justices (Scalia and Thomas) indicated their more extreme position, that race-conscious affirmative action programs cannot be justified under any circumstance (Greenhouse, 1995: 1).

Even as attentive publics were digesting this decision, a series of court actions involving affirmative action in college admissions created potential implications for equal employment opportunity policy, just as the *Bakke* case had some years before. In March of 1996, a Federal appeals court decision out of the Fifth Circuit ruled against the race-conscious admissions policies used by the University of Texas Law School, in the process explicitly rejecting the *Bakke* case's interpretation that race-conscious remedies could be appropriate. In July of 1996, however, the Supreme Court declined to hear an appeal of that ruling, thus adding to the unsettled status of affirmative action. But just as O'Connor's opinion in the *Adarand* case gave some reason to expect that the essentials of affirmative action policy might endure, so did the explanation issued by the Court when it refused to hear an appeal of the University of Texas Law School case. The Court does not, in fact, generally issue an explanation for why it does not take on a particular case on appeal. In issuing such an explanation, Justices Ruth Bader Ginsburg and David Souter signaled that the Court's denial of a review was not an endorsement of the lower court's attack on the *Bakke* precedent; instead, the denial of review stemmed from the fact that the controversy in the case in question had become moot, since the University of Texas Law School had abandoned its two-track admissions program (Greenhouse, 1996a: 1).

In acknowledgment of the controversial status of affirmative action policy and as a strategy to defuse it as an election issue, the

Meanwhile, conservative groups pushed ahead in their search for suitable court cases by which to challenge affirmative action. Activists believed that they had found such a case when the Supreme Court agreed to hear, in its 1997–98 term, the case of *Piscataway Township Board of Education v. Taxman*. In this case, the Piscataway (New Jersey) school board chose to lay off white high school teacher Sharon Taxman rather than a black teacher with similar qualifications. Before the case could be heard by the Supreme Court, however, the school board decided to settle the case out of court with Taxman.

In short, while many of the elements of affirmative action remain in place, new court rulings, state-level initiatives, and administrative policy decisions may be altering the essential character of affirmative action. At a minimum, there is evidence that affirmative action was highly politicized by the late 1990's, so much so that the groundwork to re-orient this policy more in the direction of popular acceptability was in place.

Conclusion

While based on a foundation period that established a civil rights policy responsive to developing public sentiments for a color-blind society, affirmative action policy quickly diverged from public opinion as it moved toward a model of government action that was based on acknowledgment of statistical evidence, disparate impact theory, and various race-conscious preferences as remedies for the continuing problem of job discrimination. Although there have been incremental changes that modified some of the character of affirmative action programs in practice, there is yet to be a definitive reversal of the core elements of affirmative action policy. Affirmative action policy entered a distinctly unsettled state by 1998. But it has been thirty years since policy diverged from opinion on this issue, and race-conscious, preference-based programs to maximize the diversity of the workforce are still a part of employment policy in the United States.

In this respect, affirmative action policy constitutes a genuine curiosity. Analysts of the public opinion-policy connection have acknowledged that policy sometimes drifts out of line with public opinion, but a return to the zone of acceptability is typically expected. Indeed, Lowery, Gray and Hager (1989: 10–11) suggest that non-incremental policy changes play an important role in the process of re-instituting a linkage between opinion and policy. In their view, non-incremental policy change episodes, or policy shocks, are ways of bringing policy more into congruence with opinion after periods of drifting away from it incrementally. But this has not happened with affirmative action, which has recently evidenced incremental change, not the substantial change that may be required to resolve the lingering conflicts between policy and majority public sentiment. How might we account for the relatively long-term durability of non-responsive policy in this case?

Lowery, Gray and Hager (1989: 11) acknowledge that policy is less likely to be dramatically wrested back toward public opinion if it involves "issues that are largely removed from public view, are complex, and/or are not central to the lives of most citizens." As the concluding chapter of this volume will show, this may indeed be part of the explanation for the sustained non-responsiveness of affirmative action policy. Affirmative action was initially developed outside of public view in the guidelines promulgated by administrative agencies such as the EEOC and in court decisions; and details of EEOC policies and court decisions interpreting fine points of the meaning of disparate impact are complex and arcane. While EEOC policies did not remain completely removed from public view for long, affirmative action has nevertheless *not* been a high salience issue until the 1990s.

But the relative complexity and low salience of affirmative action are not the only reasons for the sustained discontinuity between opinion and policy in this area. Why, in fact, would oppositional politicians not be immediately tempted to capitalize on the opinion-policy discrepancy by raising the salience of this issue? And, when politicians did finally raise the level of rhetoric about affirmative action, why did such little policy change result? Several different considerations might help to explain this.

First, it is important to note the continuing value of affirmative action as a wedge issue. This issue has relatively regularly been used by Republicans to place Democrats in the uncomfortable position of either endorsing a policy that is problematic to many of their constituents or of backing down from a policy that is extraordinarily important to a key component of the Democratic coalition. Because affirmative action has regularly been critiqued by Republicans, it is all to easy to conclude that it would be a top priority for reform when Republicans are empowered. But such a conclusion ignores the fact that, once transformed, affirmative action would then no longer be available as a wedge issue. And since substantive transformation of affirmative action would, despite its mass unpopularity, carry some political costs (see below), dramatic, substantive change in affirmative action policy is perhaps less to be expected than continuing symbolic attacks on it.

Second, while affirmative action cannot be totally inoculated from normal politics, it does enjoy a special status as a moral issue. While the civil rights lobby may not have found it legitimate to press for race conscious approaches in the context of the Civil Rights Act of 1964 (Skrentny, 1996), subsequent developments have made it easier for proponents to conflate affirmative action with civil rights and to interpret an attack on the former as an attack on the latter. More generally, the disjunction between mass opinion and public policy on this issue has been treated as a moral necessity rather than a problem of democracy. As Jesse Jackson has argued: "There would not have been a popular vote for the 1964 Civil Rights Act, the 1965 Voting Rights Act, or the 1968 Fair Housing Act. In our nation's history, there has never been a popular vote for racial justice, gender equality, or the rights of workers" (Jackson, 1996: 295).

But there is a third force for stability as well. Although it is often assumed that private employers are burdened by affirmative action programs and unified in their hostility to the continuation of these programs, the reality appears to be much more complex. There is, in fact, considerable evidence of business accommodation to affirmative action. Belz (1991: 196), for example, has argued that business, and especially big business, was not particularly supportive of attacks on affirmative action during the Reagan administration: "By the 1980s most large companies, having institutionalized affirmative action as part of the corporate culture, had little inclination to stir up the employment discrimination pot once again by supporting the Justice Department's anti-quota policy." More generally, corporate America has learned the value of maintaining at least a symbolic level of diversity, if not a genuinely substantive commitment to equality of results in employment opportunity. People of color are an important component of the market for the goods and services of American business; and for this reason, it is simply not good public relations to have an assailable record on the utilization of minorities in the work force. Although businesses are by no means uniform in seeing that some level of workforce diversity is in their enlightened self-interest, many have. And a numbers-based approach, showing good faith through statistical evidence of progress toward goals and timetables for minority hiring, is not only institutionalized in much of corporate America but is easier to accommodate than the potentially more threatening and intrusive approach that would be represented by aggressive governmental enforcement of individual complaints of actual discrimination. For this reason, American business has long since found a race-conscious approach to affirmative action to be preferable to a regulatory approach based upon a demand of color-blind justice (Skrentny, 1996).

4

The Regulation of Pornography

Policy Change and Non-attitudes

Introduction

Sexually explicit materials are a relatively pervasive aspect of contemporary society. From graphic song lyrics to erotic magazines to explicit scenes in mainstream films to widely available "X-rated" videos to lewd pictures and chat rooms on computer networks, the United States is arguably awash in erotic materials. But what do Americans believe about this phenomenon? In particular, how widespread is support for the legal availability of pornography, and how willing are Americans to have government restrict the access of either adults or juveniles to these materials? And have governmental policies with respect to the regulation of pornography developed in a pattern that suggests responsiveness to public views on the matter?

This chapter will argue that there are substantial reasons for suspecting that the pornography issue elicits among many people the sorts of superficial, loosely held, inconsistent, and uncertain opinions that are sometimes designated "non-attitudes." Over the long term, there has been a substantial shift in public policy concerning pornography. The contemporary period of enhanced restrictions and regulatory efforts has replaced a more liberal period in which pornography was treated much less restrictively. Unfortunately, this shift in public policy predates the availability of systematic public opinion data on pornography. Consequently, it is not possible to test how that policy shift, dating from about 1973, may or may not have related to public opinion in the period before 1973. But, in the period since 1973, there is evidence that aggregate public opinion in this area includes a far from trivial share of non-attitudes. And the very long-term stability in this pattern suggests that the same may have been true prior to 1973 as well.

In any case, the non-attitudes interpretation in this chapter suggests that, at least in the contemporary phase and perhaps before as well, policymakers have neither followed nor successfully led public opinion. The lack of a firmly grounded, majority opinion on pornography has meant that the issue is open to the mobilization efforts of competing ideological camps. Nongovernmental and governmental anti-pornography crusaders have recognized the prospects for arousing the public in the direction of their point of view through redefinitions of the issue. Consideration of the problem of erotic materials circulating through civil society have given way to discussion of child pornography, violent pornography, and pornography in cyberspace—realms where the weak, civil libertarian middle of mass opinion can perhaps more readily be moved to concern. But, despite their periodic efforts to mobilize the public on this issue, policymakers have failed to generate a successful sequence of policy learning—i.e., the pornography issue still exhibits the non-attitudes problem. This chapter explores the complexities and expert disagreements that have contributed to the failure of policy learning and the continuation of non-attitudes.

The Policy History of Pornography Regulation: A Play in Two Acts

Two very different phases of public policy toward pornography are evident in the 30-year period from the 1960s to the present: a liberal phase extending through the 1960s to about 1973, followed by a much more conservative period of toughened regulation and enforcement crackdown. This chapter will primarily focus upon the second phase, because corresponding public opinion data are not available for the first phase. However, it is important to document the character of public policy in the first phase in order to provide historical grounding for more contemporary policy developments.

The differences in the two phases are dramatically evidenced in key court cases, contrasting presidential commissions, and enforcement actions.

Pornography and the Courts

Up until the landmark Supreme Court ruling in the case of *Roth v. U.S.* (1957), most courts in the U.S. treated lewd material as legitimately subject to regulation, based on British legal doctrine which allowed for criminal treatment of material that would deprave and corrupt those who are susceptible to immoral influence. And, during this period, dicta in Supreme Court decisions such as *Chaplinsky v. New Hampshire* (1942) showed clearly that the Court viewed obscene material as falling outside the category of protected expression; hence, regulation of such expression was not presumed to be unconstitutional. The difficult issue, of course, was what expression could and should be defined as obscene.

In *Roth v. U.S.* (1957), the Court sustained the view that obscenity was not protected speech under the First Amendment, but held that prevailing legal doctrine encompassed too much in its definition of obscenity. Instead of treating as obscene any material that would corrupt those most susceptible to such influences, the Court offered the following test of whether material is obscene: "whether to the average person, applying contemporary community standards, the dominant theme of the material, taken as a whole, appeals to the prurient interest (354 U.S., p. 487, as cited in Kobylka, 1991: 3). Justice Brennan's wording in the case added an important element to pornography law. In his stipulation, material with a sexual content was not necessarily obscene if it had "even the slightest redeeming social importance" (Kobylka, 1991: 4).

Functionally, the *Roth* decision gave the Court a more pronounced role in ensuing years, as it had to interpret, in case after case, whether contemporary community standards were broached by particular material, or whether obscenity convictions were appropriate in the light of the average person's assessment and in the light of the nature of the work taken as a whole. And in the process of making such judgments, the Court, in the period from 1957 to 1971, effectively liberalized obscenity doctrine. In a number of cases, the Court objected on procedural grounds to various aspects of pornography regulation (such as warrant procedures being used to locate and seize pornographic materials and pornography controls that raised prior restraint issues). In still other cases, the test of what is pornographic was substantively developed further, in ways that made it more difficult for pornography convictions to be upheld. For example, in *Manual Enterprises v. Day* (1962), the Court held that the material at issue had to be "patently offensive" in order to be deemed obscene; and in *Jacobellis v. Ohio* (1964) the Court stipulated that the material had to be "utterly without redeeming social importance" as well as patently offensive in order to be adjudged obscene (Kobylka, 1991: 5). In *Redrup v. New York* (1967), the Court, while divided about the appropriate definition of obscenity, reversed the obscenity conviction at issue on grounds that it did not meet any of the different tests of obscenity that various justices found appropriate. And in the ensuing four years, 32 more obscenity convictions were reversed by the Court (Kobylka, 1991: 5).

This liberalizing trend was brought sharply to a halt in 1973 when the Court, including four justices appointed by President Richard Nixon, issued its opinion in *Miller v. California* (1973). The test of obscenity articulated in this case was essentially a return to the basics of the *Roth* case. Material was deemed obscene if the "average person, applying contemporary community standards" would consider the work as a whole as appealing to "the prurient interest" and if the work shows sexual conduct in a "patently offensive way" and if the work as a whole lacks "serious literary, artistic, political, or scientific value." Contemporary community standards were explicitly stated to be local, not national standards, and prosecutors were relieved of the requirement of showing that material is "utterly without redeeming social value" in order to treat it as obscene. The Court also jettisoned the doctrine, used by some justices in the *Redrup case,* that would have negated the finding of obscenity if the audience for the material consisted of consenting adults. In the wake of this tightening of obscenity doctrine, most ensuing decisions found in favor of obscenity proscriptions—a distinct change from the many reversals of obscenity convictions that had been issuing from the court (Kobylka, 1991: 7). Indeed, in his content analysis of obscenity cases before the Supreme Court, Kobylka (1991: 8) finds that the Warren Court, in the period 1957–1971, issued libertarian decisions (i.e., opposed to pornography regulators) 78% of the time, while the Burger Court, from 1972–87, issued libertarian decisions in only 22% of its obscenity cases.

Pornography and Presidential Commissions

The contrast between the liberal period of court interpretation of pornography immediately after the *Roth* case and the turn toward more conservative, pro-regulatory interpretation in the post-*Miller* period is mirrored in the very different recommendations of two presidential commissions on pornography, one constituted in the midst of the liberal period of pornography's policy history and the other constituted in the midst of the conservative period. In 1968, Congress, at the instigation of Senator McClellan (D., Arkansas) created a President's Commission on Obscenity and Pornography to investigate what Congress stipulated to be a "matter of national concern" (U.S. Commission, as cited in Hawkins and Zimring, 1988: 7). The commission was given the responsibility of analyzing and making recommendations about pornography law, researching the character and magnitude of trafficking in pornography, researching the impact of pornography on the public, especially in regards to crime and especially with regard to youth, and making recommendations about ways to control pornography within constitutional limits.

The commission, composed of a combination of lawyers, sociologists, psychiatrists, religious leaders, publishing executives, academics and librarians had a brief but stormy existence, culminating in a report which served to heighten the politicization of the pornography issue. Drawing upon a wide range of social scientific studies, many specially prepared for it, the Johnson commission found "no evidence to date that exposure to explicit sexual materials plays a significant role in the causation of delinquent or criminal behavior among youth or adults" (U.S. Commission, as cited in Hawkins and Zimring, 1988: 75). The commission ultimately recommended repeal of any legislation regulating trafficking in pornography, including hard-core pornography, to consenting adults, on grounds that no adverse effects of pornography could be proven and "the laws prohibiting the consensual sale or distribution of such materials were extremely unsatisfactory in their practical application. (Hawkins and Zimring, 1988: 133).

While the Johnson commission articulated and provided evidentiary support for a relatively permissive point of view on pornography, its recommendations were not translated into policy. Instead, it represents the swan song of the liberal period of pornography policy. In fact, its recommendations were subject to political controversy before they were even issued. Two of the members of the commission, the Rev. Morton Hill of Morality in Media and the Rev. Winfrey Link, objected to the direction that the commission was taking and conducted independent hearings in eight cities, despite the commission's policy against such an approach. As the date for the reporting of the commission's results approached, a draft of the report was obtained by the House Subcommittee on Postal Operations, which promptly scheduled hearings to trash the as-yet unreleased commission findings. Another member of the commission, Charles Keating, sued to prevent publication of the commission report because he had not been given enough time to construct a written dissent. Ultimately the Nixon administration, to which the commission reported its findings, completely rejected the findings of the commission (Hawkins and Zimring, 1988: 9–10). And, as we have seen, within a few years, the Court's ruling in *Miller v. California* would steer policy in a direction more conducive to restriction.

Fifteen years after the President's Commission on Pornography, yet another pornography commission was created. This commission, initiated by President Reagan, was formed in 1985 under the leadership of then-Attorney General Edwin Meese II. Unlike the Johnson commission, which relied primarily upon social science experts, the Attorney General's Commission took a more politicized approach, including public hearings and "working sessions" in six cities. Those hearings featured graphic testimony, not only from legal specialists but from ordinary citizens, activists, and criminals who claimed that their crimes derived from the use of pornography.

Ultimately, the Meese commission reported: ". . . we have reached the conclusion, unanimously and confidently, that the available evidence strongly supports the hypothesis that substantial exposure to sexually violent materials as described here bears a causal relationship to antisocial acts of sexual violence, and for some subgroups possibly to unlawful acts of sexual violence" (U.S. Dept.

of Justice, 1986: 326). This is not directly comparable with the Johnson commission's findings because the Meese commission focused on violent sexual materials, a category that was not extensively considered by the Johnson commission. But the Meese commission report repeatedly emphasizes that "only a small amount of currently available highly sexually explicit material is neither violent nor degrading" (U.S. Dept. of Justice, 1986: 336).

As a result of what it took as the clear demonstration of harms, the Meese commission chose to "reject the argument that all distribution of legally obscene pornography should be decriminalized" (U.S. Dept. of Justice, 1986: 363–4) and it urged that "prosecution of obscene materials that portray sexual violence be treated as a matter of special urgency" (p. 376). Complaining about under-enforcement of existing obscenity law, the commission argued that more initiatives in enforcement are needed rather than a revamping of the law. Although it cited Atlanta and Cincinnati as exceptions, where enforcement is vigorous and successful, the commission complained that "with few exceptions the obscenity laws that are on the books go un-enforced" and noted what it viewed as woefully inadequate local staffing for the enforcement of the obscenity laws (U.S. Dept. of Justice, 1986: 366).

With respect to federal law, the Meese commission issued recommendations that Congress enact legislation to allow for the forfeiture of assets used in or stemming from the violation of obscenity laws and to bar obscene cable television programming and the transmission of obscene material by telephone. The commission also recommended that the Department of Justice create a special obscenity task force and that investigation and prosecution for obscenity be more vigorously pursued, using all available legal weapons at their disposal, including the Racketeer Influenced and Corrupt Organizations (RICO) Act provisions (U.S. Dept. of Justice, 1986: 434–7).

Unlike the Johnson commission, whose recommendations fell by the wayside, the Meese commission's recommendations were eagerly taken up by government officials in the Reagan and Bush administrations and reflected in congressional action in the late 1980s and early 1990s. Indeed, the pace of policy development escalated rapidly in this period in the direction of greater restrictions against and crackdowns on pornography—as reflected in both legislative developments and executive branch actions. As the following section shows, this rapid escalation in policy developments concerning pornography, obscenity, and indecency was fostered by the proliferation of organizations active on the issue and by the spawning of diverse and threatening definitions of the pornography issue.

Congressional Action and Executive Branch Activity

The War on Child Pornography. If pornography in general does not necessarily evoke alarm and concern across broad sectors of the American public, the use of children in pornographic materials evokes a violation of innocence that transforms the issue into one that can galvanize a broader spectrum of public concern. By the late 1970s, 19 states had passed laws against involving children in the production of pornographic materials, whether or not those materials could be deemed "obscene" according to the Supreme Court's standards in the *Miller* case (Greenhouse, 1982: 1). And in the 1982 case of *New York v. Ferber*, the Supreme Court unanimously ruled in favor of such laws (Greenhouse, 1982: 1). Many other states and the U.S. government moved against child pornography that falls within the obscenity rubric. In 1977, Congress acted on this issue, passing legislation that would make it a federal crime to use children under the age of 16 in either actual or simulated sexual activities to be incorporated in obscene films or other materials sold in interstate commerce. This legislation, the Protection of Children Against Sexual Exploitation Act, set maximum penalties of $50,000 and 20 years in prison. The enforceability of this law immediately became problematic, however, as questions were raised about whether convictions would be constitutionally upheld if defendants were not aware of the age of individuals participating in the making of pornographic materials.

In the early 1980s, the "kiddie porn" issue was again the subject of congressional action. Legislation dealing with it was initiated in 1983, cleared Congress in May of 1984, and was signed into law by President Reagan as the Child Protection Act. The new act had provisions that increased the age of children protected from 16 to 18, deleted the requirement that sexually explicit materials involving children must be obscene before they can be banned, prevented the making and distribution of child pornography whether or not it is a commercial activity, increased the fines to $100,000 for the first offense, authorized the use of court supervised wiretapping in enforcing the law, established a fine of $250,000 against organizations that violated the law, and provided for asset forfeiture ("Child Pornography Bill," 1984: 225)

The crusade against child pornography continued through the remainder of the Reagan administration and was continued in the Bush administration. Child pornography legislation was periodically revisited with gestures toward toughening in the years following the passage of the Child Protection Act, typically in election years, as in November of 1988 when President Reagan signed a comprehensive crime bill including yet another version of the Child Protection and Obscenity Enforcement Act and in November of 1990 when President Bush signed a crime bill that included a Child Protection Restoration and Penalties Enforcement Act (Clark, 1991: 979). The 1990 act made *possession* of child pornography a federal offense, and it required producers of pornography to keep a log of the age of the individuals appearing in hard-core pornography, thus obviating any attempted legal defense based on the claim that participants were not known to be juveniles.

In the wake of the Meese commission's 1986 report, the Justice Department, led by Attorney General Meese, had created a new National Obscenity Enforcement Unit, later renamed the Child Exploitation and Obscenity Section. The 1984 Child Protection Act had given the Postal Inspection Service new investigative powers as well. In the late 1980s, both executive branch agencies noticeably escalated their enforcement activity, for obscenity investigations generally and for child pornography in particular. In the 1987–1991 period, the number of child pornography investigations soared to 1,422, nearly twice as many as in the 1980–84 period, while adult pornography investigations increased from 81 in the 1981–1985 period to 222 in the 1987–1991 period (Clark, 1991: 975).

The efforts of the Postal Inspection Service and the Child Exploitation and Obscenity Section of the Justice Department were aggressive enough to evoke controversy. Some commentators charged that the Justice Department unit was staffed with overzealous agents who were conducting showpiece investigations, complete with showy confiscations of erotic materials even in cases where the chances for conviction would be very slight (Dority, 1992). But there is evidence that this stepped-up enforcement effort was far more than a symbolic gesture of activity without results. Figure 4-1 shows that, by 1987, the Postal Inspection Service was generating nearly four times as many convictions in obscenity cases as it had in 1982, that by 1988 it obtained three times as many convictions as it had in any year since 1973, and that, while the number of convictions declined noticeably throughout the latter 1980s and most of the 1990s, the organization was in 1997 still generating more than four times the number of convictions that it had been in the early 1980s.

The aggressive war on kiddie porn has included some controversial tactics, however. In particular, government officials have made efforts to find conservative states in which to prosecute pornography vendors—a practice that some legal scholars have criticized as "forum shopping" and that others have called a form of entrapment (Clark, 1991: 976).

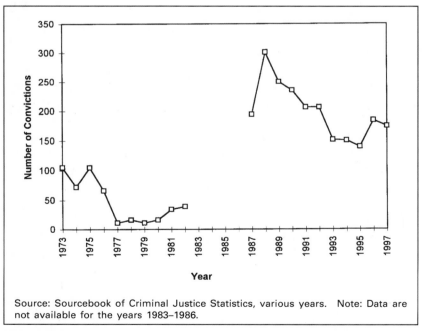

Source: Sourcebook of Criminal Justice Statistics, various years. Note: Data are not available for the years 1983–1986.

Figure 4-1. U.S. Postal Inspection Service Convictions Obtained for Obscenity or Pornography, 1973–1997

Arts Funding as a Venue for Wars Against Pornography. Still other policy initiatives relating to obscenity and pornography were sparked by the funding of controversial works of art by the National Endowment Association (NEA) in the 1980s. In particular, an NEA-supported photographic exhibition of the works of Robert Mapplethorpe, which included homoerotic and sadomasochistic themes, had created a furor among anti-pornography activists and had galvanized Senator Jesse Helms's efforts to restrict NEA funding. In 1989, Helms pressed for a measure that would have prevented the NEA and the National Endowment for the Humanities (NEW) from providing grants to support art projects that were obscene. Ultimately, Congress settled upon a softer version of this in the 1989 appropriations bill that included NEA and NEH funding. That provision banned the NEA and the NEH from funding works that, in the judgment of the endowments, could be considered obscene *and* lacking serious literary, artistic, political or scientific value ("Language on Obscene Art Hangs Up Interior Bill," 1989: 731–5).

In 1990, efforts to prevent NEA funding of objectionable art once again threw the Interior Department's appropriations bill into turmoil and the NEA was up for reauthorization as well, providing additional opportunities for the issue to be aired. The major issue entrepreneurs were Jesse Helms in the Senate and Dana Rohrabacher (R., Calif.) in the House, neither on panels with jurisdiction over NEA. In an effort to resolve the issue the Senate Labor and Human Resources Committee developed a compromise that would have allowed the NEA to fund any project it wished, but with the stipulation that any artist or organization funded with NEA money whose work was then found by a court to be obscene or in violation of child pornography laws would have to give the money back and be ineligible for further NEA monies for three years. This approach was enacted though it didn't satisfy critics such as Helms, who threatened the arts community that "You ain't seen nothing yet." (*CQ Almanac*, 1990: 433). Even Hatch, who acted as the compromiser, verbally put the NEA on notice: "If there are any of these [offensive projects] funded in the future, they're going to be in trouble, and I'm going to be upset, too," he said (CQ Almanac, 1990: 433).

And these have not been idle threats, for the budget process has provided a regular venue for the NEA and the NEH to be caught up in anti-pornography policy initiatives. Helms continued his crusade in 1991, offering an amendment to an appropriations bill that would mandate prison time for selling child pornography. He also attempted to get language in the NEA appropriation that would prevent NEA from funding art showing "sexual or excretory activities or organs." That provision was dropped in conference ("Interior Provisions," 1991: 564). But a continuing pattern has been established—one in which the NEA and NEH budgets are regularly threatened, especially when their funding of any controversial art project attracts renewed attention to the fact that tax dollars are being used to support projects that are sexually offensive.

Technology and Pornography. New policy initiatives involving pornography were spurred not only by issue redefinition which focused attention on the sensitivities of tax dollars being devoted to offensive works of art and more heinous forms of pornography such as "kiddie porn" but also by issue redefinition stemming from the proliferating venues for distribution of pornography. For example, throughout the 1980s, Congress struggled with the problem of regulating telephone sex services which, given the nature of the technology, were readily accessible by juveniles. But Supreme Court decisions have complicated the regulatory efforts of Congress in this regard. In 1988, Congress had banned obscene and indecent telephone services altogether, but in *Sable Communications of California Inc v. FCC*, the Supreme Court had allowed only the ban on obscene services, not the ban on indecent ones. In 1989, Congress renewed its effort to restrict "dial-a-porn" operations, passing a provision with language that got around the Constitutional problem by denying access to indecent messages unless a person specifically subscribed for them ("Dial-A-Porn Restrictions," 1989: 382).

Technological developments have created other challenges for the regulation of pornography and frayed the boundary between obscenity law and indecency regulations. By way of background, it should be noted that case law and policy concerning pornography had been developing on a different track from law and policy concerning decency on radio and television. Compared with the sexually explicit materials available in video parlors, adult bookstores, and the like, broadcast communications are less easily screened out by those who do not wish to hear them or to have their children hear them. The airwaves, in this sense, are a public good, and government arguably has a larger role in policing that public good. This logic lay behind governmental efforts to set a more stringent standard for regulation of sexual materials on radio and television—efforts that were set forth in Federal Communications Commission (FCC) rules on "indecent" material on the air. A high profile challenge to these rules came five years after the *Miller* case. In the 1978 case of *FCC v. Pacifica Foundation*, the Supreme Court legitimated the FCC's power to ban indecent broadcasting. As a result, broadcasters have been bound by decency standards that prevent them from using language on the air that is deemed patently offensive by contemporary community standards, at least during times of the day when children would normally be part of the audience. In the 1970s, the FCC specifically established 10 p.m. to 6 a.m. as the only period of the day in which children would not normally be in the audience, thereby creating a limited "safe harbor" for indecent material on the air (Clark, 1991: 983).

But, just as the Justice Department and the U.S. Postal Inspection Service were pursuing aggressive campaigns against pornography in the second half of the 1980s, so also was there a turn toward a more aggressive approach to decency rules by the FCC in the late 1980s. Moving away from the "safe harbor" principle that had protected broadcasters who confined their raunchier materials to the 10 p.m. to 6 a.m. period, the FCC reverted in 1987 to a broader standard that would bar indecent material at any time when there was a "reasonable risk" that children could be listening. When the FCC came under protest by broadcasters for this rules change, it was given dramatic backing by Congress which in 1988 enacted a 24-hour prohibition on indecent broadcasts (Clark, 1991: 983). But the U.S. Court of Appeals struck down the law, stating that the First Amendment requires that some portion of the day be available when broadcast programs with indecent content could be provided to a willing audience. In response, Congress in 1992 enacted a law once again creating safe harbors for indecent programming—one from midnight to 6 a.m. for commercial stations and another between 10 p.m. and 6 a.m. for both public radio and TV stations that go off the air at midnight (Greenhouse, 1996: p. A5).

Into this unsettled picture emerged yet another technologically-induced occasion for policy initiatives concerning pornography regulation—the arrival of the Internet as a commonly used vehicle for communication. The Internet, a global network of linked computers, provides the capacity for words and images, pornographic or otherwise, to be transmitted to an estimated 7 million Americans in 1995 who are on-line either through subscription services such as America Online or Compuserve (Clark, 1995: 563) or who can get on-line through institutional access at the workplace. As it became clear that many pornography-related news groups were proliferating on the Internet and that chat rooms and bulletin board services sometimes involved sexually explicit language, concern arose over the capacity of parents to shield their children, who are often more computer-sophisticated than their parents, from this material.

In response, Congress incorporated the Computer Decency Act in the comprehensive telecommunications legislation passed in 1996. Evidencing the logic that "cyberspace should be subject to the stricter regulation given television and radio," the Computer Decency Act stipulated that the provision of indecent or patently offensive material on computer networks is a serious felony carrying penalties that can include not only large fines but prison terms (Lewis, 1996: 1).

However, in June of 1996, a three-judge appeals court panel ruled against the constitutionality of the Computer Decency Act. In a strongly worded decision, the appeals panel stipulated that, by attempting to restrict a broad range of indecent and patently offensive materials, the Act was an abridgment of the free speech rights of adults. The justices noted that obscenity and child pornography were already illegal in any form of communication, and that mechanisms such as computer software are available to protect children from sexual materials that are indecent or offensive but not obscene (Lewis, 1996: 18). In a ruling on June 23, 1997 the Supreme Court agreed, striking down the Computer Decency Act as an unnecessarily broad suppression of speech directed to adults.

Pornography, Violence Against Women, and Victim's Rights. In the early 1980s, a significantly new approach to the issue of pornography emerged from a group of feminist theorists who argued that pornography should be viewed as a civil rights issue—i.e., that pornography systematically contributed to the subjugated status of women in American society. A key to this point of view is the argument that pornography directly contributes to a variety of significant harms to women—"the rapes, the battery, the sexual harassment, the sexual abuse of children, the forced sex, the forced prostitution, the unwanted sexualization, the second-class status" (Dworkin and MacKinnon, 1988: 25–6). In particular, two feminist legal theorists, Andrea Dworkin and Catharine MacKinnon, argued that the law should treat pornography as a form of sex discrimination and it should empower the victims of pornography to sue the purveyors of such sexual materials. Their arguments galvanized city officials in Minneapolis, Minnesota and led to that city's passage of a pathbreaking ordinance in 1983, crafted by MacKinnon and Dworkin, that allowed women to sue for damages against producers or purveyors of the pornography if they could show that they had been coerced into a pornographic performance, or show that they had suffered an assault directly caused by a particular piece of pornography, or that they had pornography forced upon them (Downs, 1989: 44–47). Pornography was defined for purposes of the Minneapolis ordinance as "sexually explicit subordination of women, graphically depicted, whether in pictures or in words, that also includes one or more of the following . . ." with an ensuing list that included nine different characterizations, such as the presentation of women as "dehumanized as sexual objects," the presentation of women in "postures of sexual submission," the presentation of women as "whores by nature," and the presentation of women "as sexual objects who enjoy pain or humiliation" (Dworkin and MacKinnon, 1988: 101).

Although the Minneapolis ordinance was vetoed by the mayor, attention to this approach had in the meantime spread to Indianapolis, which moved ahead with a similar ordinance. That ordinance was struck down as unconstitutional by a district judge in 1984 and by the Seventh Circuit Court of Appeals in 1985 (Downs, 1989: 136–8).

Nevertheless, the debate surrounding the Minneapolis and Indianapolis ordinances drew a great deal of attention nationally and helped to further a redefinition of the pornography issue toward an emphasis on the link between pornography and violence against women and toward the concept of victim compensation. In the mid-1980s, the Meese commission provided another institutional venue for the arguments of theorists and scholars who had claimed that pornography frequently contained violent themes and that pornography was implicated in rape and other violent crimes against women. By 1992, the Senate Judiciary Committee was considering legislation that embodied these strands of thinking. The proposed Pornography Victims' Compensation Act would have permitted rape victims to sue pornographers and pornography distributors if it could be shown that the sexual materials they provided had incited the offender's action (Dumas, 1992: 1887). Although passed by the Senate Judiciary Committee in 1992 by a one vote margin, the bill bogged down in disagreements over the legitimacy of the approach.

Pornography and Policy Change: A Summary and Transition. Beginning with the *Miller* decision in 1973, governmental policy toward pornography took a turn toward the more restrictive. Equally important for our purposes, that restrictive turn in policy has largely been sustained in the period since 1973. In some respects, policymaking with respect to pornography has escalated in volume and intensity toward a veritable frenzy of activity. A spate of legislative initiatives have led to policy developments concerning child pornography, women as victims of pornography, pornography on the airwaves, pornography on computer networks, and pornography in taxpayer funded arts; and vigorous enforcement initiatives have sustained a heightened level of prosecutions and convictions. Although the Courts have resisted some elements of this frenzy of legislative and executive branch activity, as in the recent ruling against the Computer Decency Act, court decisions involving pornography cases have moved away from the permissive standards that held in the liberalizing phase prior to the *Miller* case.

As noted earlier, there is no systematic public opinion data for the period prior to 1973 to help us to determine whether or not the initial shift toward a more restrictive stance was responsive to public opinion. The following section considers trends in public opinion concerning pornography for the period since 1973 to explore whether the continuing drive for restrictions on pornography is consistent with contemporary public opinion and whether the many policy developments concerning pornography, from presidential commissions to Supreme Court cases to high-profile legislative initiatives, have had an impact on public opinion. As the next section will show, however, what we encounter instead is aggregate public opinion that exhibits some important features of the non-attitudes model.

Public Opinion on Pornography

At one level, public opinion about governmental regulation of pornography can be described as divided, and relatively stable in that division over time. The initial evidence comes from the most consistently asked survey research question about pornography—a General Social Survey item asking respondents whether pornography should be legal regardless of age, illegal for those under age 18, or illegal for everyone. As Figure 4-2 shows, at no time in the past two decades has there been more than trivial support for the position that pornography should be unequivocally legal, and the

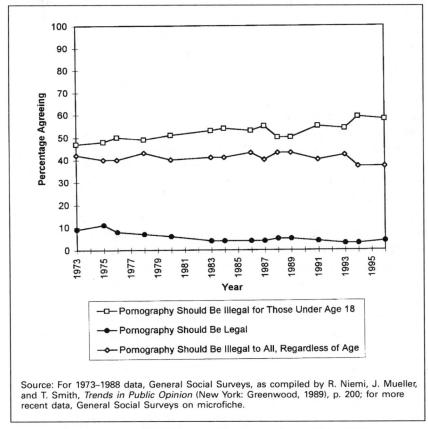

Source: For 1973–1988 data, General Social Surveys, as compiled by R. Niemi, J. Mueller, and T. Smith, *Trends in Public Opinion* (New York: Greenwood, 1989), p. 200; for more recent data, General Social Surveys on microfiche.

Figure 4-2. Public Opinion on Pornography, 1973–1996

scant 10% that responded this way in 1973 declined to less than 5% by 1994. But a plurality, and in some years a bare majority of respondents, espouse the view that pornography should be legal for adults but illegal for minors. Combined with the respondents who want pornography to be legal regardless of age, there is a substantial majority of respondents, throughout the 1973–1996 period, who prefer that pornography should be legal *for adults*. The most common response, and indeed the majority response since 1980, has been that pornography should be illegal for those under age 18. This is the viewpoint that has gained ground, but only at the very minimal rate of about ten percentage points over the last two decades. There is a sizable minority viewpoint, holding steady in the low 40% range, that pornography should be illegal for everyone.

There is thus more evidence of a *split* in public opinion than *change* in public opinion. Indeed, the continuity in this time series contrasts markedly with the continuing trend toward more aggressive regulation of pornography.

The stability of this public opinion series over time suggests that the public has been relatively immune to the many attempts at opinion mobilization that are revealed in the policy history of pornography. Presumably, this means in part that social definitions of pornography have changed. While there are no systematic data on what the public considers to be pornographic, the popularity and evident acceptability of nudity, erotic themes, and sexual content in movies, books and song lyrics in the 1980s and 1990s might lead one to conclude that the stability of public opinion about pornography regulation reflects changing standards relative to the 1960s and 1970s—i.e., the general public's growing tolerance of more and more explicit material. Other poll results, however, show how much room there is for wars on pornography to be waged in the name of public opinion. A more episodically-asked Yankelovich, Skelly, and White poll item asks respondents to agree or disagree with the statement: "The government should crack down more on pornography in movies, books, and nightclubs." The results, as compiled by Smith (1990: 42) suggest that, in both the 1970s and the 1980s, anywhere from about two-thirds to three-quarters of respondents at least partially favored a crackdown.[1] As we saw above, majorities were also favoring legal availability of pornography for adults throughout this period on GSS polls, so majority desires for crackdowns either reflect preferences for a crackdown on pornography being purveyed to minors, preferences for crackdowns on some kinds of pornography even while pornography generally is perceived to be legitimate for adults, or simple inconsistency in opinion on the part of a noticeable portion of the American public.

Indeed, further exploration suggests that the apparently stable yet divided public opinion described above is really comprised of a substantial element of non-attitudes. In the classic sense, public opinion poll results are said to amount to "non-attitudes" if expressed views are unstable or give other evidence of lack of consistency, lack of a basis in knowledge, or meaninglessness. The concept of a "non-attitude" suggests a cavalier response to an issue that is not genuinely important to the individual.

Research on the issue of "non-attitudes" typically focuses on individual respondents and on questions of individual response stability and other evidence of opinion coherence or the lack thereof. But the discussion here focuses primarily on public opinion in the aggregate. From this perspective, the temporal stability of public opinion on pornography is not necessarily evidence of rationally grounded, meaningful public opinion. Indeed, in their influential analysis, Page and Shapiro (1992) suggest that change in aggregate poll data over time is evidence of the meaningfulness and rationality of public opinion if there are social and economic trends or national and international events relevant to the issue in question and the direction of movement in collective opinion is consistent with what those trends and events suggest.

This perspective puts a new light on the relative stability of public opinion on pornography, as charted in Figure 4-2. Despite the highly contrasting conclusions of two different presidential commissions, despite the emergence of child pornography as a threatening new aspect of the issue and the rise of a movement linking pornography to violence against women, despite (or perhaps because of) the proliferation of sexually explicit materials in the United States, and despite numerous anti-pornography crusades at both the national and local levels, the percentage of individuals believing that pornography should be illegal regardless of age has remained virtually unchanged for over twenty years and the percentage believing that pornography should be illegal for those under age 18 has increased very little.

This could, of course, reflect a genuine commitment to free speech among the majority of Americans that makes them resistant to restrictions on freedom of expression even in the face of substantial threats. However, there is too much other evidence to accept such a rosy interpretation of these results. For example, despite apparent increases over time in the general public's commitment to freedom of expression, more focused research on the topic suggests that the true level of support for such democratic values is actually quite low (Sullivan, Piereson, and Marcus, 1982; McClosky and Brill, 1983).

Interestingly enough, respondents to the General Social Survey (GSS) in 1984—just as the Meese commission was about to form—were asked how firm their opinion on pornography regulation was and how much information they had about the pornography issue. In the aggregate, the responses suggest that non-trivial numbers of respondents were unlikely to change their opinion despite self-professed limitations in their information on the subject. When asked how much information they had about the pornography issue, only 35% indicated that they had either all or most of the information that they needed; the remaining respondents, constituting a substantial majority, admitted that they had only some of the information that they needed (37%), very little information (26%), or gave no response (2%). Yet, when asked "How firm are you about your opinion on the pornography issue?" only 17% indicated that they were either very likely (3%) or somewhat likely (14%) to change. In short, the aggregate responses on these items suggests that a substantial portion of public opinion on pornography consists of something like gut-level responses divorced from knowledge about the issue. And, as noted in chapter 1, genuine attitudes entail a combination of cognitive and affective elements.

A comparison of the initial GSS items on the legality of pornography with still other survey research items raises further questions about the meaningfulness of public opinion about pornography. The General Social Survey has also asked respondents whether they believed pornography (defined in an introductory statement as "books, movies, magazines, and photographs that show or describe sex activities") had any of various effects, such as leading to the breakdown of morals or leading to rape. Throughout the roughly two decade span of this time series, the majority of respondents have agreed that looking at or reading pornography does lead to the breakdown of morals. Since, as we have seen, substantial majorities throughout the years have nevertheless believed that pornography should be legal for adults, this means that at least some portion of the responding public supports the legality of pornography despite its corrosive effect on morals. Again, such a combination of views need not necessarily constitute evidence of irrational or otherwise meaningless opinion. Perhaps detrimental moral effects are deemed less important than free speech rights; or perhaps those "detrimental moral effects" are special concerns with respect to impressionable youth, hence explaining why there is so much more support for limiting the accessibility of pornography to youth than for limiting accessibility to adults. But to continue this line of inquiry further, we find that, throughout the years, the majority of GSS survey respondents (anywhere from 50–60%) have also agreed that reading or looking at pornography leads to rape. Squaring majority support for this statement with majority support for the legality of pornography is more difficult, partly because this is not the sort of negative impact that is confined to impressionable youth and partly because of the seriousness of the effect in question. Evidently, at least a portion of the responding public wants pornography to be legal to adults even though they believe that viewing it leads to rape—an illegal act and a very specific harm. There may be a variety of reasons for this combination of views other than a hyper-valuation of pornography in particular or free speech rights in general. For example, some might believe that government bans on pornography could never be effective in any case. But, by this point, we must acknowledge that we are straining to put a rational interpretation on collective opinion.

Furthermore, some individual-level analysis of survey data on pornography has been reported, and that analysis is more suggestive of the inconsistencies of non-attitudes than of rational opinion grounded in deep-seated free speech values. At the individual level of analysis, a key manifestation of non-attitudes is a lack of ideological structuring or other coherent opinion patterning (Converse, 1964). In their study of attitudes toward censorship of pornography and attitudes toward more general censorship (i.e., censorship of extreme views, politically unpopular positions, and so forth), Hense and Wright (1992: 1670) found strong evidence of ideological structuring with respect to general censorship. Attitude toward general censorship was substantially correlated with radicalism/conservatism, traditional family ideology, authoritarianism, and church attendance (r's in the range of 0.46 to 0.67). By contrast, the findings were less consistent and much weaker *with respect to censorship of pornography*. The correlation between traditional family ideology and support for regulation of pornography was only 0.23, and the correlation between authoritarianism and support for regulation of pornography was only 0.27.

In a survey study of respondents in Dane County, Wisconsin in 1986, Thompson, Chaffee and Oshagan (1990: 80) found that, after controlling for genetic, demographic, and other factors (such as experience with pornography, political orientation, etc.), the most powerful predictor of opinion about government regulation of pornography was belief about the effects of pornography. But, "Specifically, and unexpectedly, those who perceived pornography to have the greatest effects were opposed to its being regulated. These perceived effects were primarily negative, including deleterious effects on interpersonal relations between the sexes and violation of women's civil rights."

The authors interpret this as an example of the "third-person effect" thesis which stipulates that people believe others are more affected by their exposure to the mass media than they are themselves. The third-person effect might, in fact, be an avenue for explaining away what would seem to be illogical and inconsistent attitudes. That is, if many individuals believe that pornography has harmful effects on others but that they themselves are immune to such harms, they might logically oppose regulation *providing that they consider their own rights to free access or the abstract principle of freedom of expression to be more important than the mitigation of the harmful effects that pornography has on others.* But there are two problems with using the third-person effect to try to write off what would otherwise appear to be evidence of non-attitudes. First, research specifically directed toward the study of the third-person effect with respect to pornography shows that the crucial link in the forgoing argument—i.e., attitude toward free expression—is of very limited importance in accounting for opinions about the regulation of pornography. For example, Gunther (1995: 35) finds that while attitude toward free expression is a statistically significant variable, it accounts for only 3% of the variation in support for regulation of pornography. In addition, Gunther (1995: 35) suggests that the third-person effect constitutes a perceptual bias: "Either they are underestimating influence on themselves, overestimating influence on others, or doing some of both."

Erroneous or biased perceptions are not, of course, quite the same thing as non-attitudes. But the evidence that substantial numbers of Americans are cavalierly making erroneous assumptions about the effects of pornography on themselves relative to others is more consistent with a non-attitudes interpretation than with any effort to find knowledgeable and deeply held attitudes in the opinions expressed about pornography.

Finally, there is reason to believe that the pornography issue is not a particularly salient one. It never shows up with enough mentions on the "most important problem" item to warrant a separate categorization. And, in 1984, when the GSS asked specifically "How important is the pornography issue to you," 11% said "one of the most important"; 33% said "important"; 39% said "not very important"; 15% said "not important at all"; and 2% said "don't know" or gave "no answer". Thus, even when prompted with a specific question about this issue at a time when the Reagan administration was giving much attention to it, only 44% thought pornography passed the threshold of being more than "not very important". This low level of salience does not in itself mean that the public's views on pornography are non-attitudes. But it does mean that the pornography issue is a good candidate for the sort of transitory opinion-giving that is the stuff of non-attitudes. And, as the remainder of the chapter will argue, the failure of political elites to successfully mobilize media and popular attention to a compelling re-definition of this issue means that the kind of leadership necessary to transform non-attitudes into genuine attitudes through a policy learning process has been missing.

If, as is being suggested here, aggregate public opinion about pornography includes many poll responses that are loosely held and inconsistent, it is not necessarily because the American public is wanting in rational capacity. There are good reasons for collective confusion and ambivalence about the subject. A wide variety of different types of sexually explicit materials are available in American society, ranging from the very tame to the most hard-core, some incorporating violent themes and some not, and representing a wide range of media (text-only materials, still photographs, movies, etc.). There are also a variety of ways in which sexually explicit material might be made legally available, some of which make the materials more intrusive in everyday society than others. Given these multiple considerations about what is meant by pornography and what is meant by having it legally available, it is not difficult to imagine citizens having opinions on the subject that are somewhat vague, tentative, and qualified.

Furthermore, because regulation of pornography entails restrictions on free speech rights, judgments about the propriety of expanded government control of sexually explicit materials turn heavily on the question of the harms caused by pornography. This would not be equally true for everyone. American society incorporates many different strands of political culture (Bellah, Madsen, Syullivan, Swidler and Tipton, 1985). But to the extent that classical liberal ideals still permeate the society, thinking about the regulation of pornography would be framed by conceptions of whether or not pornography really causes harm to others (Easton, 1994).

But although a plethora of specialized studies have been directed to the subject, the result has been high profile disagreement among experts rather than conclusive evidence. Furthermore, the character of the debate over the evidence has damaged the credibility of ostensibly objective, social science expertise and exposed the discussion as a fight between warring ideological camps.

The disagreement among experts and the fight over whether social science has been used appropriately is not new. It dates back at least to reactions to the President's Commission on Pornography, which drew heavily upon social science research studies that correlated crime statistics over time with pornography availability and comparisons of the use of erotic materials by convicted sex offenders and others. Studies of both kinds showed results that called into question the claim that pornography contributes to sex crimes (Linz and Malamuth, 1993: 30–31), and buttressed the Commission's conclusion that pornography for adults should be unregulated. However, conservatives such as James Q. Wilson (1975: 235) critiqued the findings of the President's Commission on a variety of grounds and concluded that "social science probably cannot answer the questions put to it by those who wish to rest the case for or against censorship on the proved effects of exposure to obscenity . . ."

But the level of disagreement escalated in the 1980s. As the quantity of scientific studies of the effects of pornography has increased, the prospects for a consensus have diminished. Instead, there have been vastly divergent research results, driven by a combination of differing methodologies interpreted in different ways. For example, a number of research studies have investigated the possible link between pornography and rape by examining correlations between sex magazine circulation rates, the availability of adult theaters, or other indicators of the extent of pornography on the one hand and rape rates on the other hand (Baron and Straus, 1989; Scott and Schwalm, 1988). Some of this research shows a correlation, and some does not. And even when a correlation is found, researchers have sometimes treated the link as a spurious one, explained by underlying cultural patterns of hypermasculinity in some areas (Berger, Searles, and Cottle, 1991: 97–8).

In addition to the fact that correlational studies cannot definitively establish a causal link between two phenomena, such studies are easily challenged on grounds that the measures that they use, and in particular their measures of exposure to pornography, are lacking in precision or validity. These and other critiques have led to the generation of a host of experimental studies—studies that examine changes in the behavior of individuals, including sexual arousal as studied through measures of penile tumescence, after they are exposed to erotic and/or sexually violent materials. Rather than providing definitive evidence, these studies have further confused the issue. As Berger, Searles, and Cottle suggest (1991: 99): "The variety of experimental designs makes it very difficult to draw general conclusions about pornography and leaves much room for different interpretations of the results." At least some of the research seems to suggest that exposure to pornography with violent themes contributes to aggressive laboratory behavior directed at women. But the welter of experimental studies cannot conclusively disentangle the relative impact of erotic content and violent content; and, given the nature of laboratory research, the ability of such studies to speak to real world impacts is always subject to debate.

Given these research limitations, neutral observers might wonder whether studies are serving only as grist for pre-set ideological positions. In their assessment, Linz and Malamuth (1993: 61) suggest that interpretations of the research evidence "are guided by the powerful influence of the underlying philosophical assumptions and social values" of either a conservative-moralist ideology of obscenity, a liberal ideology of erotica, or a feminist theory of pornography; and they conclude: "Whether or not any of the scientists involved in research from the point of view of one of the three perspectives would reject their basic premises in the face of contrary data gathered from another perspective is questionable." In short, social science experts don't and can't agree, in part because their differing ideologies cause them to frame the research question differently, to focus on different variables, to value or devalue various research protocols (i.e., liberals dismiss experimental results as not being realistic enough about real, direct harms), and to interpret the findings of others differently.

Not surprisingly then, the research has been used by policymakers, but not in a neutral, objective, scientific fashion: "Policymakers, taking one or another of the positions, have tended to ignore potentially conflicting evidence from competing points of view" (Linz and Malamuth, 1991: 61). And professional disagreements about the evidence have become more acerbic as they have been transformed into internecine warfare among experts over the manner in which research evidence has been conveyed. This is nowhere more evident than in Diana Russell's scathing critique (1993: 160) of a group of pornography researchers, including Daniel Linz, Neil Malamuth, Edward Donnerstein, and others, for their refusal to acknowledge a causal relationship between pornography and rape in their testimony before the Meese commission. Noting that several of these individuals had previously reported research findings that seemed more supportive of the conclusion of a causal relationship, Russell goes on to speculate that these researchers minimized the evidence for a causal link because they were concerned that the commission would use such findings to advance a more restrictive policy agenda; while acknowledging that any scholar would be concerned about the dilemma of having their work used inappropriately, she nevertheless castigates them, indicating that "distorting the implications of one's research is not an ethical way to handle this dilemma."

Conclusion

The scholarly controversy over the social effects of pornography helps us to understand why mass public opinion on the issue shows elements of the non-attitude phenomena. Noting the scholarly controversy, Thompson, Chaffee and Oshagan (1990: 74) suggest: "Given such unequivocalness among researchers, widely varying beliefs among the public about the effects of pornography . . . are not surprising." Beyond the variation *among* members of the public, this chapter suggests that the scholarly controversy may also have contributed to weakly-held and inconsistent opinions on the part of many individuals, such that aggregate public opinion on the topic takes on many of the features suggested by the non-attitudes argument. It is not simply that reams of specialized studies have not been able to conclusively demonstrate whether or not pornography contributes to rape or other social harms. Such inconclusive findings are common in social science research and do not necessarily come to the attention of the mass public. But in this case, conflict among the experts has been more visible to the public because the scholarly debate has partly been carried out in public policy venues such as the Meese commission. And the ideological polarization of the debate among scholars and researchers may have de-legitimized expert knowledge on this issue, thus reinforcing the predilections of many citizens to either ignore the pornography issue or to deal with it superficially and from the gut-level.

This is not to say no one has genuine attitudes about pornography. Presumably aggregate public opinion on this topic encompasses segments of the population with firm and passionately-held opinions on the topic that are rooted in deep-seated religious values or organized around other important anchors. The debate among the experts may have led others to develop mixed and contingent views on pornography, in the manner suggested by Zaller and Feldman's (1992) discussion of the multiple considerations that survey respondents might bring to bear on policy questions. But the pattern of findings reported in this chapter suggests that most of the public is simply not that concerned about pornography and that when asked about it, a non-trivial portion of the public reports views that appear inconsistent, illogical, or at the very least, curious.

Developments in public policy toward pornography cannot, therefore, reflect the responsiveness model, because there is no meaningful public opinion in the collective sense to which policymakers can respond. And despite efforts on the part of both governing elites and policy advocates to mobilize public opinion on the issue, there is little evidence that public opinion in the aggregate has been affected by mobilizing efforts. Stability rather than change is the hallmark of aggregate public opinion on this topic.

5

Abortion

Strident Controversy and Policy Responsiveness

Introduction

Few topics in American politics have been as divisive as abortion. Social movements representing both sides of the controversy have been activated, elections for state and federal offices have been affected by this single issue, communities have been convulsed by strident protest activity concerning the issue, and passions over the issue have turned to violence. Given the nation's long history with this contentious issue, it is not surprising to find that there is a relative abundance of relevant polling data and a voluminous body of research on abortion policy, on public opinion concerning abortion, and even on the relationship between the two. But, just as there is no national consensus on abortion, there is no research consensus on the linkage between abortion policy and public opinion. This may be in part because interpretations of the evidence are inevitably affected by an individual researcher's assumptions and values. But it is also likely due to the inherent complexities involved.

In particular, assessing the nature of the linkage between abortion policy and public opinion is complicated by the multiple venues within which abortion policy has been developed in the past thirty years. These venues include the federal courts, state governments, the national executive branch, and Congress. If the character of policy emerging from these different venues were generally in synch, characterizing trends in abortion policy would be simpler. However, this has not always been the case. As the following section will show, for example, portions of the abortion policy history seem to involve a tug of war in which Congress or the executive branch have attempted to restrict abortion while the Court was sustaining a relatively unrestricted right to abortion. Furthermore, state policies with respect to abortion have always differed from each other. And, in the wake of recent Court decisions affirming the legitimacy of certain state-imposed restrictions, states have become an even more important, diverse, and ever-changing venue for abortion politics and policy.

Because of these complications, consideration of the nature of the temporal linkage between abortion policy and public opinion must make several accommodations. First, the analysis requires a dual focus. Consideration of the patterns of linkage between aggregate, national trends in public opinion and federal policy is one important focus. Although state policy differences are important and state-level differences in opinion may also be important, it is possible and appropriate to view abortion as a national policy issue as well, and to think of public opinion at the national level. This is in part because of the obvious significance of the Supreme Court, Congress, and the national executive branch in making policy that constrains state-level policy choices. In addition, activists on both sides of the issue are not content with whether policy in their own state is restrictive enough or too restrictive. The existence of abortion clinics anywhere in America is offensive to many pro-life advocates; and state-level restrictions affect the availability of abortion in ways that are of concern to pro-choice activists everywhere, especially since such restrictions may have consequences for medical training, willingness of providers to get into abortion service despite state-level differences in policy, and so forth. Hence, much of the chapter will consider abortion policy as promulgated at the federal level and the linkage of that with aggregate national opinion polls results. Characterizing the trends in abortion policy at the federal level, however, will require attention to the contrasting directions that the courts, Congress and the executive branch have sometimes exhibited.

Where it is available, research on public opinion and abortion policy at the state level must be incorporated as a second focus, however. Fortunately, and in contrast with the other topics treated in this volume, there is a growing research literature that does just this. Secondary analysis of the results of that research will be considered in this chapter.

The chapter begins with a policy history that shows three distinct phases of abortion policy: (1) a state-based liberalizing period in the pre-*Roe v. Wade* era (1960s–1973), (2) the era of *Roe v. Wade* hegemony (1973–1989), and (3) the post-*Webster v. Reproductive Health Services* period in which states have been empowered to play a larger role and national policymaking on abortion became stalemated. The end-points or boundary markers for each phase are defined, in conventional fashion, by key court cases. But, as the following sections detailing each phase will show, the character and content of each phase is also defined by policies emanating from Congress, the executive branch, and particularly in the most recent phase, the states.

Abortion: A Policy History in Three Phases

Phase I: State-Based Liberalizing in the pre-Roe v. Wade Era (1960s–1973)

Prior to the 1960s, state laws concerning abortion were very restrictive. States in this period typically disallowed abortion except when a physician determined that the life, or in some states, the life or health of the mother were endangered. These restrictions were largely developed at the behest of the medical profession which wanted to prevent those outside the profession from having a greater role in pregnancy-related services (Tatalovich and Daynes, 1981: 24–5).

By the 1960s, however, the American Law Institute was suggesting that abortions be permitted for the sake of the physical or mental health of the mother, when the child would have physical or mental defects, or if pregnancy resulted from rape or incest. This was motivated in part, once again, by the needs of the medical community. Physicians wished to have a more firm legal footing for performing abortions rather than continuing to rely upon acceptance of their case-by-case judgments that abortion was warranted because it was life-threatening. In the late 1960s and into the early 1970s, a reform movement reflecting the American Law Institute's proposal unfolded, and by 1973, 18 states had changed or repealed their earlier restrictive regulations (Mooney and Lee, 1995: 604).

Then came some judicial involvement, such as a California state Supreme Court case (*People v. Belous*) in which the court ruled the state's restrictive abortion law to be unconstitutional, and a federal court case (*U.S. v. Vuitch*, 1969) in which the court ruled the District of Columbia's abortion statute unconstitutional. These cases, and a flood of other state and federal cases, were attacking abortion statutes because their vagueness violated due process, they violated privacy, or the discriminatory impact of such statutes with respect to poor women violated equal protection (Tatalovich and Daynes, 1981: 27–8).

This initial period of judicial ferment over the abortion issue culminated in the Supreme Court's landmark decisions in the linked cases of *Roe v. Wade* and *Doe v. Bolton*. In those decisions, the court "held that women have a constitutionally protected right to legal abortion"—a right "found to be a specific instance of a more general 'right to privacy'" (Cook, Jelen, and Wilcox, 1992: 2). The *Roe* decision set forth a framework that rules out state restrictions on abortion in the first third, or trimester, of a pregnancy and limits state restrictions in the second trimester to those needed to preserve the woman's health. Given that fetal viability was viewed as normally occurring at the beginning of the third trimester, the Court held that only in that final trimester could abortion restrictions be imposed in the interest of maintaining the life of the fetus.

Phase II. The Era of Roe v. Wade Hegemony (1973–1989)

In a substantial string of cases following *Roe v. Wade*, the Court "encouraged a broad and uncomplicated access to abortion" against various state efforts to limit it (Canon, 1992: 643). These cases invalidated requirements of spousal consent, parental consent (without an alternative) for minors to have abortions, judicial approval for minors, hospitalization, waiting periods, and various other state restrictions. The only limitations allowed by the Court were those banning public financing of abortions.

The hegemony of the abortion rights framework laid out in *Roe v. Wade* was sustained in the face of policy developments in Congress intended to restrict abortion. This is not to say that anti-abortion forces in Congress made no headway during this period. In fact, Craig and O'Brien (1993: 103–150) outline a veritable barrage of pieces of legislation that brought restrictions of one kind or another. The best known of these is the Hyde Amendment, first enacted in 1976 as a ban on the use of Medicaid funds for abortions except if necessary to save the woman's life; then liberalized to allow Medicaid funding of abortion in cases of rape or incest as well; revised again in 1981 to limit Medicaid funding to abortions necessary to save the woman's life; and then changed again in 1993 to allow Medicaid funding of abortion in cases of rape or incest. Numerous other restrictions were enacted in this period, typically attached to various health program re-authorizations or appropriation bills. In 1973, for example, Congress enacted a provision protecting federal fund recipients from being required to perform abortions or making facilities available for abortion procedures. In 1974, federally-funded "legal aid" lawyers were prevented from helping clients to obtain non-therapeutic abortions. In 1977, Congress stipulated that employers did not have to include abortion as a health insurance benefit except as a procedure needed to save a woman's life. In 1979, Congress barred the use of foreign aid funds for abortions and in 1982 Defense Department funding was similarly restricted, thus preventing the provision of abortions in military facilities. In 1981, the congressional appropriation for the District of Columbia prevented funding for abortions except where necessary to save the woman's life or in cases of rape or incest. (Later, this ban was made even more restrictive when the rape and incest exemption was removed in 1985). In 1981, strict rules were introduced to curtail the use of Title IX monies by programs that provided abortions or abortion counseling.

Given this ream of restrictions, one can characterize abortion policy during this period as pulling in two directions—with the Court sustaining a broad-based right to abortion and Congress chipping away at that right. And, for certain categories of individuals—most notably poorer women who might need to rely upon federal funds or facilities for access to abortion—these restrictions may be far from trivial. However, the period from 1973–1989 is treated here as one of the hegemony of *Roe v. Wade* not only because the legality of abortion in the first trimester and the need to link second trimester restrictions to maternal health considerations was not successfully challenged in the courts, but also because broad-based assaults on abortion rights were not enacted by Congress.

With regard to the latter, the major hope of anti-abortion forces was the passage of a constitutional amendment outlawing abortion altogether, relegating it to the states for regulation, or at least stipulating that abortion was not a constitutionally protected right. Various amendments of this sort were proposed in the early 1980s, but none received Congressional endorsement. Alternatively, legislation that would have effectively outlawed abortion by defining fetuses as legal persons, thereby giving fetuses Fourteenth Amendment protections of due process and equal protection under the laws, was proposed by Senator Jesse Helms in 1981. That approach also failed to achieve passage (Craig and O'Brien, 1993: 140–147).

Thus, in the period from 1973 to 1989, the right to abortion that had been set forth in *Roe v. Wade* was subjected to challenge and public policy promulgated in Congress compromised the availability of abortion for a number of subgroups of the population. But the Supreme Court remained firmly supportive of abortion rights as laid out in *Roe v. Wade,* and state efforts to limit abortion through restrictive state regulations were not legitimated by the Court.

Phase III: Court Empowerment of State Abortion Policymaking and National-Level Stalemate (1989–present)

By the end of the 1980s, however, the composition of the Supreme Court had changed as a result of Reagan-era appointments—appointments that were scrutinized carefully for their implications concerning the abortion issue. As a result, the tide of abortion policy emanating from the Court turned in a more restrictive direction. Three key cases exemplify this. In *Rust v. Sullivan,* a 1991 case, the Court allowed an administrative regulation imposed by the Reagan administration that barred federally-funded family planning facilities from speaking to clients about abortion.

Of still greater importance are a pair of cases in which the Court opened the door for more restrictive state regulations regarding abortion. In *Webster v. Reproductive Health Services* (1989), the Court considered the constitutionality of a Missouri state law requiring that all abortions be performed in a hospital; that physicians do a test for viability on any fetus that they believe is 20 or more weeks old; that barred the use of public funds for abortion counseling or for abortions that were not necessary to save a woman's life; and that made it illegal for public personnel or government facilities to be involved in abortion procedures or counseling. In upholding these restrictions, the Court provided an invitation for other states to develop a variety of restrictive laws. In *Planned Parenthood of Southeastern Pennsylvania v. Casey* (1992), the Court upheld most provisions of a Pennsylvania law restricting abortions. While neither spousal notification nor reporting and public disclosure requirements were upheld, *Casey* allowed the state to require abortion counseling and informed consent from the woman, a 24-hour waiting period, and one parent's (or a judge's) consent for unmarried women under age 18. The *Casey* decision included an endorsement of the continuing validity of the basic framework of *Roe v. Wade*, including a woman's basic right to choose an abortion before fetal viability and to obtain an abortion without undue interference. However, four justices, including White, Scalia, Thomas, and Chief Justice Rehnquist, dissented from this holding.

The full impact of *Casey* is still being assessed as of this writing. It is clear that the Court's rulings in *Webster* and *Casey* have returned state governments to a key policymaking position on the abortion issue. But this has not necessarily meant a widespread and decisive turn toward more restrictive abortion policies, as many pro-choice advocates feared. In their 1993 assessment, Craig and O'Brien (1993: 282) suggest that once the *Webster* case bounced the issue back to the states, new state laws on abortion have predominantly been neither absolutist about abortion rights nor extreme attacks on the legality of abortion.

In the wake of the *Casey* decision, states have continued to move abortion policy in a variety of different directions, some adopting more restrictive policies and some making abortion more accessible. In at least 12 states, pro-choice activists have successfully used state courts to get Medicaid funds to pay for abortions, thus using the more liberal provisions of some state constitutions to circumvent national policy on the matter (Weidlich, 1995). A variety of summative scores of the restrictiveness of states' abortion policies have been developed, such as a nine-point scale developed by the National Abortion Rights Action League that rates states depending upon how many legal restrictions the state has on minors obtaining abortions and on Medicaid funding of abortion. As of 1992, states scored all the way from 0 to 8 on the scale, with states such as Hawaii, New York, Oregon and Vermont anchoring the least restrictive end and states such as Alabama, Rhode Island, South Carolina, Michigan, Missouri, and Louisiana anchoring the most restrictive end (Wetstein and Albritton, 1995: 95). In his assessment of abortion policymaking in a set of ten case study states, Byrnes (1995) emphasizes the tremendous differences that have emerged, with states such as Louisiana and Pennsylvania enacting quite restrictive policies while states such as Washington and Maryland enacted policies to shore up abortion rights against federal incursions. Moreover, after noting that the direction of state abortion policy after *Webster* and *Casey* seems to reflect the states' abortion policy orientations prior to *Roe v. Wade*, Byrnes (1995: 250) argues that the pattern is supportive of "the notion that *Roe v. Wade* short-circuited a process whereby the fifty American states were headed in the 1970s to continued diversity in terms of their receptiveness to legal abortion." As we will see below, this diversity in contemporary state policies concerning abortion has special significance from the perspective of the public opinion-public policy connection.

There have been abortion policy developments at the national level since the *Casey* decision as well. Shortly after his inauguration, President Clinton issued an executive order lifting the gag rule on abortion discussions in federally-funded family planning clinics—a gag rule that had survived Supreme Court scrutiny and attempts by Congress to overturn the rule. Other executive orders issued by Clinton rescinded Reagan-Bush era restrictions on abortions in overseas military hospitals (providing the costs of the procedure were borne privately) and on family planning programs overseas that included abortion counseling (Rubin, 1994: 285–6).

Still other policy developments in the post-1992 period were counted as "wins" by pro-choice advocates. In 1993, for example, the Hyde Amendment was once again revised to include rape or incest as well as endangerment of the woman's life as circumstances under which Medicaid could be used to pay for abortions.

But especially important developments in the pro-choice direction were policies responding to the problem of maintaining the reality of legal access to abortion under circumstances in which violence at abortion clinics intimidated providers and abortion clients alike. In particular, attention to the problem was galvanized by the 1993 fatal shooting of an abortion clinic doctor, David Gunn, outside the same Pensacola clinic that had previously been subject to bombing attacks, and the shooting of another abortion doctor in Wichita, Kansas. In response to militant protest activities and the reality or potential for violence at clinics, pro-choice advocates had adopted the strategy of getting federal court injunctions preventing pro-life protesters from harassing women entering clinics. Legally, these injunctions were based on the Ku Klux Klan Act, legislated in the Reconstruction era to protect blacks. But the Supreme Court ruled against this application of the Klan act in January of 1993 (*Bray v. Alexandria Women's Health Clinic*). In direct response to these developments, the Freedom of Access to Clinic Entrances Act was enacted by Congress and signed into law by President Clinton in 1994. The Act prohibits force, threat of force, or physical obstruction at clinic entrances that would interfere with, injure or intimidate clinic personnel or women attempting to get abortions. Civil and criminal actions could be brought by the U.S. or state attorneys general or individuals whose rights were violated, and stiff criminal penalties were established for those found guilty of violent acts against clinics. For destruction or damage of clinic property, a first offense could yield a fine of up to $100,000 and one year in prison; for personal injury a maximum penalty of 10 years in prison was set. Less severe penalties were set for nonviolent acts ("Bills Seek to Ensure . . .", p. 354).

Recent Supreme Court decisions have largely favored pro-choice advocates in their battle to maintain access to abortion in the face of the intimidation of anti-abortion protest at clinics. In the same year that the Freedom of Access to Clinic Entrances Act was passed, the U.S. Supreme Court issued a ruling in a case that challenged other sorts of regulations that local governments had devised to protect women's access to abortion in the face of clinic protests. In *Madsen v. Women's Health Center*, a 1994 case, the court ruled that restricting pro-life protesters from a 36-foot buffer zone around abortion clinics was not an abrogation of free speech rights, although regulations limiting protest displays within 300 feet of such clinics were overturned. The Court's decision in *Madsen v. Women's Health Center* was viewed as a reassuring development by pro-choice forces

(Idelson, 1994) for, although the Court in 1994 had refused to consider a challenge to the Freedom of Access to Clinic Entrances Act itself, such a challenge was viewed as inevitable. In the case of *United States v. Wilson*, a challenge to the Freedom of Access to Clinic Entrances Act was mounted, based on the argument that the Act exceeded the federal government's powers to regulate interstate commerce. In 1996, the 7th Circuit Court of appeals upheld the Freedom of Access to Clinic Entrances Act on grounds that interstate commerce was evidenced by the national organizing involved in clinic protests and the need for some women to cross state lines to obtain abortion clinic services (Nemko, 1996). And in February of 1997, the U.S. Supreme Court ruled in *Schenck v. Pro-choice Network of Western New York* that the use of a fixed buffer zone limiting abortion protest around clinic entrances is permissible.

In the fight being waged to maintain access to abortion in the face of vitriolic and sometimes violent abortion clinic protest, advocates had also taken up a legal weapon that had more commonly been used in the fight against drug trafficking and organized crime—the bringing of suits under the Racketeer Influenced and Corrupt Organizations (RICO) Act. RICO suits constitute a potent weapon because those found guilty in such suits are liable for triple damages–a penalty that is intended to be financially crippling. In the case of *NOW v. Scheidler*, the Supreme Court held that the National Organization of Women could bring a RICO suit against abortion clinic protesters on the grounds that a conspiracy to destroy abortion clinic operations constitutes a continuing criminal enterprise (Randolph, 1995).

And while some moves to restrict abortion have emanated from Congress in the post-*Casey* era, they have so far been neutralized by presidential veto. Most notable in this regard is legislation enacted in 1996 that would have made it illegal for doctors to conduct what were called "partial birth" abortions—a form of late-term abortion. While such legislation would not have had much substantive impact because most abortions performed in the U.S. are not late-term, physicians were alarmed at the precedent of congressional policy replacing the medical community's judgment on the propriety of medical procedures. Anti-abortion forces, meanwhile, saw the legislation as a means not only to restrict late-term abortions but also as a device for calling attention to troubling images about the handling of the fetus in such abortions, thereby undermining the nation's comfort level with abortion more generally. However, the legislation was vetoed by President Clinton on April 10, 1996 on grounds that it provided no avenue for medical professionals to conduct the abortion procedures that could be necessary when a woman's health was endangered.

Abortion policy in the United States has thus moved from an early phase in which states were gradually, and differentially, moving toward liberalization of very restrictive policies to a phase dominated by the Supreme Court's definition of first trimester abortion rights and its limitations on state efforts at general restrictions, to a complex, contemporary phase in which access to abortion is being both challenged by restrictive regulations in some states and protected by governmental policy, including both the Court's continued affirmation of the legality of abortion and its endorsement of federal and local policies designed to prevent intimidation and protest activity from functionally preventing access to abortion.

In order to assess whether this trajectory of public policy change is meaningfully linked with public opinion, we must first consider the evolution of public opinion on abortion and the burgeoning literature assessing it. The next section takes up this task.

Public Opinion on Abortion

Assessing the Character of Public Opinion

Just as abortion is a contentious subject in American politics, so are there conflicting assessments of how public opinion on the subject should be characterized. In part, this is due to the inevitable limitations of polling data. Although the topic of abortion has actually been the subject of a comparatively rich and varied body of opinion polling that includes at least one battery of questions asked for a long period of time, there are no poll items consistently available over time that fully tap the many contingencies and circumstances that have swirled around the abortion controversy.

Consistent with much of the research on the topic, this section relies primarily upon a series of General Social Survey (GSS) questions on abortion which have been asked consistently by the National

Opinion Research Center for many years. The battery of questions asks respondents to indicate whether they favor or oppose the legality of abortion under six different situations: there being a chance of the baby being born with a serious birth defect, the mother's health being endangered by the pregnancy, the pregnancy resulting from rape, the woman simply wanting no more children, the woman not wanting to marry the child's father, and the family not being able to afford more children. The advantages of this measure are its consistent availability over time and the fact that reactions to abortion in a variety of different situations, rather than abortion generally, are assessed.

The key disadvantage, however, is that this battery of poll items does not differentiate between earlier- and later-term abortions. Presenting data from a pair of late-1970s Gallup poll items that do make such a differentiation, Adamek (1994: 414) suggests that levels of support for the legality of abortion are significantly affected. Nevertheless, because there are no consistent poll data over time based on items like those treated by Adamek, the analysis here relies primarily upon the GSS items, conditioned by the critique that Adamek suggests and supplemented by data on additional poll items that have been asked rarely but at interesting historical moments.

With these considerations in mind, Figure 5-1 shows three striking and important features of aggregate public opinion on abortion. First is the dramatic increase in support for abortion in the period leading up to 1973. While these polling questions were asked more sporadically in this pre-*Roe* period than since, it is nevertheless obvious that an important shift in opinion was in process. For all scenarios except that of the woman's health being endangered, support for the legality of abortion shifted upward 25 to 30 percentage points from the mid-1960s to 1973. Even in the case of the mother's health being endangered, a scenario that already elicited very high levels of support for legal abortion in the early to mid-1960s, there was a noticeable shift of nearly 20 percentage points in the direction of favoring legal abortion. As a consequence, 1973 represents not only a legal keystone for abortion policy; it also constitutes a high water mark for public support for legal abortion.

The second characteristic of aggregate public opinion in Figure 5-1 is the clear distinction that has been maintained between

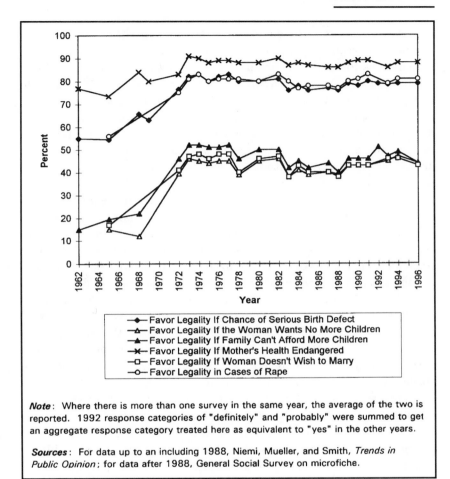

Figure 5-1. Percent Favoring Legality of Abortion Under Various Circumstances, 1962–1996

"medical" and "social" reasons for abortion, or what Cook, Jelen, and Wilcox (1992: 33) call the distinction between "traumatic" and "elective" abortion. Throughout the time series, there is at least a 30 percentage point difference between the vast majorities of the American public that favor the legality of abortion for the various "medical/traumatic" reasons and the numbers that favor legality of abortion for the various "social/elective" reasons. Indeed, only one of the latter reasons—the family not being able to afford more children—has ever evoked majority support in these polls.

The importance of these distinctive responses to different circumstances for abortion are underscored by other poll data showing that the majority of the American public is neither purely pro-life nor purely pro-choice, but instead has a contingent view of abortion. The Gallup poll has regularly assessed public opinion on abortion by asking respondents whether they believe abortion should be legal under any circumstances, legal under certain circumstances, or illegal in all circumstances. Across the roughly 20 years for which data of this kind are available, "legal under certain circumstances" was the response of more than half of the respondents in virtually all years, while "legal under any circumstances" has typically been the choice of about one-quarter of respondents and "illegal in all circumstances" has always been the choice of fewer than 10% of respondents (Craig and O'Brien, 1993: 263). For most individuals, then, opinion on abortion is situational—it depends on the reasons for abortion. And while there is near consensus about the "medical/traumatic" reasons, the "social/elective" reasons simply have not achieved the same legitimacy among the mass public.

The third characteristic is the relative stability of public opinion since 1973. Indeed, one of the most important and frequently-made observations about abortion opinion in the United States is the temporal stability in aggregate opinion on the topic. Stimson (1991: 82–83), for example, notes that the trend in public opinion about abortion does not track with the trend in his indicator of overall policy mood, as other domestic problems (welfare, urban problems and race) do: "Abortion preferences are an unusual time series. Compared to all others their variation is almost trivial." Similarly, Cook, Jelen and Wilcox (1992: 37) emphasize the long-term aggregate stability in abortion attitudes: "For eighteen years, the 'average' position on abortion has hovered near allowing abortion in four of the six possible circumstances, allowing abortions in between two and three traumatic circumstances, approving of abortion in between one and two elective circumstances."

This is not to say that there has been no change in the poll data. Figure 5-1 shows that, depending upon the reason at issue, there is a seven to twelve percentage point spread between legality-favoring levels in the years of highest support for legal abortion and the post-1973 years with the lowest levels of support for legal abortion. And the post-1973 years of least support for legal abortion, especially for social reasons, are concentrated in the mid- to latter-1980s; the years of highest support are concentrated in the mid- to late-1970s with the early 1990s showing signs of reestablishing those levels of support. In short, one might read these data as showing very high levels of support for legal abortion in the immediate post-*Roe* period, followed by an erosion of support in the 1980s, followed by a resurgence of support in the 1990s.

Such a reading is tempting. And it invites interpretations suggesting that public opinion has been driven by both social movements and policy events. That is, the dip in support for abortion in the early 1980s might be attributed to the efforts of the pro-life movement and the legitimacy accorded to anti-abortion concerns by the substantively marginal yet symbolically significant restrictions enacted by Congress in this period. Likewise, one might attribute the recent upward movement in the percentage favoring abortion legality as resulting from the counter-efforts of the pro-choice movement, reinforced by legitimating policy actions such as the Clinton administration's lifting of the gag order on abortion counseling.

However, such a reading and interpretation of the data probably constitutes over-reaching. Especially where the "medical/traumatic" reasons are at issue, year-to-year variations are small enough to be roughly within a range in which sampling error can account for differences; and although the variations are slightly greater where the "social/elective" reasons are at issue, the magnitude of these variations is nevertheless relatively modest. When viewed over the longer term of the full post-*Roe* period, the series exhibits a pattern more like substantively meaningless fluctuation around a stable plateau than meaningful trending.

If Figure 5-1 reveals important features of public opinion on abortion—its pre-*Roe* liberalizing movement, its relative stability thereafter, and its differential treatment of "medical/traumatic" and "social/elective" abortion situations—it cannot show some other features of public opinion that emerge from assessment of episodic poll data of different sorts. In particular, there is evidence of a huge discrepancy between the single-issue intensity with which some activists view the issue and the relatively low salience of the issue to the majority of the public; and there is evidence of considerable ambivalence or attitudinal conflict about the issue.

With respect to salience, there is evidence that abortion simply is not a particularly important public issue for most people. When Americans are asked to list or rank order important issues, it barely registers (Craig and O'Brien, 1993: 270). Sometimes respondents are asked about the importance of the abortion issue in the context of their vote decision. In 1989 only 14% listed a candidate's stand on abortion as a very important voting consideration. In a 1992 Gallup poll of 589 registered voters, only 13% indicated that they would only vote for a candidate for major office who shared their views on abortion and half indicated that abortion was "only one of many important factors when voting"; 36% said that abortion was not a major issue in terms of its effect on their vote choice.

Lack of awareness of abortion policies can be viewed as another indicator of the lack of salience of the abortion issue to most Americans. Rosenberg (1991: 236) notes that on Gallup poll questions commissioned by Judith Blake in 1975, less than half of the respondents were aware of *Roe v. Wade* and could correctly indicate what had been decided. Another poll, taken in 1982, revealed that 59% of respondents gave either a "don't know" or incorrect response when asked whether the Supreme Court forbids or permits women to get abortions in the first three months of pregnancy (Rosenberg, 1991: 236). A variety of similar showings of low awareness of *Roe v. Wade* and the current status of abortion law are available from sporadic poll items asked in the mid- to late-1980s (Adamek, 1994: 412–13).

All of this evidence of the low salience of the abortion issue for the mass public contrasts markedly with the intensity of mobilization of activists on both the pro-choice and the pro-life sides of the debate, feeding implicit or explicit criticisms of the way in which political debate about this topic has been anti-majoritarian. Craig and O'Brien (1993: 27), for example, note that "Compared with other issues and even standing alone, though, the political importance that the abortion issue commands is not reflected in poll responses. It seems clear that very vocal minorities on both sides have been able to keep the issue politically on stage" (Craig and O'Brien, 1993: 270).

But it is not simply that most Americans don't care at all about abortion, although they clearly care less than activists mobilized at either end of the issue spectrum. Rather, there is evidence that the majority middle of the American public is highly conflicted about it.

The very personal nature of the abortion issue may be implicated in this. Because it is such a private and delicate matter, citizens might be more likely to develop opinions about it based upon personal experiences and values rather than taking cues from political authorities, policy debates, and the positions that activist organizations take on the current status of the law. "In abortion, people think about the issue in its own terms, come to their own conclusions" (Stimson, 1991: 83).

But in doing so, many individuals are faced with the dilemma that abortion is far from an easy issue to sort out. Alvarez and Brehm (1995: 1057) have explored the extent to which the abortion issue evokes ambivalence among much of the American public—ambivalence in the sense that core values are in conflict for the respondent, thus leading to uncertainty and possibly to response instability on poll questions. Based on their analysis of 1982 survey data from the GSS, they conclude that it is quite common for individuals to hold mutually-contradictory attitudes toward abortion. Indeed, the majority of respondents expressed at least some such internal conflict, as measured by their articulation of reasons on both sides of the debate (Alvarez and Brehm, 1995: 1067). This ambivalence centers not so much around the question of whether abortion should be permitted to save a mother's life or in cases of rape or of birth defect. The social/elective scenarios asked about, however, bring out the conflict between core values. Alvarez and Brehm (1995: 1077) emphasize that, in contrast with the unequivocal positions of activists on both sides of the issue, for the majority of respondents "ambivalence and internal conflict reign over the four most difficult policy scenarios explored in this particular survey." Coupled with poll data showing the predominantly pro-choice but contingent views of the majority of respondents and their unwillingness to acknowledge it as a relevant criterion for electoral choice, research on the public's ambivalence on the topic provides important support for Craig and O'Brien's (1993: 273) overall characterization of mass opinion on abortion as "a troublesome, problematic, morally wrenching, wish it would go away, occasional necessity that I hope it never does but may someday face me, and in case it does I want the option (though I doubt I would want to exercise it) to decide what to do myself."

It is important to note, however, that the complex and sometimes contradictory character of public opinion on abortion does not mean that we are dealing with non-attitudes. Adopting the criterion that Page and Shapiro (1992) have used for assessing whether public opinion at the aggregate level is meaningful, we see that there is a meaningful pattern of public opinion, keyed to historical developments, rather than arbitrary fluctuation. Collective opinion exhibited a liberalizing trend in the 1960s, presumably reflecting recognition of the negative consequences of "back room" abortions, broad social changes in women's roles, and the reality of the practice of abortion; once abortion was legitimated through *Roe v. Wade*, however, the liberalizing trend stabilized and has remained so ever since, consistent with the essential stability in the legal status of abortion. Furthermore, research at the individual level suggests that the non-attitudes interpretation is largely irrelevant to public opinion on abortion. While there is some short-term instability in opinions on abortion, that response instability is much less than that for other issues. Furthermore, in the panel studies used to assess such short-term instability, "virtually no respondent switched from pro-choice to pro-life or vice versa" (Erikson and Tedin, 1995: 61). This and other research has led to the conclusion that, at the individual level, "abortion positions are probably the most stable of political attitude responses, rivaled perhaps only by party identification" (Erikson and Tedin, 1995: 61).

Nor is there evidence in individual-level studies of abortion opinion of the lack of ideological structuring that is a hallmark of non-attitudes. Those who describe themselves as conservatives are much less likely than self-described liberals to believe that abortion should be legal. This and the strong linkages between views on abortion and other individual-level characteristics, such as religiosity (Craig and O'Brien, 1993), are completely at odds with the lack of attitudinal consistency that sparked Converse's conceptualization of non-attitudes. The ambivalence and internal conflict that the abortion issue evokes among much of the public is better interpreted as resulting from the multiple considerations dynamic that Zaller (1992: 93) describes.

Abortion: The Opinion-Policy Nexus

The complexity of this characterization of public opinion on abortion underscores how difficult it is to assess whether public policy has been responsive to public opinion in various eras, especially since abortion policy itself is complex, including both restrictive elements and Constitutional protections throughout much of its history. But the preponderance of the evidence seems to suggest a sequence of policy development dominated by opinion-policy responsiveness. This conclusion can be derived whether one considers the policy-opinion linkage in the temporal sense that has dominated the discussion so far or in a comparative, cross-state sense—evidence for which will be presented shortly.

The Opinion-Policy Nexus: A Temporal Approach

Consider first the evidence of responsiveness in a temporal perspective. The first phase of abortion policy shows states liberalizing their abortion laws even as public opinion was becoming dramatically more favorable to legal abortion. The opinion responsiveness of the *Roe v. Wade* decision that capped off that phase has been the subject of conflicting interpretations. Some have argued that *Roe v. Wade* was an over-correction, pre-empting state efforts and establishing a nationwide policy standard that was more liberal than public opinion (Adamek, 1994; Tatalovich and Daynes, 1988: 177; Grossback, 1996: 10; Cook, Jelen, and Wilcox, 1992: 13), while others (Sackett, 1985) claim that the court's decision in *Roe v. Wade* was consistent with public preferences. But if *Roe v. Wade was* an over-correction, it was at least in the direction that opinion had been moving; and it anchored public policy on the side of ensuring legal availability of abortion—a side of the issue that incorporated the majority public view.

Even if one accepts the interpretation that the majority of the public had reservations about abortion that were not reflected in the *Roe v. Wade* framework, one must also acknowledge that in the era of *Roe v. Wade* hegemony, developments in other institutional venues were beginning to move abortion policy away from a maximally permissive mode. Thus, Phase II of abortion policy was a contested, contentious phase in which Court-based policy was consistent with the generally pro-choice tenor of public opinion but insensitive to the public's discomfort with abortion for social or elective reasons. And while congressional and executive branch policy developments moved in the opposite direction from the Court during this period, these policy developments created inappropriate instruments for satisfying the public's reservations about abortion. They gradually made abortion less accessible for some groups, but did not address the crucial issue of the public's discomfort with permissive abortion policy for social or elective reasons.

But Phase II culminated in key Supreme Court cases that, coupled with Congressional enactments and executive branch policy actions, appear to have moved policy quite close to the contingency-laced, pro-choice position that characterizes the majority of public opinion. This is not to say that every element of abortion policy in Phase III is consistent with majority sentiments. In particular, the Supreme Court's 1991 decision in *Rust v. Sullivan*, which upheld the administration's ban on doctors in federally-funded family planning clinics discussing the abortion option with a woman, was the subject of a Harris poll item in 1992. When asked whether they viewed this decision as right or wrong, 83% of respondents said it was wrong if the woman was the victim of rape or incest. In addition, 74% thought it was wrong if the future of an unmarried teenage girl might be seriously affected by having the baby, and nearly as many (72%) thought the gag order was wrong if the woman's mental health would be endangered from the pregnancy. When asked, overall, whether they favored or opposed the Court's decision, 72% opposed and 24% favored.

But, in addition to the longitudinal poll data discussed earlier in the chapter which reveals reservations about abortion in certain circumstances, some episodic poll data suggests a more focused consistency between public opinion and the particulars at issue in the *Webster* and *Casey* decisions. Polling evidence in the wake of the *Webster* ruling shows substantial support for some of the restrictions on abortion that were percolating through state policymaking systems at the time. A 1989 Gallup poll, for example, showed two-thirds favoring a requirement that teenage women get parental consent before being permitted to have an abortion, and bare majorities favored fetal viability tests before abortions on women at least five months pregnant (52%) and a ban on abortions in public hospitals except where the woman's life were endangered (54%) (Craig and O'Brien, 275).

Even more convincing are the results of some items from polls taken immediately in advance of the *Casey* decision—results suggesting that the Court's decision in that case was reasonably in accord with public opinion. In a May 1992 NBC poll, respondents were asked about a series of specific restrictions on abortion. Very strong majorities favored requiring women under the age of 18 to get a parent's permission before receiving an abortion (70%) and requiring women to wait 24 hours after requesting an abortion to have the abortion performed (69%). And nearly two-thirds of the respondents (62%) favored requiring married women to inform their husbands. Given that the Court in the *Casey* decision upheld a 24-hour waiting period and a parental consent requirement, while overruling a spousal consent requirement, one would have to conclude that the Court's willingness to allow for expanded state restrictions of these sorts while upholding the overall legality of abortion is highly consistent with majority public opinion. "Ironically, the most recent Supreme Court decision, *Casey v. Planned Parenthood*, may have come closest to the preferences of the public by sustaining both *Roe v. Wade* (and the possibility of legal abortion under certain circumstances) as well as *Webster v. Reprodutive Health Services* (which permitted significant restrictions on the availability of abortion to minors)" (Alvarez and Brehm, 1995: 1077).

The Opinion-Policy Nexus: A Comparative State Approach

Another way of assessing whether policy is responsive to public opinion focuses on whether variation in abortion policy across states at a given time systematically reflects variation in abortion opinion in those states—a topic that is especially relevant in the two phases of abortion policy history in which states were key policymaking venues (Phases I and III). Because of the lack of state-level public opinion data, most comparative state assessments focus on post-*Roe* patterns. However, in their exploration of the pre-*Roe* era in which many states liberalized their abortion laws, Mooney and Lee (1995) introduce two surrogate measures of public opinion—one intended to tap the level of demand for liberalized abortion (female workforce participation) and one intended to tap mass constraint on liberalized abortion (percentage of Catholics and fundamentalist Protestants in the state). They find empirical support for the importance of both surrogate indicators in predicting whether or not a state liberalized its abortion statute in the pre-*Roe* era, a result which is at least suggestive of a pattern of emergent state-level policy responsiveness in this period.

There is even more plentiful evidence of policy responsiveness to state public opinion in research on more recent phases of abortion politics. Cohen and Barrilleaux (1993: 210–211) find that variation in state public opinion is an important predictor of whether the state has passed legislation calling for a constitutional amendment banning abortion, though they also find that interest groups significantly affect state action. Wetstein and Albritton (1995: 102; and see Wetstein, 1996) have gone even further, demonstrating not only that states with more public support for abortion tend to have less restrictive abortion policies, but that this then translates into greater access to abortion: "Thus, public opinion on abortion helps structure abortion use through the intervening variables of policy and levels of access. Permissive publics tend to produce permissive abortion policies, and more abortion clinics can be found in these states."

But, as Goggin and Wlezien (1993: 190–191) correctly note, a full-blown model of policy responsiveness should show the public reacting to policy changes as well as policy responding to preferences. Such a thermostatic model provides signals to policymakers about whether they are within the zone of acceptability of public opinion or whether they have gone too far in either a permissive or restrictive direction. Goggin and Wlezien find evidence of a thermostatic model of abortion policy responsiveness in their state-level analysis based upon an index of the restrictiveness of state abortion laws passed between 1973 and 1989, state data from a 1990 CBS/ *New York Times* exit poll on whether abortion should be legal in some, all, or no circumstances, and state data from another CBS/ *New York Times* poll asking whether the respondent prefers that abortion policy be legal "as it is now," legal only in cases of rape, incest or life-threatening circumstances, or not legal at all. They find that in states where abortion policy is more permissive than public preferences, public opinion favors additional restrictions, while the reverse holds in states where abortion policy is more restrictive.

Conclusions: Policy Responsiveness or Opinion Mobilization?

Abortion is neither a one-dimensional policy area nor a topic about which public opinion is easily assessed. This chapter has attempted to acknowledge the complexities on both the policy side and the opinion side. Having done so, the general conclusion is that abortion policy, while not perfectly reflective of popular opinion, has largely been responsive to public opinion. There have been notable lags between some aspects of abortion policy and some aspects of abortion opinion, as in the long period in which *Roe v. Wade* pre-empted states from promulgating regulations that might have reflected the mass public's ambivalence about unrestricted, elective abortion. But even during this era of *Roe v. Wade* hegemony, the Court's position was more consistent than inconsistent with public sentiment. In more recent cases, the Court has empowered states to add some of the restrictions that the public appears to favor. And while this paves the way for abortion policy that is not consistent across the United States, a substantial body of research suggests that this variation in state policy is yet another vehicle for responsiveness.

Neither Congress nor the executive branch have been particularly instrumental in forging this responsiveness, except perhaps in the sense of generating abortion policies that churn back and forth, hand in hand with shifts in partisan control of each institutional venue, leaving abortion policy mixed and unsettled but never completely dominated by either extreme position. The history of abortion policy is littered with abortion-restricting executive orders that are later lifted and legislation that sometimes minimizes access to abortion and sometimes safeguards access to abortion. This is consistent with Tatalovich and Schier's (1993) notions of congressional action on morality issues like abortion being more shaped by ideology than by responsiveness to opinion and constituency pressures.

If anything, the states and the Supreme Court have played the lead in fostering policy responsiveness to the moderate majority of opinion on abortion. Such a conclusion is not particularly remarkable with respect to the states. But the centrality of the Court in sustaining a responsiveness connection between opinion and policy may strike some observers as curious. After all, the Court, with its non-elected members tenured for life and its decisions linked to legal considerations, is neither designed nor expected to be an engine for transformation of citizen preferences into policy. However, an ever-growing line of research has found congruence between Court decisionmaking and majority sentiments in the American public (Page and Shapiro, 1983; Mishler and Sheehan, 1993). And scholars have recently articulated a number of reasons why one might expect the Supreme Court's decisions to be responsive to public opinion, either directly or indirectly. For example, to sustain its legitimacy and effectiveness, the Court must try to avoid making decisions that are so far out of line with popular acceptability that they would be ignored or opposed by Congress and the executive branch. In addition, to the extent that judicial restraint causes justices to accord great weight to the policies promulgated by elected institutions, Court decisions will indirectly take public opinion into consideration when they uphold such laws out of a desire to avoid an activist role (Grossback, 1996: 5–6). And, of course, Court decisions can reflect public opinion still more indirectly if elected Presidents use their appointment powers in ways that shift the composition of the Court in directions more in accord with changing public opinion.

There is always the possibility, however, that whatever correspondence exists between abortion opinion and policy results from opinion being influenced by Court decisions rather than the other way around. Canon (1992: 641–2), for example, argues that the Supreme Court can play the role of a "cheerleader" in disputes over moral issues, either directly by encouraging or discouraging doctrines or further litigation *in dicta* or indirectly through the mobilizing or demobilizing effects that its decisions can have on other governmental institutions or interest groups. In particular, he argues that in the cases following *Roe v. Wade* the Court sent clear signals that it was cheering for the pro-choice point of view and that in *Webster* and the abortion cases immediately following it, the Court was giving "a clear invitation to state legislatures to see how far they could go in regulating abortion" as well as pointed hints of receptivity to doing away with *Roe v. Wade's* version of legalized abortion (Canon, 1992: 644). But this version of cheerleading in moral disputes is more directed toward court leadership of other institutions. What of court leadership of mass opinion?

Franklin and Kosaki (1989: 751–2) suggest that the Court *can* serve to educate public opinion, legitimizing certain positions and the claims of certain groups. There is no consensus in the body of scholarship that has been directed specifically at whether the Court's decision in *Roe v. Wade* functioned in this way. Some have rejected the proposition that the Court influenced popular opinion by noting that public opinion was already showing a liberalizing trend in advance of the decision (Uslaner and Weber, 1980). Others have rejected the proposition on broader grounds. Rosenberg (1991: 182), for example, concludes that the court followed rather than led social change in this case.

By contrast, Franklin and Kosaki (1989: 759) find contingent support for the thesis that the Court led rather than followed opinion in the case of *Roe v. Wade*. Their analysis shows that, even after taking account of the liberalizing trend that was already in process, this decision yielded increased approval for abortions for medical/traumatic reasons; with respect to abortions for social/ elective reasons, however, they find a different sort of result—"the Court's impact was primarily to increase the polarization of groups on the issue, with little or no increase in overall approval."

Apart from the inconclusive evidence concerning the potential impacts of *Roe*, the notion that the Court has moved opinion on abortion rather than being influenced by it is problematic in the longer perspective. As this chapter has shown, a key feature of public opinion on abortion since 1973 is its stability. There simply is not much evidence that the public has collectively changed its mind much about abortion, and the zone of acceptability for abortion policy appears to be in much the same place as it has been for more than 20 years. Law and policy concerning abortion have changed more over time than has mass opinion, and, as this chapter has shown, in ways that have gradually brought law and policy into even closer adjustment with opinion.

If there is limited evidence that the court moved public opinion rather than the other way around, one might nevertheless look for evidence of mobilization efforts in a more likely venue—the activities of elected politicians. It is clearly the case that there has been party polarization on the abortion issue since 1972 (Cook, Jelen, and Wilcox, 1992: 166), at least with respect to presidential politics. Party polarization on the abortion issue was especially clear by 1980, when, under Ronald Reagan's leadership, the GOP platform included the call for a right-to-life Constitutional amendment while the Democratic party platform articulated support for *Roe v. Wade* and for a woman's right to choose. In Congress, however, abortion has for two decades been an issue which split the Republican party, with Republicans in the Senate serving as "admirals on both sides" of the issue (Craig and O'Brien, 1993: 117).

Preliminary evidence suggests that, since 1972, efforts to mobilize the public on the abortion issue have followed an electoral cycle, one linked primarily to Republican presidents and Republican presidential contenders. Figure 5-2 shows this. Pronounced increases in presidential commentary about abortion are evident for Republican presidents Nixon in 1972, Ford in 1976, Reagan in 1984 and 1988, and Bush in 1992. There is a smaller surge in Democratic President Carter's attention to the abortion issue in 1980; however his Republican challenger Ronald Reagan spoke of the issue more than twice as many times in that election year. Only in 1976, when Carter as a challenger matched Gerald Ford's level of attention to the issue, does the election year cycling have a strongly Democratic flavor.

Conclusions about mobilization via an election-based cycling of attention to the issue are muddied, however, by evidence that the surges of attention were not necessarily instigated by presidents (or even their challengers) attempting to capitalize on the issue. Rather, pro-life and pro-choice activists may have forced presidential candidates into responding to questions and making statements about their positions, even if they were ambivalent. This was certainly the case for Ford, who "cautiously and rather ambivalently opposed Roe" but also opposed the proposal of a Constitutional amendment to undo it. Yet, "On the campaign trail Carter and Ford were repeatedly asked to define their positions on abortion" (Craig and O'Brien, 1993: 160).

Of course there is the possibility that sub-national politicians interested in using the issue to their advantage have been the primary locus for mobilization efforts. In her study of gubernatorial elections in New Jersey, Virginia, Texas, and California, for example, Yale (1993: 141) found that one-fourth of the media's articles on New Jersey's campaign involved the abortion issue and an "even more impressive" 38.2% of the media's coverage of the Virginia campaign was devoted to the abortion issue. As in the above-mentioned evidence about the abortion issue in presidential campaigns, however, one cannot discount the possibility that pro-choice or pro-life groups initiated questions to which politicians were forced to respond rather than politicians choosing to use the abortion issue to mobilize the electorate. Although the New Jersey and Virginia cases suggest, to the contrary, that politicians had found ways to take advantage of the issue and were actively initiating attention to it (Yale, 1993: 145), there may not be good grounds

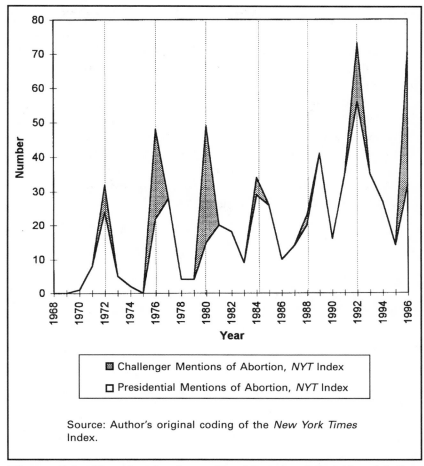

Source: Author's original coding of the *New York Times* Index.

Figure 5-2. The Abortion Issue: Presidents' and Presidential Contenders' Mentions

for positing a mobilization model in which political candidates at the subnational level frequently attempt to mobilize the electorate on the abortion issue in order to gain electoral advantage. Only under certain circumstances and only for certain groups is abortion an important electoral consideration (Howell and Sims, 1993).

In short, while it is not hard to find examples of political figures attempting to orchestrate public opinion on the abortion issue, there is not compelling evidence that the mobilization model is an appropriate characterization of any phase of the history of abortion policy and opinion. The temporal stability in public opinion on the issue means that, at best, there may have been *efforts* at opinion mobilization; but political elites have not been able to change the collective public mind or to move the zone of acceptability on abortion policy very much in over two decades. Rather than changing the public's mind about abortion, political rhetoric over the abortion issue has led people to change their partisan affiliation as party positions on abortion have become more distinct (Adams, 1997). The weight of the evidence therefore suggests that the consistency between abortion opinion and policy that is documented in this chapter is a reflection of policy responsiveness rather than a manifestation of the mobilization model.

6

Welfare

Symbols and Substance of
Policy Responsiveness

Introduction

Welfare policy can be broadly construed to include the full range of programs comprising America's unique welfare state. If so construed, the subject would include attention to income support programs ranging from unemployment insurance to the retirement support provided by Social Security to anti-poverty programs such as Head Start to the assistance payments for the poor provided under the Aid to Families with Dependent Children Program (AFDC), now the Temporary Assistance to Needy Families (TANF) program, and many other programs as well.

For most Americans, however, the term "welfare" refers only to the last of these—the targeted, means-tested program which provides cash assistance to the poor. That program, established as part of the Social Security Act of 1935, institutionalized a federal-state partnership for the provision of financial assistance to poor families with dependent children. AFDC has constituted a very small part of the nation's overall spending for social welfare. Marmor and colleagues (1990: 32–36), for example, note that in 1986, total expenditures on AFDC were $21.2 billion, compared to $479.2 billion for all social insurance programs such as the Social Security retirement program, workers' compensation payments, unemployment insurance and Medicare; and AFDC's $21.2 billion in expenditures that year constituted only 3% of expenditures for the full array of social welfare programs considered by Marmor and colleagues. Yet the AFDC program has been the most controversial program in the nation's arsenal of social welfare programs, and virtually the only one that is broadly construed as constituting welfare. To be "on the dole" in the United States is not meant to refer to those receiving earned income tax credits, Pell Grants, or Head Start benefits; to be "on the dole" is to be an AFDC recipient.[1]

This chapter focuses on welfare policy in this narrower sense. It traces the policy changes that have occurred over the life of the AFDC program. That program has been regularly subjected to reform efforts, culminating in legislation in 1996 that essentially eliminated the program, replacing its longstanding status as a federal-state entitlement program with a federal block grant that states could use to run their own assistance programs for the poor.

Even with this narrowed definition of welfare, assessment of the character and magnitude of policy change in the welfare area is complicated by four factors. One complication stems from the fact that AFDC has been a joint federal-state system, with substantial state-level discretion. Hence, while there has been important policy leadership at the federal level and while federal action impacts the states and vice versa, tracking policy is complicated by the patchwork of different state responses. This makes it difficult to pin down, at any point in time, what welfare policy in the United States actually is.

A second complication stems from the fact that, in the welfare policy domain, the ratio of symbolic to substantive policy is quite high. Symbolic policy-making involves the use of rhetoric to create images that may be as important as actual resource allocations. Symbolic policy can be used to assuage public concern with strong messages that give the appearance of problem-solving even if, in reality, problems have not been solved. And symbolic policy can be used to hide discrepancies between major policy reform programs (i.e., the law "on the books") and actual implementation. This too makes it difficult to characterize welfare policy.

Thirdly, assessing welfare policy change is especially complicated because of the intense way in which key policy indicators inevitably confound policy change with change in the policy environment. For example, change in the size of the welfare rolls is often used as evidence of tightening of eligibility to force more people off welfare. But the welfare rolls are affected by general economic conditions as well as by official eligibility standards and the discretionary efforts of welfare programs administrators, using those standards, to decrease the rolls.

But perhaps the most serious complication in any effort to characterize welfare policy and its change is the multidimensional nature of "policy" concerning welfare. There are at least three important elements of the nation's welfare program, and policy decisions at various times respond to issues involving one element but not others. One important element has to do with the financial generosity of the system. This element entails policy decisions about how liberal benefit levels will be and how strict eligibility standards will be. A second element has to do with the connection between work and welfare. This element entails policy decisions that either treat work as something that should be encouraged with services and incentives or that treat work as a requirement, with severe penalties including expulsion from welfare, for those who do not meet their obligations to find work. A third element, while related to issues of eligibility, has to do with the extent to which and the manner in which welfare recipients will be morally judged and the state will take an intrusive role in regulating sexual behaviors, child rearing, and other personal matters. This wasn't an issue during most of the early history of welfare in the United States, because those deemed the "unworthy poor" were systematically excluded from the early programs of aid to mothers with dependent children. But once individuals who formerly had been excluded came onto the rolls in large numbers in the 1960s, the moral ambiguities associated with the "unworthy poor" became central to the program (Handler and Hasenfeld, 1991).

Change in welfare policy, therefore, may involve change in (1) the *generosity of financial benefits*, (2) the *approach to the work-welfare nexus*, (3) the *extent of moral regulation* of welfare recipients, or some combination of the above. Scholarly interpretations of the nature of welfare, the extent of policy change, and the reasons for change stem in part from differential emphases on each of these elements.

For example, in their influential interpretation, Piven and Cloward (1993) posit that the role of welfare in welfare state capitalism is to minimize social dislocation and maintain labor discipline by alternately expanding and contracting with the business cycle:

> First, when mass unemployment leads to outbreaks of turmoil, relief programs are ordinarily initiated or expanded to absorb and control enough of the unemployed to restore order; then, as turbulence subsides, the relief system contracts, expelling those who are needed to populate the labor market (Piven and Cloward, 1993:3).

This thesis is used as an explanation for the dramatic increase in the number of welfare recipients in the latter 1960s. That explosive increase in the welfare rolls occurred after the transformation of Southern agriculture and the subsequent migration of blacks to northern cities created an excess pool of black laborers in urban areas. This, coupled with racial disorders in urban areas in the 1960s, provided precisely the sort of threat to the social order that, in the Piven and Cloward interpretation, the welfare system had to handle through program liberalization that enabled substantial numbers of families to get on the welfare rolls.

Piven and Cloward (1993: 371–374) suggest that there has been substantial policy change in the opposite direction in the period from 1970 through the 1990s, with a general tightening of access to benefits to re-establish workforce discipline. The period from the Carter administration onward, and especially the period from 1980 onward, is characterized as an inevitable reaction to the liberalization of welfare in the latter 1960s.

From the perspective of Piven and Cloward's thesis, primary emphasis is on the generosity dimension of welfare policy—i.e., expansion and contraction in welfare rolls and benefits via changes in eligibility requirements and benefit levels. The other two elements of welfare policy are not overlooked, but they are treated as secondary and merely supportive of larger policy goals having to do with the scope of the welfare program. Thus, for example, Piven and Cloward acknowledge the introduction of work requirements which, while not particularly successful at placing large numbers of welfare recipients in employment, have the symbolic purpose of reasserting the social value of work and demeaning welfare recipients by forcing them through work "rituals" (Piven and Cloward, 1993: 381).

Mead (1992) also sees substantial change in welfare policy but his emphasis is upon the transformation from a period of "progressive politics" to one of "dependency politics." The progressive politics of the 1960s cast the welfare debate around issues of adequacy and capacity to provide opportunities out of poverty. But, according to Mead (1992: 167): "Since the late 1960s, the drift of antipoverty policy has been away from providing opportunity and toward enforcing moral standards. Increasingly, welfare recipients are not encouraged to work by special payoffs but required to work as a condition of eligibility. It is an effort to restore, through government, some of the social authority that used to enforce the work ethic." In short, Mead portrays welfare policy as moving from a period in which the generosity elements of the program were at issue to one in which that element of welfare policy is submerged by attention to the other two elements: the work-welfare nexus and moral regulation.

In contrast with the cyclical model offered by Piven and Cloward, Mead (1992: 167) suggests that this change was prompted by elite and popular reaction to the failures of earlier welfare policy approaches. "The movement originated in the disappointment over the outcome of voluntary programs and the rising frustration of voters over the worsening work problem." And, in something like a stage model of welfare policy change, Mead suggests that the replacement of generosity issues with issues surrounding the work-welfare nexus was eventually supplanted by an emphasis on moral regulatory elements: "In the 1970s the work issue remained important, but debate over how to raise work levels focused mainly on barriers that seemed to prevent work . . . By the 1980s, how work programs would operate received more concrete attention, reflecting the emerging paternalism in social policy" (Mead, 1992: 186).

If Piven and Cloward see *cyclical change* revolving around the generosity element of welfare policy and Mead sees *staged change* in which the work-welfare element and then the moral regulation element replace the emphasis on generosity issues, other theorists portray *continuities rather than change* in welfare policy. In particular, Handler (1995) along with his co-author Hollingsworth (Handler and Hollingsworth, 1971) portray welfare policy as consistently revolving around issues of moral worthiness. According to these theorists, welfare policy always has a core concern of distinguishing the truly needy from the unworthy poor. In order to deter the unworthy poor and insure that only the truly needy get assistance, welfare programs have always relied upon a variety of methods of "moral degradation" to make living "on the dole" so miserable that only the truly desperate would tolerate the situation. This is the principle of "less eligibility." Of course, this means that the worthy poor are held hostage to the perceived need to deter the unworthy poor. But the principle of "less eligibility" is of such overriding importance that welfare programs have always been structured to segregate, stigmatize, and sanction the poor on the assumption that the poor are morally degraded and that the state can and should regulate their morality.

From this perspective, work requirements in contemporary welfare reforms are not particularly new. They are simply the latest variant of largely symbolic work requirements that can be found in the meaningless labors assigned to individuals in early 19th Century poorhouses in England and the United States. And from this perspective, penalties for additional pregnancies or for inadequate supervision of a child's school attendance, requirements that welfare mothers name the fathers of their children so that the fathers can be required to help provide support, and other contemporary regulations of welfare family arrangements are simply the latest variants in a long line of welfare state intrusions on the reproductive behavior and family life of the poor. Keeping welfare benefits minimal (relative to what one would get as a low-wage laborer) is also an important element of the "less eligibility" principle, of course. So the generosity element of welfare policy is tacitly portrayed as consistently maintaining benefits at very stingy levels. But the key to the perspective offered by Handler and Hollingsworth (1971) is the way in which the other two elements of welfare policy—work requirements and moral regulation—have consistently played an important role in maintaining the "less eligibility" principle.

The three sets of theorists summarized above emphasize different aspects of welfare policy and consequently portray welfare policy change in dramatically different ways, ranging from cyclical change (Piven and Cloward) to developmental change (Mead) to continuity rather than change (Handler and Hasenfeld). And because they emphasize different elements of welfare policy without clearly acknowledging the possibility that change in one element might be distinctive from change in the other elements, these interpretations implicitly ignore the possibility that welfare policy might be consistent with public opinion on one dimension but inconsistent with opinion on others. "Welfare policy" is not unitary, but rather is composed of policies concerning generosity, policies concerning work requirements, and policies concerning moral regulation. And it is entirely possible that public opinion about the generosity of welfare benefits is distinct from public opinion concerning work requirements or moral regulation. Because these distinctions are not carefully maintained, global characterizations of welfare policy development can "talk past each other."

But despite their differences, Teles (1996: 6) argues that theorists such as these can all be categorized as "consensus" theorists. That is, their interpretation of welfare policy is based upon the premise that "public values are expressed in our nation's [welfare] policies" and that government is "completely functional, incapable of misperceiving, misadministering, or twisting public values for its own purposes."[2] By contrast, Teles (1996: 12–17) argues that welfare policy is more appropriately interpreted from a theory of dissensus politics. From this theoretical perspective, policy-making is the result of conflict among intellectual and political elites. In this conflict, each side attempts to discredit the other by emphasizing a key cultural value to the exclusion of the others, even though all are realistically a part of a more multifaceted value consensus in American society. The result is welfare policy that does not necessarily reflect the societal consensus.

This chapter takes up the task of considering whether welfare policy has been consistent with public opinion, as the consensus theorists suggest, or driven by elite dissensus that has prevented it from reflecting public opinion, as Teles's dissensus politics theory suggests. In order to make that diagnosis, it will be important to disaggregate welfare policy into its three distinctive elements, consider the question of opinion-policy linkage separately for each, and finally to consider the interrelationships among the elements.

While the very long time frame used by many analysts provides an important historical perspective, systematic public opinion data on the topic is only available for the period since about 1970 (and even so is more sketchy for some elements than for others). Interpretations that adopt a longer time frame draw conclusions about the linkage of welfare policy to broad public values or cultural themes, but it is difficult to evaluate how such characterizations might mesh with the concept of mass public opinion per se.

This chapter will focus primarily upon welfare policy development from roughly 1970 to the present. A brief review of earlier periods provides historical foundation for the examination of contemporary welfare policy, including attention to key events such as the creation of the Aid to Dependent Children program and amendments to that program in 1967. But the quarter century since 1970 is almost universally acknowledged to be the era in which the nation's welfare program assumed its modern form and became a subject of periodic political controversy and popular concern. The repeated episodes of reform effort that have characterized the AFDC program, culminating in the 1996 reform that essentially restructured the program, are the focus of this chapter.

The Historical Foundation of Contemporary Welfare Policy

Prior to the passage of the Social Security Act in 1935, there was no national program of aid to the poor in the United States. However, by 1912, 21 states had enacted programs modeled after the principles set forth in a 1909 White House Conference on children in poverty, and by the early 1920s, 40 states had such programs. These "mothers' pension," or Aid to Dependent Children (ADC) programs, were modest in benefits. As exemplified by the Illinois program, they were also structured in a way that provided a very aggressive role for the state in moral regulation. Cases of women with dependent children were referred to the juvenile court by county or town officials, local courts, friends, or relatives of the family, and the courts made the determination of which families were eligible for ADC. Eligibility was based not only on need but on whether the mother was deemed fit to properly care for the children. Grounds for being an unfit mother included drunkenness, bad moral habits, or other factors judged to constitute a poor environment for raising children. In cases where the mother was deemed unfit, the court could take the child away from the mother and place the child with another family or in a state institution. Those receiving ADC under this early system of mothers' pensions were primarily white widows; mothers who had never married, divorcees, and African-Americans were much less likely to receive such aid (Handler, 1995).

During the depression, federal policy discussions were primarily focusing upon the poverty problems of the elderly poor and dislocated workers, and those discussions were hewing closely to a social insurance conception of a solution. There was little interest in federalizing the state ADC programs. But those programs were struggling financially. Something needed to be done to sustain them, but they did not readily fit into the contributory, social insurance scheme that was being developed. The result was two-pronged social security legislation that created a non-means tested, contributory program of income support for retiring workers and a separate program of federal grants-in-aid to states to shore up their ADC programs. The essential features of existing state ADC programs were preserved under this arrangement, but federal involvement did bring with it some federal mandates. State ADC programs had to be available statewide, a controversial provision in Southern states that were attempting to keep their ADC programs out of predominantly black counties, and benefits had to be paid in cash. However, states and the county governments administering the program for them retained substantial discretion to restrict eligibility through definitions of whether potential recipients had a "suitable home" (Handler and Hasenfeld, 1991: 103–105).

From 1935 through the mid-1960's, welfare entered what Berkowitz (1991: 95) describes as a "benign era" and Teles (1996: 34) describes as the "era of normalcy." Both terms characterize the lack of controversy and low visibility of the welfare program in these early years of its development. A key change in the Social Security Act, however, would have important implications for the ADC program. In 1939 amendments to the Social Security Act, Congress created a special program of "insurance"-type benefits for the widows and children of individuals who would have qualified for retirement benefits. As a result of this change, a group that was easily defined as epitomizing the "worthy poor" was removed from the welfare program and covered instead under an entitlement program. The removal of this group would have a negative impact on the political legitimacy of the ADC program, which was left to deal with a population of recipients who were much less easy to characterize as symbolizing the "worthy poor" (Teles, 1996: 34–6).

In 1962 amendments, the ADC program was changed to the Aid to Families with Dependent Children program (AFDC) in recognition of the perverse incentives of an ADC program that provided no aid to poor families if the father were present but did provide aid to poor families if the father were not present. Now, states had the option of providing welfare assistance to poor families if the father were present but unemployed through the Aid to Families with Dependent Children-Unemployed Parent component of the program (Teles, 1996: 39).

By the advent of the Nixon administration, welfare policy had matured into a sizable program, with a recipient population that was much different in racial and family structure characteristics than was true of the program at its founding. It was also in the throes of a period of explosive growth. Compared with a 17% increase in the welfare program in the previous decade, the welfare rolls increased by 107% from the end of 1960 to early 1969 as 800,000 families were added (Piven and Cloward, 1993: 183). The emergence and political organizing of a welfare rights movement, spearheaded by the National Welfare Rights Organization (NWRO), is an important part of the explanation for this explosion in the welfare rolls, as NWRO mobilized many eligible families that had not applied to get on the welfare rolls (Piven and Cloward, 1993: 331). Piven and Cloward argue more generally that racial disorders in American cities created the context for the liberalization of programs for the poor, including a broad array of Great Society programs and a breakdown in local welfare agencies' capacity to sustain restrictive rules that would discourage the poor from coming onto welfare (Piven and Cloward, 1993: 198). Court decisions helped to fuel the welfare explosion as well, or at least to provide a legal framework that would make it more difficult for states to maintain a restrictive posture (Teles, 1996: 106–109).

Contemporary Welfare Policy History:
The Generosity Dimension

If the 1960s witnessed an explosion of growth in the AFDC program, the 1970s and 1980s constituted an era of stability or even retrenchment after the explosion. Viewed from the perspective of raw numbers, the sharp increases in welfare enrollments during the 1960s leveled off by the mid-1970s and remained stable for a decade and a half (see Figure 6-1). Only in the 1990s is there evidence of sharp growth again in the welfare rolls—a subject to which we will return later. Average monthly benefits for individuals and for families on welfare slowly increased in raw dollars from 1970 to about 1990, and then leveled off or declined slightly.

However, a more realistic portrait of the generosity dimension of welfare policy in this period probably requires standardization of these raw figures. Such standardization suggests that in the 1970s and 1980s policy decisions accomplished more than a stabilization

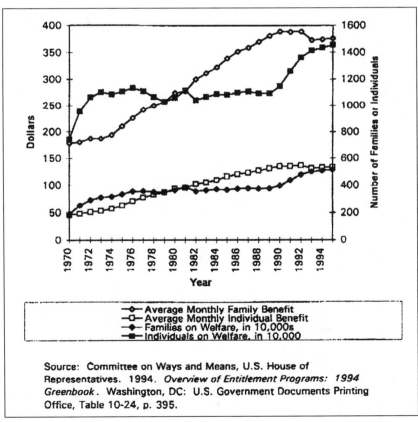

Source: Committee on Ways and Means, U.S. House of Representatives. 1994. *Overview of Entitlement Programs: 1994 Greenbook*. Washington, DC: U.S. Government Documents Printing Office, Table 10-24, p. 395.

Figure 6-1. Welfare Policy Trends: Enrollments and Average Payments

of the welfare system. In fact, the program shrank. After reaching a high-point in 1973, the count of individuals on the welfare rolls per 100,000 population dwindled to a low point in 1989, a decline of 15% (see Figure 6-2). Again, however, a noticeable resurgence of growth in the welfare rolls is evident in the 1990s. Welfare payments to individuals did not quite keep up with inflation in the 1970s and 1980s, and the dollar value of the average payment to a welfare family eroded noticeably (see Figure 6-3).

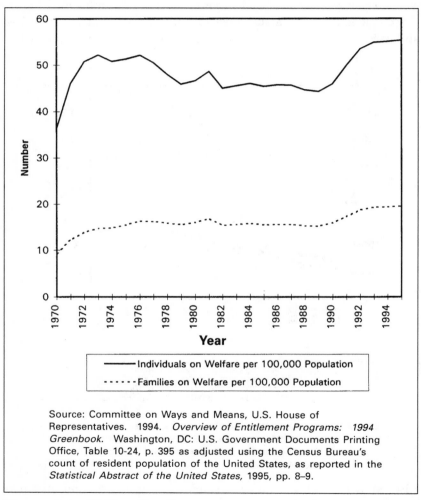

Source: Committee on Ways and Means, U.S. House of Representatives. 1994. *Overview of Entitlement Programs: 1994 Greenbook.* Washington, DC: U.S. Government Documents Printing Office, Table 10-24, p. 395 as adjusted using the Census Bureau's count of resident population of the United States, as reported in the *Statistical Abstract of the United States,* 1995, pp. 8–9.

Figure 6-2. Welfare Enrollments, per 100,000 Resident U.S. Population, 1970–1995

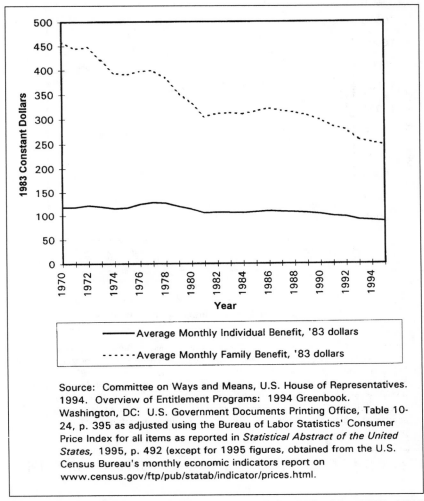

Figure 6-3. Welfare Payments, Adjusted for Inflation, 1970–1995

The net result of these trends is that overall spending on the AFDC program, in constant dollars, peaked in the mid-1970s, declined sharply, and remained relatively stable at a diminished level until the 1990s (see Figure 6-4). On the generosity dimension, then, there is evidence here of a policy shift by the latter 1970s—a shift in the direction of tightening and retrenchment.

But what policy initiatives or decisions account for these outcomes? Unlike the major, visible pieces of legislation that have

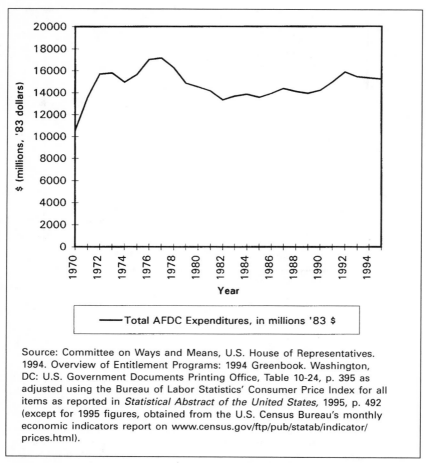

Source: Committee on Ways and Means, U.S. House of Representatives. 1994. Overview of Entitlement Programs: 1994 Greenbook. Washington, DC: U.S. Government Documents Printing Office, Table 10-24, p. 395 as adjusted using the Bureau of Labor Statistics' Consumer Price Index for all items as reported in *Statistical Abstract of the United States,* 1995, p. 492 (except for 1995 figures, obtained from the U.S. Census Bureau's monthly economic indicators report on www.census.gov/ftp/pub/statab/indicator/prices.html).

Figure 6-4. AFDC Spending, Adjusted for Inflation, 1970–1995

dealt with issues of the work-welfare nexus and moral regulation (see sections below), these changes on the generosity dimension of welfare policy were largely accomplished through low-key, administrative changes (Brodkin, 1995: 215) coupled with even less visible legislative "nondecisions." With respect to the former, Handler and Hasenfeld (1991: 120) document how welfare program costs were reined in through the introduction of technologies and administrative practices that amounted to a wholesale tightening up of the program. These changes, introduced in the name of "quality control," involved converting from social workers to closely monitored clerical workers, introduction of strict rules and computerized data bases, and policies that penalized states, individual welfare workers, and their supervisors for excessive error rates. Ironically, the transformation of welfare agencies from social work institutions to clerical, claims-processing entities would have repercussions for later welfare reforms, because the claims-processing approach left these agencies ill-equipped to deal with later challenges of providing supportive services to help transition recipients from welfare to work (Brodkin, 1995: 215).

With respect to legislative actions that incrementally and invisibly moved welfare in a less generous direction, state legislatures adjusted the need standard that should be used to determine when a family qualifies for AFDC and benefit levels were deliberately left to erode relative to the cost of living (Handler and Hasenfeld, 1991: 121–122). Congressional action also contributed to the retrenchment of welfare, and in a similarly low-visibility fashion. Substantial cuts in welfare were enacted "under the rubric of budgetary reform" in the Omnibus Budget Reconciliation Act of 1981 (OBRA), which specified that only those with incomes under 150 percent of state-set need standards were eligible for AFDC. Since the majority of states had by this time set their need standards lower than the official poverty line, this manipulation of eligibility effectively restricted welfare to only the extremely poor (Brodkin, 1995: 216).

But by 1990, welfare spending had begun to notch upward again. As earlier evidence suggests (see Figures 6-1 to 6-3), that reversal had more to do with the inability of the welfare system to contain new enrollments, and especially the enrollment of large numbers of children on welfare, than any policy choice to make welfare payments more generous. In fact, the inflation-adjusted value of welfare benefits continued to erode in the 1990s, though not as sharply as in the high inflation 1970s. But in the 1990s, for the first time since the peak years of AFDC in the early 1970s, the number of families on welfare relative to the population as a whole moved noticeably upward and the number of individuals on welfare moved sharply upward.

The Opinion-Policy Nexus: Welfare Generosity

On the generosity dimension, then, welfare policy in the past two-and-a-half decades exhibits four phases—a phase in the first half of the 1970s that was the culmination of a longer, explosive growth period in the AFDC program carried over from the latter 1960s, a retrenchment phase of sharp reductions in real spending from 1977 to 1982, a period of stable or very slow growth in the remainder of the 1980s, and, beginning in 1990, a phase of re-newed growth in real AFDC spending. Is this cycle consistent with trends in public opinion?

It is easier to assess public opinion with respect to the generos-ity dimension of welfare than with respect to the other dimensions. This is because the generosity dimension is relatively well repre-sented by the standard General Social Survey item on popular preferences with respect to welfare spending—an item which asks whether we are spending too much, not enough, or the right amount on welfare. Figure 6-5, which charts the results against the actual pattern of AFDC spending, reveals a striking pattern of correspon-dence. The percentage of respondents saying that we are spending too much on welfare grew to its high point during the same period that real AFDC spending grew to its high point.[3] Even the tempo-rary drop in spending that occurred during that growth phase is mirrored by a dramatic and equally temporary drop in popular opposition to welfare spending. The reversal of welfare's growth phase is accompanied by an even more dramatic slide in the pro-portion believing that too much was being spent on welfare. In-deed, that decline in popular opposition to welfare spending continued even after the decline in spending hit a plateau in the 1980s. And only as AFDC spending again began to rise does popu-lar opposition to welfare spending also show a sharp rise.

One cannot definitively establish from the evidence in Figure 6-5 whether opinion drives policy or policy trends are shaping public opinion, or indeed whether both trends are responses to other fac-tors. For most of the series, reversals in public opinion occur simul-taneously with reversals in spending trends. The important point here is that the two move virtually in tandem, suggesting the possibility of a peculiarly sensitive thermostatic model of opinion and policy change. But there is another possibility as well. The relatively long-term decline in public concern about welfare spend-ing that is exhibited in Figure 6-5 may reflect the public's acknowl-edgment of other aspects of welfare policy change instead of or in addition to the retrenchment in welfare generosity. The following two sections detail the introduction of symbolically important policy

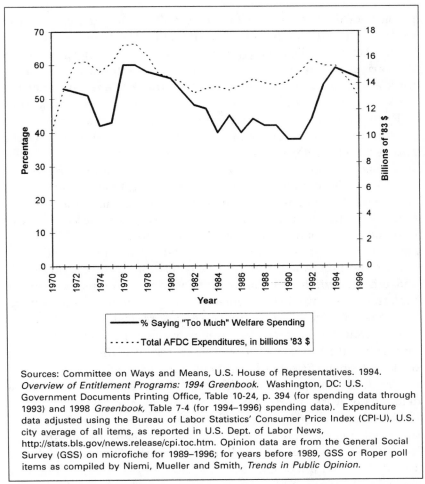

Figure 6-5. Welfare Spending and Spending Preferences, 1970–1996

changes involving the welfare-work nexus and moral regulation of welfare recipients—policy changes that may be at least as important to the public as real changes in welfare spending.

Contemporary Policy History: The Work-Welfare Nexus

There have been several waves of welfare policy reform directed at issues of work incentives, work requirements, and solving the problem of dependency, all part of a quite different dimension of welfare policy: the welfare-work nexus. This dimension, which Mead (1992: 21) calls "dependency politics, " requires that we examine the various program changes that have been intended to influence work effort, or at least to give the appearance of ensuring that the work ethic was sustained instead of eroded by welfare programs.

By and large, the program changes and policy debates surrounding the work-welfare nexus involve different understandings of the nature of welfare dependency and corresponding differences in policy solutions. On the one hand, welfare dependency can be understood as the result of individual deficiencies that have a bearing on employability. That is, individuals do not have the skills, orientations, and other resources that are necessary for successful entry into the labor force. The policy solution attached to this understanding has been a *service-oriented* strategy, in which social workers or other program agents provide education, training, job search, and other services to enhance the individual's employability. On the other hand, welfare dependency can be understood as a rational choice for individuals under some circumstances. When the income that can be received through welfare payments compares favorably with the income that can be received through low-wage work and when the other benefits of being on welfare (e.g., eligibility for food stamps and health care benefits; freedom from the demands of work) more than compensate for the costs of being on welfare (e.g., occupying a socially demeaning status and enduring the hassles of meeting bureaucratic requirements to sustain eligibility), individuals choose welfare over work. The policy solution attached to this understanding has been an *incentives strategy*, in which the benefits of low-wage work are enhanced and the costs of depending upon welfare are increased, perhaps via work requirements that demand some work or efforts to find work as a condition of eligibility for welfare.

As the following review shows, much of the history of welfare policy involves a marriage of these two strategies. At times, it has seemed an easy marriage. Various services such as day care and job training can and have been treated as incentives for work. But services such as day care and job training are relatively expensive to provide for the welfare recipient population as a whole, so welfare-work programs based on this fusion of the service-strategy and the incentive-strategy have, after being launched with great fanfare but inadequate resources, foundered in implementation.

Out of that failure has emerged a new policy strategy. Like the incentive strategy, it assumes that the welfare-work tradeoff is a matter of rational choice for individuals comparing the costs and benefits of low-wage work versus welfare. And like the service strategy, it assumes that job training, day care, and other services can be used as incentives to encourage work over welfare. But to this mix is added a new element: time limits on welfare receipt for individuals and a mandatory cutoff when that time limit is reached, whether or not the individual has successfully found work or other means of support. In short, this new approach, which we might designate the *cutoff strategy*, assumes that a combination of carrots and sticks must be used to deal with issues of work and welfare dependency, and the threat of definitively losing welfare benefits after a set time period serves as the big stick.

The earliest efforts to reform welfare to deal with problems of dependency and lack of work effort came in 1967 with the establishment of the WIN program, which required that all "appropriate" welfare recipients over the age of 16 enroll in a work program. The legislation exempted recipients with disabilities, those whose children were in school, who were functioning as caregivers for an aged or ill family member, and those whose children would, in the judgment of the state welfare agency, be harmed by their parents' required involvement in the program.

The WIN program merged service-strategy and incentives-strategy thinking by treating training and day-care funding services as work incentives. In addition, the 1967 legislation that created the WIN program also institutionalized another welfare policy change directed toward incentives. Rather than losing one dollar in welfare benefits for each dollar they might earn, welfare recipients would be allowed to have the first $30 per month and one-third of the remaining monthly wages that they earned not count against their welfare eligibility (Handler and Hasenfeld, 1991: 142).

In a pattern that would be repeated in later welfare reforms, the service-strategy portion of this early WIN program actually reached very few welfare recipients. The program was meagerly funded at the federal level, and many of the necessary job training and child care services simply were not available at the magnitude that would be required for full-scale implementation. State welfare agencies had much latitude to exempt individuals from the program and that discretion was used to make the WIN program in practice little more than a symbolic exercise. A little less than one-quarter of the welfare recipients that state agencies processed were determined to be appropriate for the program, and less than 20% of that number actually enrolled (Handler and Hasenfeld, 1991: 140–141).

Revisions to the WIN program were included in 1971 amendments to the Social Security system. The revamped WIN program essentially stiffened the paper requirements for work. Those eligible for the program included women with children over the age of 5, registration for the program was made mandatory, and job placement services were emphasized over education and training services. But the revised WIN program suffered from many of the same disappointments in implementation. States did not have the resources to provide job placement services to all eligible welfare recipients, but were able to comply with the mandatory registration requirement simply by processing paper for recipients but keeping them in a holding category with no employment services. Evaluations of the revised WIN program found that state programs were rationing their services by directing them to the most employable, thus leaving unresolved the broader problems of moving welfare recipients to work (Handler and Hasenfeld, 1991: 154 and 157–8).

The WIN program thus illustrates the essential dilemma of fusing the services and incentives strategies. Without adequate funding to carry through on requirements for mandatory participation in job-oriented programs, such a policy strategy becomes no more than a paper exercise that leaves the incentives of large numbers of welfare recipients unaffected. On the other hand, as Piven and Cloward (1993: 381) argue, work requirements, while not particularly successful at placing large numbers of welfare recipients in employment, had the symbolic purpose of reasserting the social value of work and demeaning welfare recipients by forcing them through work registration rituals.

Meanwhile, the issue of welfare as a work disincentive had prompted a series of reform ideas and national experiments focusing on what many economists argued would be the virtues of a pure income strategy rather than the combination of social services and cash grants of traditional welfare programs. As early as the Johnson administration, economists' critiques of the dependency-fostering problems of welfare programs had led to the commissioning of large-scale experiments designed to determine what mix of benefits and tax rates would minimize work disincentives (Handler and Hasenfeld, 1991: 144). While the results of the experiments were mixed, controversial, and inconclusive, the concept of avoiding welfare dependency by maximizing the incentives to work was not. In 1969, the Nixon administration put forth a bold and complex plan based upon this concept that would have provided a guaranteed annual income for *all* the poor, along with the provision that the first $720 of earned income would not count in the computation of an individual's assistance and that additional earnings would be taxed at a 50% rate. This Family Assistance Plan was never enacted. It fell victim to its own complexities, which left conservatives too worried about the potential costs and liberals worried that the financial provisions were not generous enough (Berkowitz, 1991: 127–130). The political failure of the Family Assistance Plan meant that federal policy would continue to provide for the non-working poor (welfare recipients) but not the working poor. To deal with this embarrassing discrepancy, proposals to offer a tax credit for the working poor were circulated in Congress and enacted into law in 1975 as the Earned Income Tax Credit (EITC) program (Handler and Hasenfeld, 1991: 159).

The installation of Ronald Reagan as president in 1981 ushered in a new approach to the problem of transitioning welfare recipients to work. Through a combination of cuts in the existing WIN program (Handler and Hasenfeld, 1991: 172) and the facilitation of state experimentation with alternative work programs, the Reagan years witnessed a proliferation of innovative welfare-to-work programs at the state level. Because Congressional support was not forthcoming for this decentralized, state-centered approach to welfare reform, the Reagan administration, in his second term, made use of provisions of the 1962 Social Security Act amendments that allowed for executive branch discretion in authorizing demonstration projects that might improve the AFDC program. As long as the demonstration did not involve added costs for the federal government or violate health or safety requirements or displace already employed workers and was based on voluntary participation and a few other minimal requirements, the federal government could waive the normal requirements of the AFDC program in order to empower a state to experiment with an innovative program. This power to grant waivers had lain largely dormant since 1962, but in the mid-1980s the Reagan administration elevated it to prominence. A special, White House-based panel to expedite review of waiver requests—the Low-Income Opportunity Advisory Board, was created and states were encouraged to request waivers (Teles, 1996: 122–124).

While waivers would later be used for much more controversial purposes having to do with the moral regulation dimension of welfare policy (see below), during most of the Reagan years waivers were largely granted for demonstration programs that allowed states to pursue imaginative approaches to the combined service strategy and incentive strategy. In New Jersey, for example, a system of intensive case management (which allows welfare caseworkers to tailor a set of services for each recipient family and to better monitor the recipients' obligations to follow through) was attempted. In Wisconsin, financial incentives were given to encourage school attendance, under the presumption that the latter was critical to developing the employability of recipients (Teles, 1996: 139).

One of the best-known of the early waiver demonstrations is California's GAIN (Greater Avenues to Independence) program which was enacted in 1986, implemented as a pilot program in 10 California counties in the period from 1987–1989, and implemented statewide in 1991. The GAIN program, which was a forerunner for ensuing welfare reforms at the federal level, epitomized the fusion of a service strategy and an incentive strategy. AFDC recipients were required to participate in job placement-related programs or else lose their benefits. The program provides an extensive array of services, however, including "job search workshops, adult basic education, GED classes, English for non-English speakers, job clubs, training, and work experience" (Waste, 1995: 59). The GAIN program has generated some positive results, especially in Riverside County where program administrators have emphasized job placement more heavily than longer term educational services. But overall, the results of the GAIN program have been disappointing. The differences in wage earnings between those who completed the GAIN program and those who did not have been relatively minor.

More important for our purposes, the GAIN program has exhibited much the same problem that has plagued previous welfare-to-work programs—resource limitations, combined with the need to exempt certain classes of recipients because of their age, family circumstances, and the like, mean that the program reached a very modest proportion of the AFDC recipient population. About 66% of typical registrants in the program failed to make it into the job search and training phase of the program (Waste, 1995: 62).

In addition to disappointing results from many demonstration programs, there were continuing problems with welfare that were not resolved by the waiver approach. Although they constituted a back-door, decentralized approach to welfare reform, waivers were technically to be limited-duration experiments that required states to request federal permission for innovations on a piecemeal basis. Such an approach was not ultimately satisfying to governors and state legislators wishing to have more definitive authority to deal with the issue of the welfare-work nexus. Similarly, proponents of national standards for welfare programs were predictably unhappy with a piecemeal approach that allowed executive branch discretion and state-level initiatives to substitute for a definitive statement of what could be required of welfare recipients and what services should be provided to enable recipients to move from welfare to work. Finally, the resource issue that had always haunted federal programmatic efforts to move welfare recipients into the work world was at least as insurmountable at the state level. Job training, education, child care, and job placement services are more expensive than the simple provision of welfare checks. State governments could only hope to carry out serious welfare-to-work programs without running afoul of budgetary constraints if the programs could be successful enough quickly enough to reap savings in welfare spending via reductions in the welfare rolls as individuals moved into employment. But the waiver demonstration programs did not have that magnitude of success, in part because budgetary constraints prevented full-scale investment in the service elements of welfare-to-work programs.

With continued pressure from the nation's governors, the debate about welfare reform at the federal level continued in the second half of the 1980s. The National Governor's Association, under the leadership of then-Governor Clinton, developed a proposal that articulated a Democratic vision of national welfare reform, stressing the responsibility of government to provide education, job training and placement services to welfare recipients and the promise to devote savings derived from reduced welfare rolls to enhancement and equalization of benefit levels across the nation. The Reagan administration, however, insisted that welfare reform should emphasize workfare—that is, work in exchange for welfare benefits (Brodkin, 1995: 216–7). In short, the Democratic vision retained an emphasis on a service strategy while the Republican administration's vision articulated a new view which went beyond both the service strategy and the incentive strategy. In contrast with the traditional service strategy, work would be required immediately, not deferred while the recipient was made more job-ready through training and education services. And in contrast with the incentive strategy, which had involved the manipulation of program elements in a way that would make work an attractive *choice* compared to welfare, the new conception of "workfare" treated work as something that the recipient would be *mandated* to do in exchange for welfare benefits.

Despite these contrasting visions, pressure for welfare reform culminated in a bipartisan compromise with the passage of the Family Support Act in 1988. That act, touted as a comprehensive welfare reform, established yet another program of work requirements for AFDC recipients—the Job Opportunities and Basic Skills, or JOBS program. Under the JOBS program, eligible AFDC recipients were required to participate in education or job-training activities or work programs, as appropriate for their circumstances. Education could include high school completion, or remedial education. Job-training could include skills training or job location activities. And work programs could include on-the-job training programs, work for a state-subsidized public employer, community work experience or other work experience programs under which the recipient would work in exchange for their welfare benefits. The issue of child care was strongly addressed in this legislation, which mandated that states provide child care for participating AFDC recipients with young children. Federal funding support for child care was authorized on the same entitlement funding terms that governed Medicaid (which varies from a 50% to an 80% federal match of state funds, depending on the state). States were mandated to sanction AFDC recipients who refused to fulfill the obligations of participation or to accept legitimate job offers when given by withdrawing the adult's share of the welfare payment and directing the portion of the welfare check intended to support the dependent children to a third party ("After Years . . .", 1989: 353–4).

But, consistent with so many previous efforts at work requirements, the JOBS program included a host of exemptions, implementation extensions, and other provisions that insured that this supposedly comprehensive reform would, in practice, be of limited impact. Recipients were exempted if they were ill, aged, beyond the first trimester of a pregnancy, or incapacitated, if they were serving as a caregiver for a family member who was ill or incapacitated, if they were under age 16 or attending school full time, if they were the primary caregiver for a child under the age of 3, or if they were caring for an older child and their state's JOBS program had not provided child care in their area. In addition, states were only required to get 7% of non-exempt recipients into the JOBS program by 1991 and only 20% by 1995 ("After Years . . .", 1989: 353–4).

In addition to those self-limiting features of the legislation, the Family Support Act (FSA) was unfortunate in the timing of implementation relative to economic conditions nationally. The pressures of a recessionary economy made wholesale conversion of welfare recipients into the workplace highly problematic at the turn of the decade. And the FSA's limited federal funding for education, job training, and job development services was soon matched by state cutbacks in those services as a result of broader pressures for financial retrenchment at the state level. Not surprisingly, the welfare rolls began to climb shortly after the enactment of FSA (Brodkin, 1995: 217).

By 1992, there was considerable frustration with repeated efforts at welfare reform that failed to resolve the dilemma of the welfare-work nexus in a way satisfactory to either conservatives or liberals. Not surprisingly, welfare reform was featured in the presidential campaign that year, with then-Governor Bill Clinton representing a "new Democratic" vision of reform that could "end welfare as we know it." Clinton's reform package retained the service strategy that has been so crucial from the perspective of the liberal viewpoint on welfare while offering tough-minded elements appealing to conservatives. Most important, it embraced an element that would provide a crucial transition to a more full-blown version of the cutoff strategy. After having participated in employment service programs, AFDC recipients would have a time limit of two years to obtain employment, after which they would be required to work at public sector jobs in exchange for any further benefits (Brodkin, 1995: 218).

Had this set of proposals been pushed as the top priority in the newly-installed Clinton administration, the AFDC program might still exist. But the initial years of the Clinton presidency were preoccupied with health care reform efforts. In the 1994 elections, Republicans captured control of Congress, were newly-installed in many state legislative chambers and governors' mansions as well, and brought an aggressively conservative agenda to the fore. In the aftermath of these developments, welfare reform took a distinctly different turn.

In particular, the Personal Responsibility and Work Opportunity Reconciliation Act, enacted in July of 1996 and signed by President Clinton amid outcry by liberal Democrats, ended AFDC as a federal entitlement program. The longstanding arrangement by which the federal government guaranteed cash benefits to needy dependent children and their parents was scrapped in favor of a block grant arrangement that empowered states to constitute their own welfare programs with greater freedom to make their own arrangements for solving the issue of the welfare-work nexus. Two of the most controversial provisions of the legislation were stipulations that a family would lose its entire welfare check if the family head did not work within two years of going on welfare and the institution of a lifetime cap of five years for receipt of welfare benefits. While states could exempt 20% of their caseloads from the 5-year lifetime limits, they were also empowered to set even stricter limits (Pear, 1996a: A10). State governments had been pushing in the direction of such cutoffs for some time and encountering resistance from the Clinton administration in the 1993–1996 period. Massachusetts, for example, passed legislation in 1995 that, among other provisions, limited welfare recipients to two years of cash assistance. But despite extensive negotiations, then-Secretary of Health and Human Services Secretary Donna Shalala refused to approve a waiver for such a two-year cut-off (Kilborn and Verhovek, 1996: A8). With the signing of the 1996 legislation, the federal government too embraced the cut-off strategy.

The 1996 legislation contains a number of other important provisions having to do with the moral regulation dimension of welfare policy. These will be discussed in the next section. Before turning to that dimension, however, it is important to consider whether and how policy changes involving the welfare-work dimension of welfare policy fit with public opinion on this matter.

The Opinion-Policy Nexus: Work-Welfare Nexus

As the preceding policy history suggests, concerns about welfare dependency and work disincentives have a longstanding place in discussions of welfare, and work requirements of various kinds have long been a part of welfare policy. But there has been a shift in policy. For a long period, welfare incorporated a largely symbolic commitment to work requirements. "Mandatory" participation in various service programs would make recipients more employable while simultaneously reversing disincentives for work. But limited resources meant that the services were available to relatively few and requirements for participation and work were not practically enforceable. In the 1990s, however, institutionalization of the cutoff strategy resolved this dilemma, albeit in a way that opponents such as Daniel Patrick Moynihan would refer to as a "horror." Whether they had any real prospects for employment or not, all cash benefits for welfare families would be ended after two years unless recipients found their way into the ranks of the working poor; and no one could accumulate more than 5 years of cash benefits.

How consistent is this policy shift with public opinion? Unlike the long-running series of questions on the public's preferences concerning welfare spending, poll data on work requirements are not as readily to be found. However, a number of pieces of poll data do have a bearing on the welfare-work nexus. For example, central to the welfare-work nexus are issues of dependency and willingness to work. Characterizations of welfare recipients as relying on welfare whenever they could, with more effort on their part, get by without it are manifestations of concern about the welfare-work nexus. In episodic surveys dating from 1976, the *New York Times*/WCBS poll asked "In your opinion, do you think that most people who receive money from welfare could get along without it if they tried, or do you think that most of them really need this help?" As Table 6-1 shows, there has been remarkably little change in the results when this question has been asked from 1976 to 1994, except on occasions when the allowance of mixed responses altered the overall structure of the response categories. Generally, modest majorities of respondents have indicated their belief that most welfare recipients could get along without welfare if they tried—a pattern that is in broad contours consistent with the nation's long-standing efforts to incorporate welfare program provisions that direct recipients into work.

Teles (1996: 55) also argues that embedding work requirements in welfare programs is highly consistent with the public's long-term values. Indeed, he argues that work requirements are popular because they tap into all three strands of the nation's political culture: ". . . they seem to engage all sides of the public's mind: its egalitarian desire to help those in need, its hierarchical desire to enforce a central societal norm, and its individualist desire to foster independence and self-reliance." Furthermore, Teles (1996: 56) points to yet another set of public opinion data that suggests consistency between policy and opinion on this matter. The percentage of respondents who believe that women should not work has dropped noticeably since 1972. While the poll questions behind that data are not specifically couched in terms of welfare recipients or even necessarily of women with children, Teles (1996: 58) nevertheless

Table 6-1. Perceptions of Whether Most Recipients Really Need Welfare

	Percentage Responding:			
Poll Date	Most Could Get Along Without It If They Tried	Most Really Need It	Both Responses Are Right	Don't Know/ No Answer
8/76	52	38		10
10/76A	51	36		13
10/76B	53	40		7
7/77	54	31		14
11/80	51	39		10
9/81	55	32		15
1/86	40	35	20	4
5/92A	45	45		10
5/92B	29	50	16	4
1/94	48	35	13	4
12/94	57	36		7

Source: New York Times/WCBS poll results on microfiche, Dec. 9, 1994.

marshals an impressive array of public opinion data to support the argument that cultural beliefs that "society has an interest in keeping women out of the workforce" have eroded. The new consensus that women can work without significant harm to their family obligations provides an important source of popular support for the work requirements of the AFDC program, which after all are largely directed at women on welfare, many of whom have children. The earliest work requirements, such as those in the WIN program, exempted women with children under age 16; the Family Support Act exempted women with children under age 3. That change in the target of work requirements is consistent with a sea change in public opinion about women in the workplace, and indeed the dramatic increase in the number of women, even women with small children, who are working.

By the second half of the 1980s, the debate over work requirements had, as we have seen, begun to incorporate a tougher language of "workfare"—i.e., welfare recipients being required to work in exchange for welfare benefits, even if it was work at a menial job that netted them no pay beyond their benefit check. States began to implement such provisions under waiver programs even before the Family Support Act provided more general approval for such an approach. And there is some scattered poll data showing substantial popular support for this more stringent form of work requirement. In a December 5, 1985 poll by the Joint Center for Political Studies, respondents were asked: "Some states have laws requiring people on welfare who have completed job search and training programs and still can't find jobs to work at public service or nonprofit jobs without additional pay. Would you like to see such a law in your state or not?" Over two-thirds (69%) favored such a law, 25% opposed the idea, and 6% had no opinion. In response to an item on the 1990 General Social Survey asking whether they favored or opposed "requiring that people work in order to receive welfare" 81% said they favored or strongly favored the requirement. In a Gallup poll from November of 1991, 79% of respondents favored "requiring all able-bodied people on welfare, including women with small children, to do work for their welfare checks." And in a *U.S. News and World Report* poll from December, 1993, 17% somewhat favored and 76% strongly favored "requiring job training for those on welfare and after two years requiring them to work"—for a total of 93% in favor of this workfare item.

But if broader cultural values have long supported work requirements and changing notions of women and work fit with ever more
inclusive definitions of which AFDC recipients are subject to them,
what of the more recent and dramatic change in policy concerning
the welfare-work nexus—i.e., the shift to a cutoff strategy? Is there
anything approaching a public consensus for the sorts of strict time
limits that a number of state governments wanted to implement in
the 1990s and that the federal government ultimately embraced in
the 1996 reform legislation? The fragmentary opinion poll data
that exists suggests that there is something approximating majority support for some versions of the cutoff strategy, but that the
public is divided and cautious about this approach. In the December, 1993 *U.S. News and World Report* poll mentioned above, respondents were asked about whether we should "limit welfare
benefits to 2 years and then not allow people to get back on welfare
for at least 5 years." Half of the respondents were in favor—about
one-third strongly so; but 38% were opposed, and 11 percent were
unsure. Although this poll contained no question that precisely
matched the 5-year lifetime cutoff that was incorporated in the
1996 legislation, a follow-up question asked about cutting people
off after two years and never letting them back on welfare. Only
22% favored this lifetime cutoff, while 73% opposed it.

In short, the evidence suggests a high level of consistency between public opinion and policy on the work-welfare aspects of
welfare policy. Admittedly, the symbolic aspect of policy—i.e., the
tough language of work requirements as stipulated in welfare reform legislation—is much more consistent with public opinion than
the substantive realities of policy, in which resource limitations
meant that policy as implemented was only a pale imitation of
what the rhetoric of the policy enactment promised. Nevertheless,
the content, direction and intention of welfare policy with respect
to work requirements is aligned with a broad popular consensus
about the matter; and even implementation limitations may be
viewed as responsive to the constraints established by the public's
tolerance level for spending on welfare. In this case, the symbolic
aspect of policy (i.e., the affirmation of the importance of work and
society's lack of toleration for long-term un-excused absence from
the workforce) may be as or more important to the general public
than the substantive aspect of policy as implemented.

Contemporary Policy History: Moral Regulation

There is yet a third dimension of welfare policy—one having to do with the intervention of the state into the realm of welfare recipients' decisions about child-bearing and other matters of sexual behavior, family composition, and child raising. While there has been considerable controversy over contemporary reforms that include these matters, such a moral regulatory posture is not new. Until the latter part of the 1960s, "welfare was conditioned on such actions of the poor as the stability of their ties to the local community, their sexual practices, and the quality of the care they provided to their children" (Corbett, 1995: 28). Handler and Hasenfeld (1991) show that poverty programs have long been premised on moral constructions in which officials distinguish "fit" from "unfit" mothers based in large part on sexual behaviors. The state-level mothers' pension programs that were the pre-1935 precursors of contemporary welfare programs were heavily dependent on moral standards for implementation. Mothers who neglected their children or who engaged in any sexual activity outside the domestic code of the time were deemed unfit for such assistance. Moral judgments continued throughout the early years of administration of the Aid to Dependent Children (ADC) program. For example, the "man-in-the-house" rule that was used in the ADC program until 1962 disqualified a woman if a man were found to be regularly present in the home. The rule was enforced with unannounced, late night searches of the homes of welfare recipients. While partly relevant to eligibility and cost issues that are a part of the generosity dimension of welfare policy, the man-in-the-house rule also had a more explicitly moral purpose—"to ensure that welfare assistance reached only the 'right sort of people'" (Teles, 1996: 101).

But there was a distinct turn away from the moral regulatory approach to welfare in the late 1960s, a stand-down that lasted until the 1980s. Teles (1996) suggests that this retreat from moral regulation occurred because of the emergence of a rights-oriented approach to welfare—an approach fostered by liberal intellectuals, legal theorists, and federally-funded poverty warriors who waged an aggressive and successful war in the courts. Man-in-the-house rules were the opening front for this war. Although the federal government had, in 1962 amendments to the Social Security Act, done away with such rules, states were not necessarily inclined to so easily give up on their historic role of separating "fit" from "unfit" mothers on these grounds. In its first-ever decision on the AFDC program, the Supreme Court ruled in the 1968 case *King v. Smith* that Alabama's AFDC regulation concerning substitute fathers was a violation of the federal government's prerogative to determine eligibility in the program. By defining a substitute father as any individual cohabiting with the mother and by cutting off benefits to women found to have such cohabitation arrangements, Alabama was found to have improperly imposed an eligibility rule beyond those stipulated in the federal government's 1962 amendments (Teles, 1996: 107–108). This decision was followed by others which struck down residency requirements and established the rights of welfare recipients to due process hearings. While these cases were not explicitly about welfare provisions involving moral regulation, they shored up a rights-oriented body of case law involving AFDC and federal preeminence on eligibility, both of which undermined states' ability to enforce moral standards through their administration of welfare. Most important, Teles (1996: 117) suggests that this movement away from moral regulation constituted a disjunction from public opinion:

> The Court ratified an understanding of public assistance out of step with public and governmental opinion and thus helped to put that understanding, rather than the mix of financial generosity and behavioral stringency that conformed with public norms, at the center of the welfare debate.

We will shortly investigate whether the scattered poll data that are available support the notion that a stand-down from moral regulation was out of kilter with popular opinion. First, it is important to acknowledge the substantial sea change that has occurred back in the direction of moral regulation.

The States and Moral Regulation

Much of the impetus for the return of moral regulation beginning in the 1980s came from the states. The waiver process (discussed above) that empowered states to institute more aggressive policies with respect to work requirements also unleashed a series of state policies focused on what Teles (1996: 139) describes as "more controversial matters, including family composition and structure."

Wisconsin was an innovation leader in this regard. In response to growing caseloads and the perception that the state's history of relatively generous benefits might have cast the state in the role of a "welfare magnet," welfare had become a crisis issue in Wisconsin by the mid-1980s. The election of Republican Governor Tommy Thompson in 1986, who had campaigned on a pledge to reform welfare in the state, ushered in a series of welfare reforms that quickly received national notice (Corbett, 1995: 33–37). While welfare reform in Wisconsin involves a complex array of programs and provisions, the most high-profile elements involve the moral regulation dimension. For example, Wisconsin's Learnfare program, implemented after federal waiver approval in 1987, requires that teenage recipients of AFDC attend school regularly. If they do not, they cannot be counted in the calculation of the family's welfare benefit. In short, Learnfare uses welfare benefits as a mechanism to enforce parents' responsibility to see that their children get to school. In 1992 Wisconsin obtained federal waiver approval for its Parental and Family Responsibility Initiative, which was designed to "encourage family formation, discourage subsequent births for those on assistance, and provide income support through AFDC to young working heads of two-parents families" (Corbett, 1995: 25). Specifically, this initiative, popularly dubbed "Bridefare," provided more generous benefits to mothers under age 20 who lived with the father of the child. The program also instituted a cut in the benefit increase for additional children delivered while on welfare.

By 1992, a more stringent version of this "family cap" was featured in New Jersey's welfare reform. New Jersey's Family Development Plan mandated that women who give birth to children while on welfare be denied any additional cash benefits for the additional child. In contrast with the Wisconsin initiatives which were spearheaded by an activist Republican governor, New Jersey's foray into a moral regulatory approach was the "personal project" of Wayne Bryant, an African-American Democratic state assemblyman with impeccable credentials as an advocate for the poor (Goertzel and Hart, 1995: 110). The family cap is only one of several welfare reform provisions that Bryant successfully pushed through the state legislature. Another provision attempts to encourage marriage by modifying AFDC eligibility rules to favor a mother who marries even if the man is not the father of her children. These moral regulatory elements of New Jersey's welfare reform are embedded in a host of other provisions that create a relatively expansive, service strategy approach to the welfare-work side of the state's policy. For example, job development, educational and training services are provided, as are support services such as child care and a 2-year extension of Medicaid eligibility as the individual begins work (Goertzel and Hart, 1995: 114). But, as in Wisconsin, it is the moral regulatory elements that have given New Jersey welfare reform a high profile nationally.

Elements such as family caps, encouragement of marriage, and mandates that teenage recipients live with their parents were taken up in the 1990s by a number of other states. For example, Vermont adopted the concept of requiring teenage welfare recipients to live with their parents (Teles, 1996: 139). Georgia's "Personal Accountability and Responsibility Project included a family cap (Kass, 1995: 6) and, by 1994, more than 30 states were attempting to adopt some form of a family cap for welfare beneficiaries (Cockburn, 1994: 18). States also used the waiver process to implement new methods for increasing child support enforcement, including requirements that women name the father of their child as a condition of getting welfare benefits (Thompson and Norris, 1995: 7). By 1995, at least 51 different waiver demonstrations were in place in 27 states, many with multiple elements, and many including at least some aspect of moral regulation ("Welfare by Waiver," 1995: 4).

Perhaps the most controversial element of the moral regulatory program at the state level involves efforts to check welfare births by means of incentives for contraceptive use. Though typically cast in terms of incentives rather than requirements, proposals such as a 1994 Florida bill that would have provided an additional $200 per year for women on welfare if they used contraceptives or Colorado state representative Bill Jerke's proposal to provide a bonus of $100 to welfare mothers with three children who would accept contraceptive implants (Cockburn, 1994: 16–17) constitute a not-so-subtle form of coercion for birth control. Proposals such as these are especially volatile because they evoke themes that can be tied to the ideas of the eugenicists who, in the early decades of this century, pushed for the sterilization of the feeble-minded, sexual perverts, and individuals such as "the congenitally idle and other burdens on the public patience and the public purse" (Cockburn, 1994: 16). The availability of the contraceptive implant called Norplant, which would allow authorities to verify contraceptive use in ways that would not be possible with other contraceptive methods, may have sparked much of the interest in steering welfare mothers to contraception. But Norplant has generated problems for a number of users who experienced unexpected side effects or who encountered substantial problems in having the implants removed. As a result, at least one class action lawsuit has been filed against the makers of Norplant. The combination of controversies surrounding contraceptive implants has, at least temporarily, derailed initiatives to add bonuses for contraception to the growing arsenal of moral regulatory tools that states have devised for welfare recipients.

More generally, the institution of moral regulatory elements into welfare reform has not come without controversy. Opposition comes from those who fear that state encouragement of family formation might translate into pressures for poor women to marry men who are abusive or irresponsible. Right-to-life groups have had concerns that family caps might encourage abortions (Goertzel and Hart, 1995: 111). Required paternity declarations have been viewed with alarm by women with concerns about the potential that such a requirement might place a woman at risk for retaliatory abuse. Despite their controversial nature, many of these elements of moral regulation became more securely entrenched as part of the nation's approach to welfare policy as the federal government embraced parts of them in federal welfare reform and ultimately empowered states to run their own welfare programs.

The Federal Government and Moral Regulation

While federal policy has not embraced the most extreme elements of state-level initiatives and proposals for moral regulation of welfare recipients, many of the provisions that began as state-level initiatives have gradually been incorporated, albeit sometimes in a softer form, in federal policy. For example, the federal government has not adopted required paternity declarations. However, in an effort to encourage child support from the fathers of welfare children, a 1984 law used an incentive approach rather than outright regulation. That law instituted a bonus, usually of about $50, that a welfare mother received in any month in which the father of her children made a child support payment. But this incentive-based approach was very troublesome to administer and generated no substantial evidence that it had an impact on the extent of child support (Kilborn, 1996: A1).

The Family Support Act of 1988 continued the pressure for paternity establishment while delegating to the states the hard choices about how to accomplish the task. The legislation mandated that, within four years, the states either establish the paternity of at least half of children born out of wedlock who were getting state services or meet one of two alternate targets for paternity establishment. The methods that the states might use to meet these targets were left unspecified. For example, no provision suggested that welfare mothers be required to name the father. But the paternity establishment targets, along with a provision that offered federal match money to help pay for lab tests in cases of contested paternity, encouraged aggressive approaches to paternity establishment. An additional provision relating to paternity establishment also suggests the extent to which the privacy and personal autonomy of welfare recipients is discounted. The legislation mandated that states "require the child and all other parties in a contested paternity case to submit to genetic tests upon the request of any party" ("After Years of Debate . . . , 1989: 352).

With the total revamping of the welfare program in 1996, the federal government provided additional tools and mandates to the states regarding paternity establishment. The Personal Responsibility and Work Opportunity Reconciliation Act of 1996 requires states to have arrangements by which the implementing state agency will make determinations about whether welfare recipients are cooperating in good faith with state efforts to establish paternity and obtain financial support from the absent parent. The Act also permits any state to cut off assistance payments to individuals who refuse to cooperate with the state in establishing paternity or obtaining child support unless the individual has small children needing child care or the individual can show cause to be exempted from the requirement for assistance with paternity establishment.

The matter of enforced family living arrangements for teenage recipients had been incorporated in the Family Support Act of 1988,

which gave states discretionary power to implement AFDC requirements that would prevent any teenage (i.e., under age 18) parent
from receiving benefits unless they lived with a parent, relative or
adult legal guardian or in an adult-supervised institutional living
arrangement. That requirement was softened, however, with language that exempted teenage parents in a variety of circumstances,
including a state agency determination that the "physical or emotional health or safety of the individual or her child would be jeop-
ardized" (After Years of Debate . . . , 1989: 356). The Personal
Responsibility and Work Opportunity Reconciliation Act of 1996
went one step further in this regard. Rather than permitting states
to have such requirements, the 1996 act mandated that states
impose adult-supervised living arrangements on unmarried teenage parents in order for them to qualify for assistance.

Taking a cue from state initiatives such as Wisconsin's Learnfare
program, the 1996 reform also included a stipulation that the federal government would not prohibit states from sanctioning a welfare family if the adult recipient fails to ensure that their minor
dependent children meet state requirements for school attendance.
In addition, the reform act incorporated requirements that unmarried teenage parents attend high school or equivalent training
programs or else lose their benefits.

The 1996 reform did not include a "family cap" provision such as
New Jersey's controversial cutoff of additional payments to women
who have additional children while on welfare. Instead, the 1996
legislation offered states a back door method of compensating recipients who had been cut off through family cap provisions instituted at the state level. Specifically, the legislation amended the
social service block grant (Title XX) so that it could be used to
provide vouchers for services to families denied cash welfare benefits
because they had additional children while on welfare. On the other
hand, the legislation did add a federal incentive to already-existing
state-level pressures to manage the reproductive decisions of welfare recipients. In particular, the 1996 reform provided additional
grant fund bonuses to states that showed reductions in illegitimate
births.

Through a combination of demonstration programs implemented
by the states under federal waivers and two federal reform pack-
ages that reflected many of the ideas from those waiver experiments, welfare policy in the United States had by 1996 taken on

much of the moral regulatory content that had been eschewed in the latter 1960s. Through a complex array of incentives and regulations that coerce welfare mothers into marrying, naming the father of their illegitimate children, sending their children to school, living with their parents, and limiting the number of children that they bear, these policies assert the power of the state into some of the most personal decisions that women make. Some of the power of the new moral regulatory approach to welfare is also aimed at the fathers of dependent children, for they are now being sought out much more aggressively for child support payments. But welfare's new face of moral regulation introduces particularly significant elements of state power into the child bearing, child rearing, and family living decisions of poor women.

As noted above, some of these elements of moral regulation have been quite controversial. Is this because the reintroduction of welfare-specific moral regulation after a stand-down from it in the 1960s is at odds with public opinion? Or is Teles (1996: 117) accurate in his assessment that the American public was in the 1960s and is now inclined to support such moral regulation? If the former is correct, this dimension of welfare policy has recently become unresponsive. If the latter is correct, the moral-regulatory elements of welfare that have been introduced in the late 1980s and 1990s constitute a return to responsiveness after a period of policy-opinion incongruity from the late 1960s to the early 1980s.

The Opinion-Policy Nexus: Moral Regulation

Not surprisingly, public opinion data on the moral regulatory element of welfare is even more difficult to find than opinion data on the other elements of welfare. After all, the moral regulation aspect of welfare involves highly sensitive matters that had become confounded with racial politics by the late 1960s and early 1970s and perhaps therefore too explosively controversial for polling organizations to handle. However, there is evidence that public opinion in the earlier part of the 1960s was supportive of a moral regulatory role for welfare policy.

As early as 1961, there was widespread popular sentiment in favor of forced paternity declarations. In a July 1961 Gallup poll, 73% of respondents thought it was a "good idea" to "get a court order to require the mother of an illegitimate child to name the father and then to require him to pay the extra relief cost for the child." This is not an ideal survey item because it is a double-barreled question. It is possible that respondents may have been mostly in favor of getting child support from the father but not particularly enthusiastic about the requirements that would need to be imposed on the mother. But even if that were the case, it is revealing that nearly three-quarters of respondents swallowed any reservations they may conceivably have had on the mother's behalf and endorsed the idea.

Other poll questions asked in the 1960s suggest that widespread empathy for welfare mothers was not likely to have been hidden in the double-barreled question above. In a January, 1965 Gallup poll, respondents were asked: "Sometimes unwed mothers on relief continue to have illegitimate children and get relief money for each new child born. What do you think should be done in the case of these women?" This open-ended question elicited a variety of largely punitive responses. "The suggestion offered most frequently by about half of the persons interviewed in this survey was to 'stop giving them relief money.' Next most often mentioned by roughly one person in five was 'sterilize the woman.' Other suggestions were rehabilitation and job training, supplying birth control information, jail terms, fines for any illegitimate children born, and compulsory psychiatric care" (Gallup, 1972: 1921). This survey question also has a potential flaw. At least in the light of contemporary standards, the prefatory statement might be said to make it a biased or leading question. With that reservation in mind, however, the responses suggest near-majority support for financial penalties that are even more draconian than contemporary family caps. And the other responses, and most notably the 20% that favored sterilization, suggest a strong undercurrent of hostility to welfare mothers and support for the adoption of drastic measures of moral regulation.

While those favoring sterilization constitute a noticeable minority, there was also widespread support in the 1960s for less drastic forms of welfare state involvement in the reproductive decisions of women on welfare. In a January, 1967 Gallup poll, respondents were asked if birth control pills "should be made available free to all women of child-bearing age on relief." Sixty-three percent favored this, while 28% opposed and 10% had no opinion. These results are particularly interesting in light of the substantial uncertainty about the health dangers from birth control pills that existed at that time. In the same January, 1967 Gallup poll, respondents were asked "Do you think these pills can be used safely—that is, without danger to a person's health?" Only 43% respondent affirmatively; more than one quarter (26%) said no and another 31% were unsure. The juxtaposition of these two sets of results suggests that non-trivial numbers of respondents favored the free dispensation of birth control pills to women on welfare even though they had reservations about the health effects of those pills.

There is thus at least some poll data to substantiate the interpretation that public opinion in the 1960s incorporated moral judgments about the sexual behaviors of welfare recipients and was supportive of welfare policy elements that would place the state in a strongly interventionist role with respect to this sphere of welfare recipients' lives. This means that the late-1960s retreat from a moral regulatory version of welfare policy was indeed inconsistent with public opinion.

But was mass opinion reshaped in the ensuing decade-and-a-half? That is, were the mass public's moral regulatory impulses neutralized by the symbolic messages given out through those changes in welfare policy, or perhaps by the rhetoric of the anti-poverty elites that were instrumental in giving welfare policy its new, rights-oriented face? These questions cannot be answered because public opinion about welfare recipients and government's role in regulating their sexual behavior and family arrangements disappeared from the map. Questions on welfare recipients' child-bearing practices and government's role in shaping contraception and child support arrangements, for example, were no longer asked, presumably because polling organizations believed them to be inappropriate.

But more contemporary data suggest that if moral regulatory impulses were muted during this hiatus in public opinion polling on the matter, the change was decidedly impermanent. By the second half of the 1980s, concerns about the sexual behaviors and family arrangements of welfare recipients were again showing up in survey research on welfare. A battery of questions on the 1986 General Social Survey, for example, asked respondents whether they agreed or disagreed with a series of statements about the impacts of welfare. Sixty percent either agreed or strongly agreed that welfare "encourages young women to have babies before marriage"; and 58% agreed or strongly agreed that welfare "discourages young women who get pregnant from marrying the father of their child." A 1988 survey by the Joint Center for Political Studies asked respondents how often "poor young women have babies so they can collect welfare." The majority of both black and white respondents (57% of blacks and 54% of whites) answered either "often" or "almost always" rather than "seldom," "almost never," or "don't know."

By the 1990s, polls were incorporating some questions that reflected at least some of the more prominent forms of moral regulatory policy that were being implemented through waiver demonstrations or being proposed by state governments. A December 4, 1993 *U.S. News & World Report* poll, for example, asked respondents whether they favored or opposed various suggestions to reform the welfare system. More than two-thirds (65%) favored (strongly or somewhat) the equivalent of New Jersey's family cap— i.e., "do not increase welfare benefits when people on welfare have additional children"; nearly half (48%) *strongly* favored the cap. Other poll results suggest substantial but less than majority support for the family cap. Polls conducted by *Time/CNN* in May of 1992 and 1994 presented respondents with a list of changes "many people would like to make in the current welfare system" and asked whether respondents favored or opposed each idea, among them, to "end increases in welfare payments to women who give birth to children while on welfare." In 1992, 36% favored the idea, and in 1994 42% favored the idea. Questions about toughened requirements for child support from welfare children's fathers were also being asked, although without reference to the issue of requiring welfare mothers to cooperate in paternity determination. In the 1992 and 1994 *Time/CNN* poll questions on proposed changes to the welfare system, for example, 93% and 95% of respondents respectively favored the idea of "taking money out of the paychecks and tax refunds of fathers who refuse to make child support payments that a court has ordered." There was substantial, though not majority support in the 1992 *Time/CNN* poll for requiring unmarried teenage mothers to live with their parents in order to receive welfare.

While sketchy, the available public opinion data therefore suggest that many of the same concerns about the child-bearing choices and family arrangements of welfare recipients that were prevalent in the 1960s are still prevalent in the 1990s; and the data also suggest substantial levels of support for at least some of the policy changes that have emerged in the contemporary phase of renewed emphasis on the moral regulatory face of welfare. In short, the return of a moral regulatory approach appears to be a policy shift in the direction of responsiveness to popular opinion, reversing a period in which policy was inconsistent with prevailing opinion.

Alternative Interpretations and a Conclusion

Whether welfare policy is consistent with public opinion depends in part on the point in history at issue. As this chapter has shown, it is also important to consider whether the answer depends on what aspect of welfare policy is at issue. Throughout the past two-and-one-half decades, changes in the *generosity* of welfare have been tightly coupled with changing public opinion about welfare spending. And for most of this same period, policies concerning the *welfare-work nexus* have been at least symbolically consistent with longstanding public values concerning welfare and work; in recent years, however, the limitations of a largely symbolic approach have led to the adoption of a harsher, cutoff strategy that, if fully implemented, would take welfare policy into a realm without a popular mandate. With respect to moral regulation, welfare policy exhibits a long-term thermostatic sequence. Although this element of welfare policy was apparently inconsistent with the mass public's attitudes throughout the 1970s, it gradually came back into line with popular opinion in the latter 1980s and early 1990s; and the mass public's reservations about the more extreme elements of moral regulation suggest a moderating signal in this policy direction.

But, as has been noted several times in this volume, opinion-policy consistency and policy responsiveness to opinion are not necessarily the same thing. In order to interpret consistency as responsiveness, further evidence must help to rule out rival interpretations.

One rival interpretation is that public opinion simply reflects non-attitudes and that any observed consistency between opinion and policy is therefore bogus. That interpretation can be relatively easily dismissed. For one thing, aggregate public opinion about welfare does change in ways that reflect a reasonable response to actual events. Popular concern over welfare spending escalated to its highest point in the wake of the massive increases in the nation's welfare rolls in the late 1960s, abated when growth in the number of individuals on welfare leveled off, and moved sharply upward again when the number of individuals on welfare began another dramatic rise in the 1990s. Furthermore, individual-level research suggests that public opinion on welfare does *not* exhibit the lack of ideological consistency and coherent structuring that are characteristic of non-attitudes. Sanders (1988: 319), for example, finds that party identification is a significant predictor of attitudes on welfare spending; in fact, party identification is more strongly related to attitudes on welfare spending than it is to any of the other areas of government spending examined in his analysis. In addition, a considerable body of individual-level research shows that attitudes toward welfare are coherently connected to respondents' economic self-interests—i.e., whether or not they are economically disadvantaged (Cook and Barrett, 1992; Kluegel and Smith, 1986; Gilens, 1996) and to their attitudes on individualism (Kluegel and Smith, 1986; Gilens, 1996). Finally, racial attitudes have been found to be "a powerful influence on white Americans' welfare views" (Gilens, 1996: 601).

As with crime and imprisonment issues, there is evidence that the mobilizing efforts of key political figures may be instrumental in calling public attention to trends in spending on welfare and to other aspects of the welfare issue. But, while public opinion sometimes reacts to the mobilizing efforts of political figures, it is sometimes quite immune to such mobilization. Figure 6-6 illustrates this with reference to presidents and presidential candidates. High levels of popular concern about welfare spending corresponded with enormous levels of attention to the issue by Nixon and McGovern in the 1972 presidential election; and after a noticeable dropoff, popular concern about welfare spending peaked again in conjunction with notable attention to the welfare issue by Carter and Ford in 1976. But thereafter, popular concern about welfare spending began a steady drop-off that was sustained even after Reagan's high-level emphasis on the issue in 1981–82 and continuing attention to the issue by Reagan and Bush in the latter 1980s. Popular concern about welfare spending rose sharply from 1992–1994, hand in hand with Clinton's full-blown efforts at agenda-setting on the issue.

Figure 6-6 is obviously only a partial look at mobilization. Other political elites, most notably governors and members of Congress, have served as issue entrepreneurs with respect to welfare; and public concerns about welfare dependency and the moral regulation of welfare recipients are at least as important targets for opinion mobilization as are their concerns about welfare spending. If systematic data on all these actors and all these dimensions of

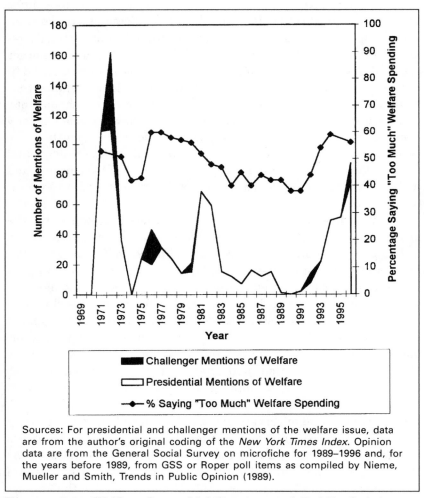

Sources: For presidential and challenger mentions of the welfare issue, data are from the author's original coding of the *New York Times Index*. Opinion data are from the General Social Survey on microfiche for 1989–1996 and, for the years before 1989, from GSS or Roper poll items as compiled by Nieme, Mueller and Smith, Trends in Public Opinion (1989).

Figure 6-6. Welfare Issue Mobilization and Public Opinion on Welfare Spending

public opinion were readily available, they might well exhibit even more evidence of mobilization than that evidenced in Figure 6-6.

The important point, however, is that the mobilization of public opinion about welfare has either been ineffective (i.e., levels of popular concern about welfare remained unaffected by agenda-setting efforts) or has occurred at times when the actual magnitude of the welfare rolls or of welfare spending were unusually high, thus leaving it unclear whether movements in public opinion are responding to policy trends a la the thermostatic model, to the mobilizing efforts of political elites, or a combination of the two (i.e., political elites calling attention to policy trends). In any case, the predominance of the evidence in this chapter favors an interpretation of welfare policy development as occurring in sequences dominated by policy responsivness, either of a sustained nature or, in the case of the moral regulatory aspect of welfare policy, in a responsive-unresponsive-responsive sequence that is suggestive of the thermostatic model.

7

Social Security

Promises They Can't Deliver

Overview

This chapter focuses on policy development surrounding the nation's Social Security program, the system that by the end of 1995 was paying retirement and disability benefits to 43.4 million individuals (Board of Trustees, 1996). Originally enacted in 1935, Social Security now includes related funds to pay for disability insurance and for the hospital insurance component of the Medicare system. While these are important additions that may have a bearing on the overall financial viability of the Social Security system over the long haul, this chapter will focus primarily upon the old-age pensions that are arguably the original core of the Social Security system.

Social Security has been called the "third rail" of politics—a colorful phrase suggesting that any politician who dares to cut this highly popular program would be politically electrocuted, and that, knowing this, few or none dare to touch the program (Light, 1995). The phrase suggests that, in the case of Social Security, the linkage between public opinion and policy is simply one of responsiveness. Social Security is sacrosanct, and policymakers act accordingly. But how did Social Security become sacrosanct? And, have there been any periods in the now 60-year-old Social Security program in which the connection between opinion and policy has been anything but directly responsive? Is there, in fact, meaningful public opinion on Social Security to which policymakers might be responsive?

This chapter will show that the development of the Social Security system in the United States exemplifies a special version of the broken thermostat sequence. Public opinion was first manipulated to create broad support for a new program—but support that was based on limited public understanding and unrealistic expectations. Once popular support was established, policy was for a long time responsive to the broad contours of the opinion that had been created. But eventually, retirement security policy was unable to keep up with the unrealistic expectations that had been fostered and policy reform was required in order to sustain the program and to deal with its inherent problems. In order to accomplish this reform, an interim period of policymaking with some unresponsive elements was required. Policymakers had to find ways to make painful adjustments in a popular program—adjustments that would by no means be viewed as popular solutions by the mass public. In order to accomplish this, policymakers used very low-visibility decision-making venues, coupled with continuing efforts at opinion manipulation to make the public more receptive to the reforms while sustaining underlying support for the program as a whole. In short, the policy history of Social Security involves a sequence of opinion manipulation, followed by a sustained period of responsiveness that becomes increasingly problematic as policymakers find it difficult to deliver on the expectations that they themselves have created.

The extended policy history of Social Security development can be broken down into four periods that help to highlight changing patterns of policy-opinion connection. These are: the founding period (1935–1939); the expansionary period (1939–1976); the period of initial financial crisis (1977–1983); and the post-reform period (1984 to present). The chapter begins with a brief policy history of these four periods. Incorporated within the discussion of each period is available evidence and interpretation concerning the nature of public opinion on Social Security at the time and evidence of officials' efforts to shape that opinion.

Social Security: A Policy History in Four Acts

The Founding Period

There has been considerable scholarly attention to the founding of Social Security, but it has generated sharp disagreement rather than consensus about the extent to which the old-age pension program that emerged was responsive to societal demands for such a program. The context of events would seem to suggest that there was a ground-swell of support for income security programs for the aged. After all, Social Security was legislated in the midst of the Great Depression, the severe economic dislocations of which cast the problems of the elderly poor into sharp relief while simultaneously eroding confidence in the private sector. Further evidence that the emergence of Social Security was responsive to both social problems and public demand can be derived from the history of the Townsend Movement, a social protest movement of the Depression era that, beginning in 1933, pushed for a plan that would provide all Americans over 60 years of age with a $200 pension each month, which had to be spent during the month. The Townsend Plan proposed to finance this pension scheme with a national sales tax (Amenta, Carruthers, and Zylan, 1992: 315). While the Townsend plan was criticized by experts and politicians on both the left and the right, and while the Townsend movement is sometimes characterized as a minor, fringe movement, it was in many ways more substantial than this. By 1935, it had 450,000 members and dues-based receipts of $905,000 (Amenta, Carruthers, and Zylan, 1992: 318). While the Townsend plan was never enacted, "the movement formed a political backdrop, putting pressure on the administration to propose something and on Congress to vote for something for the aged, accounting for some of the popularity of federal funds for old-age pensions (Amenta, Carruthers, and Zylan, 1992: 321).

Furthermore, while poll data for 1935 are very limited compared to contemporary poll data on public issues, responses to a November 1935 Gallup poll suggest that large numbers of Americans "viewed a government program to provide retirement income as a pressing national need" (Brain, 1991: 123). No poll from 1935 or earlier asked about support for social security in the social insurance form that was ultimately enacted; but a December, 1935 poll indicated very widespread support (89%) for social assistance for the needy elderly (Brain, 1991: 128).

While all of this suggests general support for some form of income security to head off the problem of the destitute aged, there is room for interpretations of the historical record that suggest something quite different from a responsiveness model of opinion and policy. Freeman (1988: 159) argues that, while some scholars have used various versions of a "democratic politics" model to understand the emergence and development of social security, that approach is flawed: "All three versions [of the democratic politics interpretation] tend to exaggerate the extent to which social security policy was the product of societal political pressures. They either overstate the degree and clarity of public opinion in favor of specific programs, oversimplify the process by which such preferences can be translated into a policy mandate, or overemphasize the roles particular sectors of the public have actually played." Instead, Freeman and others offer interpretations which stress state-centered views of the development of Social Security—i.e., interpretations that emphasize the autonomous goals and ideologies of bureaucratic specialists and other policy elites.

Carolyn Weaver (1982), for example, suggests that policymakers deliberately used a variety of deceptive strategies to get popular consent for a Social Security program that was well beyond broad-based societal demands. In particular, President Roosevelt pushed for a pension program that featured compulsory payroll contributions from a relatively broad sector of American workers (i.e., a social insurance scheme) rather than benefits targeted only to needy elderly and financed out of more progressive sources such as the income tax (i.e., a social assistance scheme). In Weaver's interpretation, Roosevelt's programmatic approach was inconsistent with broad societal sentiments for a need-based approach, as evidenced by enactment of need-based pension programs in many states in the Depression years and the rejection of compulsory old-age insurance plans by state legislatures in the pre-Depression period.

While 1935 and earlier polls do not permit a direct assessment of this allegation, polls from 1936–1938 seem to suggest that Weaver's interpretation is too extreme. While there are lower levels of support when the public was asked questions about pension programs that involved "compulsory contributions" or "taxes" for financing than when they were asked in 1935 about help for the needy elderly, the support for compulsory contribution-based pensions was still substantial, ranging from 69% to 73% in several polls (Brain, 1991: 128–129). And a dropoff in support is always to be expected when language about the financing component of a program is added to a survey item.

Nevertheless, there are three reasons for accepting the argument of Weaver and others that the initiation of Social Security was done through manipulation of public opinion rather than responsiveness to it. First, there was (and to an extent still is) a lack of sophisticated knowledge about social security policy details among the mass public, thus providing the equivalent of a "blank slate" upon which policymakers could write preferences consistent with elite opinion. Second, there was an elite policymaking group with a clear agenda of its own and the motivation to shape public opinion to accept that policy agenda. Third, there is evidence that policymakers used strategic behavior and symbolic manipulation not only to gain passage of the legislation but also to foster favorable myths about the emergent social security system and to obscure problematic aspects of the program among the mass public.

With regard to the first of these, there is of course the same problem of sketchy data about knowledge of social security policy options as was the case concerning support for social security. In a thorough review of the scattered poll data available for the early years of the Social Security program, Schiltz (1970) concludes that in this early period, there was very limited knowledge about social security among the mass public, including limited awareness of the difference between a contributory social insurance approach and a means-tested approach.[1] In Skocpol's (1994: 22) interpretation, popular concern, coupled with this lack of sophisticated policy knowledge, gave policymakers substantial opportunity for action that is, in a very loose sense, responsive to public opinion.

However, as we will see in a moment, policymakers did not simply passively accept the maneuvering room that was given to them by the lack of popular knowledge about public insurance programs. They moved to transform that amorphous public sentiment into strong support for the social insurance approach that was being promulgated. But what was the elite policymaking group with this agenda? The key role that President Roosevelt played as a policy entrepreneur for a federal, old-age pension program of the contributory sort is acknowledged by many writers. Berkowitz (1991: 14), for example, notes Roosevelt's deep commitment to a contributory social insurance approach and his desire to avoid a welfare approach to the problem of the elderly poor. Given these commitments, Roosevelt determined to counter the opposition of Republicans, who opposed the idea as unnecessarily burdensome and inappropriately compulsory. But Roosevelt "resolved to spend some of the political capital that had accrued over the first two years of his term and push for legislation that he knew would bring negligible political rewards" (Berkowitz, 1991: 14). To develop the complex legislative proposal that would achieve his social policy vision, Roosevelt appointed an independent advisory panel, the Committee on Economic Security, consisting of key cabinet members such as Secretary of Labor Frances Perkins, Treasury Secretary Henry Morgenthau, and Federal Emergency Relief administrator Harry Hopkins, supported by technical experts and academics (Weaver, 1982: 65). Not surprisingly, the intellectual kinship and shared policy orientations of this group resulted in a proposal for a social insurance-style old-age pension system for most industrial workers, coupled with a separate title that would have provided federal assistance to states for means-tested programs for the impoverished elderly. The latter was necessary because the proposed social insurance system would not have included farm laborers, domestic servants, the self-employed and those who retired before 1937 (Berkowitz, 1991: 24).

The argument that the creation of the Social Security system was manipulative of the public rather than responsive to popular demands derives also from the strategies that policy entrepreneurs used to get the program enacted, institutionalized and popularized—strategies that can be viewed as obfuscating the true costs of the program and systematically discouraging political opposition by increasing the costs of opposition relative to the benefits of opposition. Charlotte Twight (1993) catalogues these strategies of "transaction cost augmentation." For example, opposition to the compulsory provisions of the pension program was made more difficult because of proponents' strategy of packaging those provisions together with other, popular elements of an omnibus Social Security bill (such as unemployment insurance and maternal and child health programs), with the administration refusing to accept individual parts of the omnibus bill for signature (Twight, 1993: 515; Weaver, 1982: 74–76; Derthick, 1979: 219–220). Once enacted, the management of the program was placed in the hands of the Social Security Board, an independent agency whose staffing was largely restricted to experts and activists who had served on the Committee for Economic Security. This ensured that technical information and interpretation necessary for further policymaking concerning the Social Security program was controlled by Social

Security insiders, who shared in the philosophy that had gone into program planning (Weaver, 1982: 103–105). The decision to split the cost of the program between payroll taxes paid by employees and payroll taxes paid by employers effectively diminishes the apparent cost of the program to the individual taxpayer (Twight, 1993: 516).

These strategic advantages were used to secure passage of the Social Security Act in 1935, an act that included a compulsory federal program of old-age insurance that was quite limited by contemporary standards. It covered only about 60% of the workforce and promised to pay modest monthly benefits, beginning in 1942, ranging from $10 to $85. The program was to be financed out of payroll taxes (1% each from employer and employee) on the first $3,000 of wages, with scheduled increases in this tax rate to a combined 6% rate in 1949. In the meantime, a large surplus was expected to have accumulated, providing the reserve fund that would ensure the long term viability of the program (Weaver, 1982: 93).

But in many respects, this was only the camel's nose under the tent. By 1939, program proponents had further used their monopoly of technical information, coupled with Republicans' fears of the implications of government control of a large, reserve fund, to successfully get the Social Security program amended. The 1939 Amendments expanded benefits by changing the benefit formula and by making benefits available to the surviving spouses and dependents of retired workers. In the 1935 legislation, the principle had been established that the magnitude of benefits received should be linked to contributions made; but to provide adequate income for those whose earnings and contributions were low, the original benefit formula was weighted in favor of lower-paid workers. The 1939 Amendments made this weighting even more substantial (Ball, 1988: 25). The amendments also functionally moved Social Security away from the model of a funded system, financed with an accumulated reserve; instead, the program was set on a trajectory to a pay-as-you-go model, in which current benefits are paid out of current revenues. This was accomplished by repealing the payroll tax increase that had been scheduled for 1940 while simultaneously expanding benefit commitments as outlined above.

Perhaps the clearest evidence of opinion manipulation in this founding period comes from the public relations strategies that were used by Social Security insiders. In response to Republican challenges to Social Security in the 1936 election, for example, the chair of the Social Security Board resigned to undertake an active public relations effort, including the production of the movie "We The People and Social Security" and the creation and dissemination of 8 million copies of an information circular (Weaver, 1982: 107). Skillful use of symbols toward the building of favorable program myths was important throughout the founding period. Roosevelt's insistence that Social Security be financed out of payroll taxes was, in large part, based on recognition that such a model would constitute an important symbolic "buy-in" to the program for the average American. And, as Weaver (1982: 123) notes, the reassuring terminology of the insurance industry was made an official part of the program in the 1939 Amendments—"old age benefit payments were renamed 'insurance' benefits, and Title VIII income and excise (payroll) taxes were repealed and replaced by 'insurance contribution' in the Federal Insurance Contributions Act (FICA), part of the Internal Revenue Code..."

With these and similar uses of political symbolism, the Social Security program was very quickly encrusted with myths that have been critical to its expansion and durability. Sixty years later, critics snort at the "legions of people" who "think that somewhere in the depths of the system is an account bearing each person's name and number, containing the exact amount of taxes paid over a lifetime, in cash or readily cashable securities, to be paid back penny for penny on retirement" (Church and Lacayo, 1995: 29). The important point is that the Social Security system was structured from the outset to create what Herman Leonard (1990: 59–60) calls "the logic of righteous entitlement:" That righteous entitlement was "born of their having made payments they view as contributions to an insurance program . . . Having taken that pledge in hard-earned dollars every payday of his or her working life, the payroll taxpayer is not about to stand idly by and watch the awaited benefits be swept away" (Leonard, 1990: 60).

The Expansionary Period (1939–1976)

No sooner was the Social Security system established than a remarkable series of expansions in it were enacted. These expansions included steady increases in the percentage of workers insured under Social Security, from 55% in 1939 to 91% in 1975 (U.S. House of Representatives, 1996: 8). Beginning with the Social Security Amendments of 1939 and periodically throughout this period, there has also been expansion in the sense of new types of benefits or beneficiaries. Retirement benefits were extended to include wives aged 65 or older and children age 18 or younger who were survivors of an insured worker, women retiring early (ages 62–65), men retiring early, widows aged 60–64 and widowers aged 60 or older (Brain, 41).

But perhaps the most dramatic expansions have involved increases in benefit levels. While some such increases were necessary to keep the value of benefits from eroding due to inflation, the regularity of the increases, the magnitude of some of them, and the timing of the increases in the election cycle, all suggest that more was at work than straightforward adjustments. Brain (1991: 43) counts more than 20 separately legislated benefit increases in the period from 1935 to 1974 and notes that most of them were larger than the Consumer Price Index. Furthermore, the timing of Social Security benefit increases suggests that election-year credit-claiming was very much at work: seven of the ten increases legislated in the period from 1950 to 1974 occurred in election years. The way in which Social Security increases were caught up in election year politics is no more clearly exemplified than in the substantial benefit increase legislated in 1972. As documented by Derthick (1979: 362–368), congressional Democrats were poised to outbid President Nixon on proposed Social Security increases, and the arms race to larger benefit increases was exacerbated by the fact that Wilbur Mills, chair of the House Ways and Means Committee, had decided to run for the presidency.

The year 1972 marks another important expansionist milestone for Social Security, for in that year Congress legislated automatic cost-of-living adjustments (COLAs) in Social Security, to begin in 1975. Automatic COLAs were viewed by some as an improvement over the irregularity of individually legislated increases. Apparently generous increases could and often were followed by several years without increases, during which benefits again lost ground relative to prices (Bernstein and Bernstein, 1988: 23). To fiscally conservative Republicans in Congress, automatic COLAs were attractive because they institutionalized the timing and magnitude of Social Security increases, thus removing the matter from the election-year dynamics that had led to what many viewed as overly generous increases (Derthick, 1979: 357).

The various policy decisions that have liberalized the Social Security system, coupled with the increasing life span of the U.S. population, have translated into a steady increase in program spending. As Figure 7-1 shows, cash benefit payments from the Old Age,

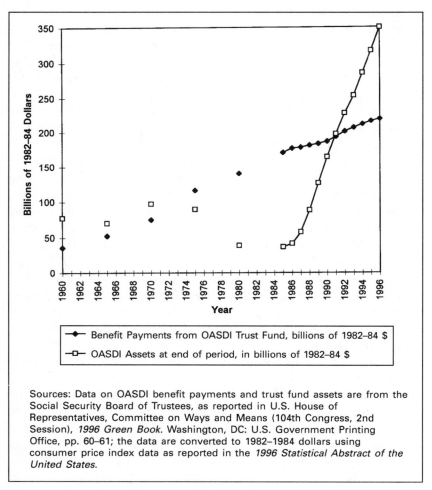

Sources: Data on OASDI benefit payments and trust fund assets are from the Social Security Board of Trustees, as reported in U.S. House of Representatives, Committee on Ways and Means (104th Congress, 2nd Session), *1996 Green Book*. Washington, DC: U.S. Government Printing Office, pp. 60–61; the data are converted to 1982–1984 dollars using consumer price index data as reported in the *1996 Statistical Abstract of the United States*.

Figure 7-1. Social Security (OASDI) Benefit Payments and Trust Fund Assets, 1960–1996

Survivors, and Disability Insurance trust fund grew considerably, even in inflation-adjusted dollars, from roughly $36 billion in 1960 to $116 billion in 1975.

There is much evidence that this period of program expansion was consistent with public opinion, albeit public opinion that had been shaped by the strategies and myths of the program's founders. Pulling together data from 15 polls conducted in the earliest portion of the expansionary period (1939–1952), Brain (1991: 146) concludes that "Clearly the program was supported by overwhelming majorities and the public was willing to finance both the program and its expansion." When poll questions were worded to "explicitly link current 'savings' by workers with their future retirement income" there was virtually unanimous support (96–97%), and there was also near unanimity when the question wordings pointed to benefits for the "needy" (89–93%). But there were also extraordinarily high levels of support even when question wordings referred only to old-age pensions or social security (78–92%). Question wordings which refer to "equal compulsory contributions" or "taxes" to pay for the program receive less support, but capture the support of an overwhelming majority (69–77%). Other poll items suggest that there was overwhelming support for expansion of the social security program to categories of workers not initially covered (Brain, 1991: 137–8); and while increases in social security benefits were favored by bare majorities in most early (1939) polls, large majorities favored such increases by the 1960s and 1970s (Brain, 1991: 132).

By the 1960s, various polls were asking the public if the nation was spending too little, too much, or just the right amount on "help to older people or the elderly" (poll items more specifically directed at spending on the Social Security program became available in later years). As Figure 7-2 shows, substantial proportions felt that old-age spending was too little. This, combined with the roughly 25% or more that felt spending on the elderly or Social Security was "about right," amounted to a very substantial consensus in favor of the expansionist regime of the period.

In the terms of our analysis, this is clearly a period of responsiveness of policy to opinion. But lest that responsiveness be over-interpreted, it is important to acknowledge the continuation of opinion-shaping strategies and tactics that sustained the initial consensus that program proponents had built among the mass public.

Figure 7-2. Public Opinion on Government Spending for Retirement Security, 1961–1996

For example, one of the things that helped to sustain popular support for the expansion of Social Security is the incremental nature of that expansion—an incrementalism which Twight (1993: 502) characterizes as strategic and manipulative of the public image of the program: "By reducing at each step the apparent marginal benefit to an individual of opposing payroll tax increases . . . such incrementalism significantly increases the transaction cost of organizing political resistance to resultant taxation." Moreover, through much of the expansionary period, Social Security also benefited from economic and demographic conditions that made expansion seem very low-cost, at least in the near term. With low unemployment and inflation, rising wages, and birth rates to assure plenty of future workers to support the system, the coverage and benefit increases enacted in the period were very politically painless (Berkowitz, 1991: 66–7). Finally, the high levels of popular support for Social Security during the expansionary phase were undoubtedly assisted by the high level of elite consensus that developed around the program in the 1950s. Berkowitz explains:

> Neither welfare nor insurance, neither socialism nor capitalism, it represented a pragmatic middle ground, a consensus on which social policy could rest. It exemplified what some observed as America's singular ability to rise above ideology and solve social problems (Berkowitz, 1991: 64).

During this period, then, Social Security policy can be said to have been responsive to mass public sentiments. Those sentiments may have been established in the first place by adept uses of myth-making, political symbolism, and strategic action in the founding phase of the program. And the sentiments, while favorable to Social Security, are likely to have been divorced from any sophisticated understanding of the program's technical aspects or long-term implications. One might even acknowledge that the positive character of public sentiments was regularly sustained by the incremental character of program expansion, by benefit increases that dwarfed apparent costs, and by continuing use of the reassuring symbols of an actuarially-sound insurance system. In this respect, the responsiveness of the expansionary period was overlaid on a continuing current of opinion manipulation. But it was a period of responsiveness, nonetheless. Elected policymakers had become accustomed to reaping the political gains of regularly enhancing benefits, with the help of economic prosperity, program administrators had found ways to accommodate this while keeping the financing reasonably sound, and Social Security had become "as

American as apple pie" (Berkowitz, 1991: 65). This tight coupling of opinion and policy, however, would constitute a major problem, when Social Security began to confront financial difficulties.

Period of Initial Financial Crisis (1977–1983)

In the latter 1970s, the Social Security system entered financially troubled times—troubles that grew to crisis proportions by 1983, precipitating a dramatic episode of Congressional development of a "fix" for the system. The financial troubles emerged within five years of the 1972 amendments, which contained inaccurate projections of program earnings and a flawed system of indexing. Consequently, the financial health of the trust fund deteriorated so that, by 1976, the Social Security Board was projecting that the Trust Fund would be exhausted by 1984. In 1977, Congress passed legislation to remedy the situation by increasing the wage base subject to social security taxation and authorizing increases in the social security tax rate in the future, along with some other minor adjustments such as a correction of the indexing mistake (Brain, 1991: 72–74).

But these changes didn't adequately fix the system, partly because of unexpectedly high inflation and unemployment and partly because the 1977 rescue package scheduled the largest tax increases for later years (1981, 1985, and 1990) while the financial pressures were immediate. By 1980, the system's reserves were so low that only three months worth of benefit payments were available as a cushion (Light, 1995: 88).

In response, the newly elected Reagan administration proposed a set of reforms which would have boosted the trust fund by $30.6 billion from 1982–86; but most of this boost would have come through benefit reductions ($34.5 billion), combined with $2.6 billion in revenue increases and $6.5 billion in benefit increases (Brain, 1991: 81). The audacity of this assault on a politically popular program is largely explained by the desperation of the Reagan administration to find substantial and immediate overall budget savings—a desperation born of the fact that budget director Stockman had gotten Congress to pass a budget that included $40 billion in unspecified savings that now had to be found (Light, 1995: 111–115). The federal government was still operating under a unified budget, meaning that the Social Security system's assets and payment obligations were combined with non-Social Security revenues and expenditures in determining the "bottom line" of the federal budget. Cuts in the benefits that Social Security was obliged to make would not only shore up Social Security trust funds, but would make the overall budget appear to balance, even though trust fund monies would not be directly spendable on non-Social Security items. Not surprisingly, Congress greeted this proposed "fix" with hostility.

As documented in Paul Light's case study (1995), the immediate crisis in Social Security was ultimately resolved in 1983 with a package of reforms that included a deferral of cost-of-living increases from July back to January, increased payroll taxes, and an increase in tax rates for the self-employed. All nonprofit and new federal employees were brought into the system, a move that in the short-term would bring in more revenues through their payroll contributions. In addition, for upper income recipients, half of Social Security benefits were made subject to income taxation, generating $27 billion in immediate savings and even larger savings in the future (Light, 1995: 176–177). The automatic cost-of-living adjustment was also changed, such that when the reserves in the trust fund fell below 15%, the cost-of-living adjustment would be based on the lower of the two indicators of cost-of-living: wage increases or price increases (Light, 1995: 209). The legislative package also included an increase in the retirement age, to 67, and the recommendation that Social Security no longer be included in the unified budget, though this was deferred till 1993 (Light, 1995: 208).

In his analysis of this period, Brain (1991: 191) concludes that policy and opinion were still largely in synch—that "public support endorsed changes which would allow the system to continue the role which the public had come to expect of it." And it is true that some elements of the 1983 reform package were consistent with public opinion. The public had, in some late 1970s and early 1980s polls, been substantially in favor of increased payroll taxes as a way to keep the Social Security system going, although the softness in this support is reflected in slippage toward divided opinion on the matter at the height of the 1983 crisis (Brain, 1991: 175). Polls in the 1978–1983 period had shown substantial, majority support for bringing in workers not yet covered by the system (Brain, 1991: 181–182), as the reform package would do with nonprofit and federal employees. And polls in 1982 and 1983 showed over 60% of respondents approving of taxing the Social Security benefits of those with higher incomes (Brain, 1991: 181).

But, in some ways, the reform package was in direct opposition to public sentiment. For example, in polling questions from 1981 and 1982, anywhere from 58% to 72% of respondents had indicated opposition to reduced cost-of-living adjustments in retirement benefits as a way to help the Social Security system; and polling questions asked in 1982 and 1983 showed that at least 46% and, more typically, well over 50% of respondents were not willing to postpone cost-of-living increases in Social Security benefits to reduce the size of the federal deficit (Shapiro and Smith, 1985: 571). More generally, the public had long shown more willingness to increase taxes than to decrease benefits as a way of keeping Social Security afloat. And while the 1983 legislative package relied heavily on tax increases and other revenue enhancements, the rescue could not be accomplished entirely with such methods. So, despite popular opposition, benefit cuts were incorporated in the package.

There is considerable evidence in Light's case study of policymaker awareness of decisions being outside of easy public acceptability and of efforts to disguise what was being done so as to avoid the wrath of the public. Despite the poll results noted above, taxation of Social Security benefits was assumed to be a lightning rod for opposition, and decisionmakers spent much energy on methods for avoiding responsibility for the choice. Other unpopular aspects of the reform package were disguised behind confusing language: "tax increases were called 'tax acceleration'; COLA cuts were called 'permanent delays'" (Light, 1995: 177). All of this "artful work" is, in Light's analysis, an inevitable element of policymaking when cutbacks in a popular program are at issue: "It was a way to disguise the pain, a way to help the public accept cuts. If there was a lesson here for other dedistributive policies, it was to confuse, not educate" (Light, 1995: 177). Ironically, the same sorts of symbolic manipulation and public relations subterfuge that had initially been used to build the foundation of popular support for Social Security were being used to make unpopular cuts in the program, albeit cuts that were necessary to keep the program afloat.

In this episode, then, there is a mix of policy responsiveness and unresponsiveness to public opinion, along with ample evidence of efforts at opinion manipulation. On balance, the period is one of continuing policy responsiveness. Clearly, policymakers were constrained in their search for a Social Security rescue by the broad contours of public opinion—public opinion which demanded that Social Security remain the trusted source of retirement income that it had become, but which put decided limits on policymakers' ability to maintain the fiscal health of the system through benefit cuts. In the many ways that the rescue of 1983 was designed with sensitivity to these constraints, policy was still driven by opinion. But the financial realities of a maturing retirement system, with ever-growing obligations to beneficiaries and payroll tax rates that were becoming quite substantial, were conspiring to make it more and more difficult for policymakers to adhere totally to popular preferences. Some benefit cuts had to be introduced. This might have been accomplished with an overt public relations campaign to make the public understand the financial problems clearly and to be more receptive to the need for benefit cuts. That would have been a form of opinion manipulation, albeit one directed toward making opinion better grounded in the hard realities of the maturing program. Instead, benefit cuts were smuggled into the mix in a way designed to minimize public awareness that they had been enacted. This too is a form of opinion manipulation—one consistent with the myth-making upon which the program had been founded. Even the interest groups representing senior citizens appear to have recognized that the anti-cut sentiment of their membership was unreasonable given the lack of real alternatives to save the program. Consequently, groups such as SOS and the National Council of Senior Citizens joined in the subterfuge by fighting COLA cuts publicly even though "they had already signed off in private" (Light, 1995: 190).

Post-Reform Period (1984–present)

In some respects, the aftermath of the package of 1983 reforms has been one of success. As a result of the legislated increases in the payroll tax, the Old-Age and Survivors Insurance (OASI) trust fund began to grow dramatically (see Figure 7-1). Total end-of-year assets of the OASI trust fund were \$36.8 billion in 1985 (in 1982–84 constant dollars), \$126.4 billion in 1989, \$285.3 billion in 1994 and \$349.7 billion in 1996 (U.S. House of Representatives, 1996: 60–61). Social Security does indeed appear to be accumulating a substantial reserve in preparation for the retirement of large numbers of baby boomers in the second decade of the next century.

However, Social Security constitutes a continuing problem in several respects. For one thing, despite the near-term fix that the 1983 legislation created and the reserves that are accumulating, the longer-term prospects for the system are still quite problematic. In its 1996 report, the Social Security Board of Trustees reassuringly estimates that the Old-Age and Survivors Insurance (OASI) Trust Fund is on track to pay benefits for the next 35 years, through the first three decades of the 21st century (Board of Trustees, 1996). If this is accurate, and there is of course considerable debate about the economic assumptions that underlie the Trustees' estimates, the Social Security trust fund will not be exhausted when the first wave of baby-boomers reaches retirement age. However, even the Social Security Trustees are not sanguine about the longer-term. Their report acknowledges that the OASI fund is not in long-term actuarial balance.

But there is more to the problem than these long-term estimates. The reserve that is now building in the Social Security trust fund is itself problematic. While the growing surplus is intended to prepare for the large number of claimants that will appear when the baby-boomer generation retires, there is no guarantee that the funds will be available for that purpose. This is because the existence of the surpluses cannot be separated from the political dynamics of budgeting in a time of deficits (Leonard, 1990: 58). Although the concept of a "trust fund" suggests that Social Security funds are earmarked and untouchable for other purposes, the surpluses are held in the form of federal bonds. Functionally, this means that the resources are available in the non-Social Security part of the federal budgeting process ("Social Insecurity," 1993: 6). They can be and are used for other government spending. In short, the existence of the Social Security surpluses has arguably made it even more difficult for the federal government to rein in its deficit spending. In order for the trust funds to be available for baby-boomer retirement benefits, the U.S. government will have to pay back the borrowed funds, something that became ever more complicated as the deficit remained unresolved and as opposition to increased taxes mounted.

The issues outlined above, coupled with the even more substantial financial problems of Medicare, suggest that the nation's ability to make good on the promise of Social Security in its present form will require very substantial tax increases at the very least. Critics note that in the fine print of its reports the Social Security Administration acknowledges that, under pessimistic economic projections, combined employee-employer payroll tax rates of 40% would be required (Borden, 1995: 2). While this may be an unrealistic worst case scenario, the combined employee-employer tax rate for the retirement portion of Social Security alone is already 10.52% and scheduled to rise to 10.7% in 1997–1999. With the disability and Medicare components of the payroll tax added in, total employee-employer payroll taxes for Social Security are already over 15% (Board of Trustees, 1995). In future years, as relatively smaller cohorts of workers are asked to pay ever higher taxes to support very large cohorts of retirees, the implicit social contract that has since 1935 allowed current retirees to receive benefits financed by the payroll contributions of current workers may begin to unravel.

And there is already evidence that public opinion on Social Security is beginning to change. Referring back to Figure 7-2 we see that since the 1980s, polling questions about the appropriate level of spending on Social Security have generated smaller proportions of respondents who think spending is too little, and somewhat larger proportions who think spending is about right. The combination of these two favorable responses to Social Security spending still constitute an overwhelming majority of those polled; but since the early 1980s, only bare majorities at best favor *increased* spending on Social Security.

But this slippage in support for more Social Security spending is less dramatic than the decline in confidence in the future of the Social Security system (data not shown in Figure 7-2). When it was first asked in 1975, 63% of respondents indicated that they were either very or somewhat confident in the future of Social Security. By 1981, this was down to 32%. In the aftermath of the 1983 rescue of Social Security, public confidence rebounded somewhat, so that by 1990 and 1991, about half of the American public polled was once again either very or somewhat confident in the future of the Social Security system. But, not only did this rebound not reach the nearly two-thirds level of confidence that had existed before; it was also temporary. As the Social Security system was once again caught up in budgetary battles at the national level, confidence slipped and stood at 40% very or somewhat confident in 1994 (Baggette, Shapiro and Jacobs, 1995: 427). And in fact there is systematic evidence that media coverage focusing on worry about Social Security or proposals for change in it has had important effects on public confidence over time (Fan, Shapiro, Jacobs, and Watts, 1995).

Even more important than the overall decline in confidence in Social Security are the generational differences in opinion on Social Security. Commenting on the 1983 financial crisis, Berkowitz (1991: 66) notes that "the episode left behind a bitter taste, particularly among the young, who began to examine Social Security more closely and to discover that the program depended on good economic conditions and effective political restraint for its long-range survival." Light (1995: 233) notes that, when opinion poll respondents were asked in 1990 whether they thought the Social Security system will have the money available to provide the benefits they expect for retirement, only 18% of 18–29-year-olds and 22% of 30–44-year-olds responded affirmatively, compared with 53% of 45–64-year-olds and 70% of those over 65. Critics of Social Security have latched onto poll results such as these, noting that "more young Americans believe in UFOs than believe they will receive Social Security benefits" (Borden, 1995: 2).

By the 1980s, in fact, public opinion about Social Security was becoming enmeshed in the broader issue of "intergenerational equity"—a complex issue involving arguments about the fairness to youth of bearing the burden of programs for the elderly and about the extent to which older generations are enjoying public benefits at the expense of younger generations. Media attention to this issue became especially noticeable in 1988, and the theme has episodically appeared in newspapers and magazines ever since (Cook, Marshall, Marshall, and Kaufman, 1994: 91). The emergence of the issue in the media is no accident, of course. It has been fostered by issue entrepreneurs such as Senator Dave Durenberger (R-MN) who founded Americans for Generational Equity (AGE) as an organizational catalyst for challenging old age benefit programs, and by academics and foundations (Cook, Marshall, Marshall, and Kaufman, 1994: 92–95).

The post-reform period thus represents two important disjunctions from the previous era—one involving an implicit policy change and one involving an opinion change. With respect to opinion change, the high level of popular consensus surrounding Social Security that had obtained for so long was beginning to soften. In the wake of the financial crisis of 1983, the myths that had been so carefully constructed during the program's formative and expansionary period had worn thin around the edges from the stress of critical attention to undeniable problems, with important consequences for overall popular confidence in the system and for the opening of a wedge between the young and the old on the issue. So, even as program outlays move inexorably upward (see Figure 7-1), reflecting a long-standing link between expansionist policy and popular endorsement of that expansion, the linkage is beginning to come undone as public opinion begins to move.

But the linkage between opinion and policy is also becoming strained because of the interaction of Social Security with overall budget politics. The reassuring continuities in Figure 7-1 obscure the fact that Social Security had been transformed into something like a cash cow to help support continuing deficit spending. This may not have been the intention of the crafters of the 1983 rescue legislation (Buchanan, 1990: 55). But it is a result that has left the future of Social Security clouded in ways that sustain a mood of deepening public disquiet about the system. That mood can only have been exacerbated when, in December of 1996, yet another federal advisory panel established to explore the problems of the Social Security system issued a divided report that gave at least partial support to the idea of privatizing Social Security (Pear, 1996: 1). One faction of the advisory panel proposed broad-based investment of the Social Security trust fund in the stock market, another faction proposed the creation of a new 1.6% tax on wages covered by Social Security and the requirement that individuals invest those monies in one or more funds sanctioned by the government, and another faction proposed that individuals be required to invest 5% of their Social Security wages in stocks of their choice (Sloan, 1997: 24).

Even as the seemingly radical nature of these proposals reverberated across the American consciousness, the difficulty of reforming

Social Security yet again with more technical, incremental fixes was underscored. In 1996, official acknowledgment that the existing Consumer Price Index overstates inflation by about 1.1% had created an opportunity to reduce spending obligations and long-term deficits in Social Security (and other entitlement programs) by making cuts that are not officially cuts. A special commission led by economist Michael Boskin suggested that revisions in the index could save $1 trillion by the year 2008 ("Statistical Guessing Game," 1996: 25), much of it from notching back the growth in Social Security payments that would occur under cost-of-living adjustments based on the existing consumer price index. But even this seemingly minor, technical fix was far from politically painless; and as a result, proposals to adjust the inflation index were put on hold in 1997 (Uchitelle, 1997: 8).

Thus, despite eroding confidence in Social Security and noticeable declines in support for increased spending, public opinion is still fundamentally supportive of the program. In addition to the overwhelming majorities favoring as much or more spending on the program as now exists (see Figure 7-2), episodic poll questions underscore what politicians still take very much for granted—that Social Security remains the third rail of politics. A *New York Times/ CBS* poll conducted in August of 1995, for example, revealed that, by a ratio of 3 to 1, the public would prefer to continue imbalanced budgets rather than change the existing Social Security program (Apple, 1995: 8). Similarly, a *Time/CNN* poll in May of 1995 showed that 84% of respondents believed it to be more important to prevent cuts in Social Security than to make significant cuts to balance the budget. Thus, despite the changes in public opinion that are acknowledged above, the "broken thermostat" sequence is still an apt interpretation. For Social Security, the heat is still on for politicians to somehow keep coming up with system "fixes" that allow for continuity in what so many Americans have come to see as an entitlement. But those fixes are becoming increasingly more difficult to devise.

Non-Attitudes and the Broken Thermostat

This chapter suggests that the "broken thermostat" sequence, which we first observed in relation to policy development concerning incarceration (Chapter 2), may actually have several variants. In both cases, there is ample evidence that opinion mobilization by governing elites serves to sustain popular pressures and demands, even when efforts to be responsive to those pressures and demands are becoming increasingly strained and difficult in the light of budgetary realities and other constraints. In the case of Social Security, though, there is also evidence that opinion mobilization was instrumental in initiating those pressures and demands by creating a popular consensus about the importance and desirability of a national program for retirement security along the lines of a social insurance model.

But if, as this chapter has argued, public opinion about Social Security has been largely built upon myths and symbols, is it possible that this case should be interpreted within the non-attitudes framework? While there are some elements of what a non-attitudes model would suggest, including some important gaps in the public's knowledge about Social Security, the evidence on the whole does not support a non-attitudes interpretation. The public may be unreasonable in its expectations, less than fully knowledgeable about some of the aspects of the Social Security program, and confused about the best way to ensure the long-term viability of the program. But these limitations do not mean that non-attitudes are at work. In contrast with the characterizations on which the non-attitudes interpretation is based, opinion on Social Security reflects coherent aggregate-level change over time and, at the individual-level, coherent patterns of linkage to other attitudes. With respect to the former, it is important to note that the dramatic drop in both support for more Social Security spending and confidence in the future of Social Security are associated with the 1983 crisis in Social Security financing and that, while both rebounded after the resolution of that crisis, continuing unresolved issues about the viability of Social Security through the retirement years of the baby boom generation have prevented a return to the highest levels of confidence and support of the pre-1983 years.

High levels of overall support for Social Security mean that there is relatively little variation in individual-level responses on questions about Social Security. But research at the individual level suggests that what variation exists is patterned in ways that exemplify attitude consistency rather than random and meaningless responses. There are, for example, clear differences across age groups in attitudes about government spending on Social Security. Older groups, already receiving or about to receive benefits, are presumably much more comfortable about the status of the program and they are noticeably more likely than younger groups to believe that spending on Social Security is "about right"; meanwhile, the youngest group (age 18–29)—those for whom the benefits of the system are the most in doubt—are by far the most likely to favor increased spending on Social Security (Rhodebeck, 1993). Research also suggests coherent linkages between attitudes on Social Security spending, benefit, and taxation items on the one hand and ideological orientation, partisan affiliation, and self-interest variables on the other hand, though these results are much more evident for the elderly than for younger groups (Rhodebeck, 1993; Day, 1993). And while the mass public may be under-informed or misinformed about certain aspects of Social Security, there are impressive levels of popular knowledge about the program as well. Even in 1979, before the 1983 crisis raised the profile of Social Security, there was evidence of substantial public awareness of program specifics. Light (1995: 58), for example, cites poll data showing that very substantial majorities knew about features of the program such as joint contributions by employees and employers, the absence of a means test, benefit eligibility by the families of deceased workers, and the like.

In short, the public may hold a variety of misconceptions about Social Security and the high levels of popular support for the program may be built upon years of myth-making and opinion manipulation by political elites. But individuals' views on the subject appear to be strongly held, based on self-interests as reflected by their age and economic circumstances, and coherently linked to deep-seated political orientations. Responses to detailed, technical questions about what might be done to shore up the Social Security system might very well elicit non-attitudes. But the broader framework of public opinion on the subject does not fit well with the non-attitudes characterization.

Conclusion

Robert Ball (1988: 20) argues that the development of Social Security represents elaboration on an "original understanding" that represents a general public and elite consensus around fundamental program features: "insurance against wage loss, compulsory, contributory, independently financed, without a test of need, and with eligibility and benefits based on past earnings." But that consensus was not a given—it was constructed. Social Security was founded in policy choices that shaped and manipulated public opinion at least as much as responding to it. As a result, whatever consistency between opinion and Social Security policy that one observes is attributable to the efforts of policymaking elites to sell the idea of contributory insurance to the public and to foster myths, such as the myth of governmentally-maintained "individual retirement accounts" (Skocpol, 1994: 22). Skockpol further argues that this was not a totally one-sided process of manipulating the public into something inconsistent with general values, but rather a process of playing upon those general values. These and similar voices would suggest that the policy history of Social Security has been one of responsiveness. But, as this chapter has shown, efforts to sustain the general consensus about Social Security through continuing opinion manipulation have created a politically untouchable program that is very difficult to reform, even when fiscal crises loom. The result is a peculiar form of the broken thermostat sequence—one in which elites appear to be actively stoking popular support for the status quo, in part by smuggling non-responsive elements into reform efforts, in order to stave off erosion in the general consensus.

Critics of Social Security would argue that the myths and opinion manipulation behind the development of Social Security are far from innocuous, because they have empowered the growth of a program that is not in the best interests of the American public and not sustainable in its current form despite constant reassurances. Ball and other defenders, by contrast, argue that the system has served America well and basically works well, although continuing adjustments will inevitably be needed (Ball, 1988: 36). Whether the broken thermostat sequence makes it impossible over the long term to generate the necessary adjustments is the key question for the future of Social Security.

8

Public Opinion and Social Policy Change

Sequences and Contingencies

The policy histories outlined in this book suggest that while there is substantial continuity in social policy in the United States, there have also been numerous instances of change, even dramatic change, over the past thirty years. Whether those changes are substantial enough to qualify as non-incremental ones is an interpretive matter, especially since change does not always involve easily quantifiable policy outcomes such as budgetary commitments. But without getting bogged down in debates over incremental versus non-incremental change, it is worth noting that there have been important shifts in policy in a number of the topical areas covered. Federal and state policy concerning crime and punishment took a dramatic turn away from an indeterminate sentencing approach rooted in rehabilitation ideals to a determinate sentencing approach rooted in incapacitation and retribution ideals, with major consequences for the size of prison populations. With respect to the generosity of eligibility standards and benefits, welfare policy exhibited a decided retrenchment after a period of explosive growth in the 1960s, and elements of welfare policy involving moral regulation of recipients have receded and then re-emerged over the course of the past three decades. *Roe v. Wade* represented an important policy shift that established the legality of abortion; and while there has been substantial continuity in abortion policy since then, recent court decisions have empowered states in this policy area and a number of them have responded with a variety of requirements that make the legal status of access to abortion different in important ways from what it was in the immediate aftermath of *Roe v. Wade*. Pornography policy exhibited a sea change from a liberal phase in the 1960s and early 1970s to a much more conservative period of toughened regulation and enforcement crackdown.

This acknowledgment of major changes that have occurred in American social policy might seem inconsistent with notions of policy lock-in, path dependency, and the conservatism of subsystem politics that are staples of political science discourse. But, as Bryan Jones (1994) has convincingly argued, public policy development in the United States exhibits substantial periods of continuity that are periodically disrupted by major episodes of change. Much of the time, public policy is controlled by sub-systems of affected interests that are left alone to make mutually satisfactory adjustments in policy. This situation, which Jones designates "parallel processing," limits policy development to incremental change because affected interests generally share the same evaluative criteria for the policy problem and because the bureaucratic organizations, Congressional sub-committees and organized interests that are the predominant actors in the parallel processing mode act in an institutional context dominated by decision rules or solution sets that channel discussion into a limited number of acceptable outcomes. But under some circumstances, policy-making changes into a "serial processing" mode in which more central political figures (the president, Congress as a whole) weigh in on an issue and major breakthroughs in policy-making are possible. These "serial shifts" depend on the invocation of alternative issue definitions by political entrepreneurs who can successfully make use of communications media to mobilize broader publics and to construct coalitions around a new issue focus.

But what role does public opinion play in all this? Parallel processing of issues through policy sub-systems clearly does *not* lead to a close link between public opinion and policy. Instead, the outcomes "forged by affected interests can be dramatically different from the overall populist policy equilibrium, in which mass preferences balance policy outputs" (Jones, 1994: 158). However, the serial policy shift described by Jones provides the potential for broader publics to weigh in on issues, albeit in reaction to the mobilizing efforts of policy entrepreneurs. At a minimum, entrepreneurs wishing to change the focus of an issue debate must be aware of the contours of public opinion and offer new dimensions for issue evaluation that are consistent with those contours.

In a very general sense, public opinion is frequently portrayed as a crucial element in shaping policy change. Characterizations of the role of a broad "public mood" are critical to such analyses. John Kingdon (1995: 146–7), for example, describes how many activists in and around government at the national level characterize the connection between policy development and public opinion as a matter of governing elites sensing a broad climate of opinion or national mood that fosters certain issues on their agenda and constrains them from pursuing others. Other empirical work (Stimson, MacKuen and Erikson, 1995; Erikson, Wright, and McIver, 1993) has shown that the development of policy is consistent with public opinion in this sense of a broad "national mood" or "climate of opinion" reflected in aggregate shifts along a traditional liberal vs. conservative dimension. And if public policy does tend to move toward the conservative side of the ideological spectrum when public opinion does and likewise to shift back in a liberal direction when the public mood turns more liberal, then policy responsiveness of a sort is evidenced.

But, as Kingdon (1995: 148–9) goes on to explain, the nation's policy mood is operationally not really the same thing as mass public opinion. For governmental practitioners, the national mood that matters is the sentiment that officials glean from "attentive publics, activists, and political elites out in the country"—not soundings of the mass public as gleaned from public opinion polls. While this may or may not be an accurate characterization of policymakers' orientation toward mass public opinion, it is *not* the conceptualization of responsiveness on which this book is based. Discussions of policy responsiveness inevitably hinge upon the question "responsive to who," and for the purposes of this volume, the "who" is the mass public.

· This book differs from analyses of policymaking and the national climate of opinion or policy mood in another way as well. The policy mood is a relatively general concept, typically keyed to broad left-right shifts along the ideological spectrum. But trends in general policy mood are not necessarily the same as trends in public preferences on more particular policy issues. Best (1995), for example, shows that Stimson's treatment of policy mood obscures three distinctively different trends in public opinion. The trend in the mass public's preferences with respect to government spending issues is different from the trend in mass preferences with respect to racial issues, and mass preferences with respect to social issues reveal yet a different trend. As we have seen, trends in public opinion on specific issues of social policy are even more variegated. The mass public's support for more spending on retirement security eroded nearly thirty percentage points since 1972, while preferences for harsher treatment of criminals and more spending on crime escalated after 1972 to a high level that has been sustained ever since. The public's view of the legality of pornography has changed very little during this same period, while concerns about too much welfare spending peaked in the late 1970s, declined about twenty percentage points over the next fifteen years, and rebounded in the early 1990s to late 1970s levels. After a dramatic trend toward liberalization that peaked in 1972, views on the appropriateness of legal abortion have changed very little in the ensuing decades. In short, a traditional characterization of the public mood as trending in either a liberal or conservative direction simply misses too many important differences that would have a crucial bearing on the nature of the linkage between opinion and policy on specific topics.

So in order to claim that public opinion is important in accounting for policy change, this book asks for more than a link between policy decisions and what governing elites think that attentive publics want; and it asks for more than a generalized consistency between trends in public policy and trends in a broad public mood. It requires evidence that *mass* public preferences with respect to *particular* policy issues are driving forces in policy development on those particular issues.

But perhaps it is polyanna-ish to expect such policy responsiveness. In a complex society with a far-from-perfect system of representative government, there are indeed a variety of other possibilities. This book began with the premise that on theoretical grounds at least three other connections between public opinion and public policy might be observed. Instead of policy responsiveness, it is possible that policy change is largely insensitive to mass public opinion (non-responsiveness), that public opinion is orchestrated into alignment with what policy-makers have already chosen to do (manipulated opinion), or that responsiveness is not possible because no meaningful public opinion exists (non-attitudes).

The book also began with the assumption that, in many cases, no one of these possibilities may be adequate to depict the policy-opinion connection across the entire history of a policy issue. Instead, different sequences of these opinion-policy connections are to be expected. One possible sequence is a *thermostatic* one involving a dynamic view of responsiveness with opinion and policy each moving in reaction to changes in the other. Another possible sequence is a *policy learning* one, with a non-attitudes phase, followed by the manipulation of public opinion in the constructive sense of public education, followed by responsiveness of policy to mass opinion. Yet another sequence is a *Downsian* one, in which policy responsiveness is ultimately supplanted by non-responsiveness. Finally, we might hypothesize the existence of a *broken thermostat* sequence in which responsiveness to opinion, coupled with opinion manipulation that further stokes popular demands, leads to a never-ending spiral of policy commitments that are responsive but public opinion that does not acknowledge those policy commitments.

Two of these sequences are obviously more desirable than the others. In particular, both the thermostatic and the policy learning sequences are consistent with the principles of a representative democracy while the Downsian and the broken thermostat sequences are problematic or flawed. The thermostatic sequence is desirable because it incorporates a negative feedback mechanism that allows for both policy responsiveness and necessary adjustments if policy goes too far in any direction. But in a democratic polity, the public may not always provide appropriate guidance for policymaking. On issues that are technically complex, for issues of low salience to the general public, or even on gut-level issues that elicit superficial reactions, public opinion may consist largely of non-attitudes rather than meaningful opinion. The policy learning sequence is desirable because it incorporates an important leadership role for political elites in educating the public and hence transforming non-attitudes into meaningful preferences that can reasonably be expected to anchor policymaking.

The Downsian sequence begins auspiciously enough with a phase of problem discovery, popular enthusiasm for a governmental solution, and governmental action consistent with the contours of popular concern and preferences. And, as Jones (1994: 193) has noted, such bursts of attention to a problem can lead to shake-ups in entrenched and under-performing policy subsystems. But in a Downsian sequence, this phase of responsiveness is followed by a phase of non-responsiveness as revamped or newly-created institutions settle into normal sub-system patterns of attentiveness only to internal interests and action based on the organizational and professional imperatives of sub-system activists. The result is policy that drifts further and further from the zone of mass public acceptability. Finally, the broken thermostat sequence is problematic because the positive feedback system that it approximates creates havoc for social policy implementation. Having created a feeding frenzy of concern about a policy problem, political elites are forced to make greater and greater commitments in a particular policy direction. With the absence of a moderating trend in popular pressure, public officials are constrained to downplay the opportunity costs of further moves in that policy direction and to ignore evidence of the need for policy reform.

When viewed against this normative framework, the findings presented in this volume are encouraging in one respect—of the six topical areas of social policy traced, at least two—welfare and abortion—exhibit preferred sequences of either continuous responsiveness or something like a thermostatic response. The responsiveness that we observe may not be as complete as one would like, and indeed in the case of the work requirement aspect of welfare policy, it is to some extent responsiveness primarily at the symbolic level being used to disguise an inability to be fully responsive substantively. But at least there is evidence that policy either remains closely aligned with majority sentiments or returns after a period of non-responsiveness to a zone of popular acceptability.

But if the good news is that preferred sequences are evident for two of the policy topics, the bad news is that flawed policy sequences are evident for the other four topics. We can take at least some comfort in the fact that in only one of these four topical areas is there evidence of the Downsian sequence in which policy drifts away from the zone of popular acceptability and remains disconnected from mass opinion for a sustained period. Affirmative action is a distinctive case in this regard; and recent developments suggest that this Downsian sequence is coming to an end as policy becomes more responsive to the mass public's hostility toward the most race-conscious aspects of affirmative action. More typically, when there is inconsistency between policy and opinion it is not because policy has moved away from public opinion. Rather it is either because manipulation has created a demanding pattern of public opinion that does not moderate despite policy moves in that direction, or because there is no meaningful public opinion to respond to.

But there is relatively cold comfort in this acknowledgment that social policy is not usually impervious to the dominant preferences of the public. On normative grounds, the broken thermostat sequence leaves much to be desired; and the fact that no policy learning sequence is to be found is disappointing, especially since the pornography issue provides the potential for just such a leadership role for political elites.

On the Role of Policy Type as a Contingency

Whether a flawed sequence is observed or not *is* contingent upon the type of policy at issue, though this is not at first apparent. As this section shows, neither the character of the stakes nor the divisiveness of the issue are important contingencies. However, the salience of the issue to the mass public is highly significant.

Material versus Symbolic Stakes

In Table 8-1, for example, the various policy issues examined in this volume are arrayed according to whether the stakes at issue for the mass public are predominantly symbolic or predominantly material ones. Most of the topics deal primarily with symbolic stakes, especially *from the viewpoint of the mass public*. Although the pornography issue has substantial economic implications for pornography vendors, for example, and occasionally for property owners adjacent to adult entertainment zones as well, for the general public the issue of the legal status of pornography is one that evokes moral considerations, free speech rights, concerns about the status of women, and similar matters. Similarly, the abortion issue has material stakes for the medical establishment; and when limiting access to abortion raises the costs of the procedure or threatens women's access to the workplace by interfering with their control over pregnancy, material stakes are partly at issue. However, even though there are such economic implications for women, the issue has been treated primarily as a symbolic one, involving a clash between moral considerations and reproductive rights. Imprisonment is a symbolic issue because, despite the obvious dollar costs of crime to society and the tremendous budgetary costs of imprisoning large numbers of offenders, criminals are condensation symbols for a variety of fears and the topic of imprisonment evokes a cluster of concerns about justice, rights, the meaning of the social order, and the status of criminals. The moral regulatory dimension of welfare is clearly a symbolic issue involving concerns about the intimate choices and personal behaviors that separate the "worthy" from the "unworthy" poor.

By contrast, the generosity dimension of welfare is best categorized as an issue with material stakes (i.e., having to do with the financial implications of varying levels of eligibility and benefits). Similarly, Social Security is a classic example of a program with predominantly material stakes, though recent discussions of intergenerational equity may eventually transform this issue into

Table 8-1. Findings on Opinion-Policy Sequencing, by Type of Issue Stakes

	Dominant Policy Issue Stakes		
	Material		Symbolic
Exhibits Preferred Policy Sequence	Welfare[2]	Welfare[1]	Welfare[3] Abortion
Exhibits Flawed Policy Sequence	Social Security		Imprisonment Affirmative Action Pornography

Welfare[1] = the work requirement aspect of welfare policy
Welfare[2] = the generosity dimension of welfare policy
Welfare[3] = the moral regulation aspect of welfare policy

a symbolic one emphasizing conflicting rights and justice across generations.

Not all of the topics can be cleanly placed in either the symbolic or the material stakes category, however, even if the categorization relies upon a rough rule of thumb concerning which stakes are predominant. Affirmative action, for example, is in part a classic issue of symbolic stakes—i.e., the status and rights of minorities. Arguably, however, the general public also reacts to this issue in terms of material stakes, as reflected in perceptions that affirmative action involves a zero sum game of allocating scarce jobs, promotions, and the like. To reflect this difficulty of categorization, affirmative action is shown in Table 8-1 as spanning the boundary between material and symbolic issues. Similarly, the work incentives dimension of welfare involves both material stakes (i.e., how much government spending is devoted to work support programs, the costs to taxpayers of extended welfare dependency) and symbolic stakes (i.e., the moral worthiness of those on welfare who could work and the symbolic value of work).

Excluding those two ambiguous policy issues from consideration, it is clear from Table 8-1 that the kind of opinion-policymaking sequence that develops does not depend on the character of the mass public's stakes in the issue. Of the two issues with predominantly material stakes, one (i.e., welfare generosity) illustrates a preferred, responsiveness-dominated sequence while the other (i.e., Social Security) illustrates a flawed, broken thermostat sequence. Similarly, the four policy issues involving predominantly symbolic stakes are evenly divided between preferred and flawed policy sequences.

Obviously there are not enough cases for a sophisticated quantitative assessment of the impact of policy type on policy-opinion sequence. And it is possible that, were this volume to have examined disability rights, Medicare, protective services for foster children, and many other social policy issues, a somewhat different set of results might emerge. The important point here is that for this set of social policies—a set that includes not only a diverse array of policies and programs but also the majority of the nation's most visible, expensive, and important areas of social policy-making—policy type in the sense of the dominant stakes at issue does not appear to serve as an important contingency in whether there is a preferred or a flawed sequence of policy development vis a vis public opinion.

In many ways, this is surprising. One might have thought that flawed patterns would be more evident when policies with symbolic stakes are at issue because the deep-seated emotions attached to matters of rights and morality provide such easy raw material for political elites to inflame public sentiment. Hence, symbolic policies might have been expected to be more subject to opinion manipulation in the worst sense of demagoguery. And opinion manipulation in that form is an important building block for one of the flawed sequences—the broken thermostat.

The nation's approach to imprisonment epitomizes this scenario. For that symbolic policy, fear-mongering by generations of politicians has created an endless cycle of increased incarceration and a public that is unwilling to signal a preference for a stand-down. But the case of Social Security suggests that much the same scenario holds for that material-stakes policy. From its creation to the present, rhetorical devices have been used to disguise the true character of the program and to obfuscate the nature of the reforms promulgated to prop it up. And as a result, despite periodic crises that have eroded public confidence in the program among the young and caused some decline in overall support for heightened Social Security spending, there is sustained pressure to maintain the program.

Structure of Public Opinion: Consensus and Salience

As noted in chapter 1, however, the structure of public opinion concerning these issues may significantly shape the prospects for policy responsiveness, and hence the opinion-policy sequences that develop. With respect to the structure of public opinion, policy issues can be differentiated along two dimensions: (1) the degree of popular consensus about a preferred policy direction and (2) the salience of the issue to the general public. In contrast with the situation concerning material and symbolic stakes, however, policy issues cannot be sorted into high versus low salience, or consensual versus divisive categories on a once-and-for-all basis. As the preceding chapters show, the degree of popular consensus about a preferred policy direction has changed over time for at least one of the policy topics considered in this volume; and while evidence concerning the salience of each of the policy topics has yet to be presented, as we will shortly see it too exhibits change over time. Fortunately, the notable shifts in popular consensus and in salience are such that the analysis that follows can appropriately be confined to three distinct eras: the early 1970s, the period from about 1973 through the late 1980s, and the period from the early 1990s to the present.

As a rough rule of thumb, the policy topics considered in this volume are categorized as consensual if aggregate public opinion reflects 60% or more of respondents revealing the same policy preference during the period in question; policy topics that do not meet this standard are classified as non-consensual issues. The imprisonment issue, for example, is a highly consensual one in each of the three periods. For nearly thirty years, over two-thirds of the public have responded that the courts are not harsh enough in sentencing criminals. Affirmative action is also a highly consensual issue, provided that we ignore the systematic differences in the responses of black and white Americans. There is a general consensus against job discrimination, but at the same time overwhelming majorities of survey respondents have since the early 1970s consistently opposed the giving of preferences in employment to minorities. While the evidence is somewhat more sketchy, public opinion about the moral regulatory aspects of welfare also appears to have been very substantially weighted in all three eras in favor of a strong role for government in enforcing moral standards on welfare recipients; and public opinion has consistently shown a consensus level of preference that welfare recipients be required to make efforts to transition to work. Abortion for medical reasons is also a consensual issue in all three periods, generating very high levels of support for the legality of access to abortion. Pornography comes close to but does not quite meet our criterion for being a consensus issue. If those believing that pornography should be legal for everyone and those believing that pornography should at least be legal for adults are combined, just under 60% of the American public are typically in agreement. In most years, only a bare majority of the public agreed with the most popular of the options—that pornography be legal for adults but illegal for those under age 18.

By contrast, public opinion on two of our issues—abortion for non-medical reasons and the generosity dimension of welfare—has been non-consensual in each of the three periods. Indeed, the topic of abortion for social reasons (such as a woman not wanting any more children) is often characterized as a divisive issue par excellence. While the other aspects of welfare policy have been developed in the context of a broad-based consensus, there is much less consensus about the generosity of welfare; in all three eras, public opinion has been divided among a plurality who believe we are spending too much, about a third believing spending levels are about right, and about a fifth who prefer enhanced spending.

Only one of the policy topics considered in this volume has shifted over time with respect to the consensual versus non-consensual dimension. Social Security has been the subject of a transformation in public opinion from extraordinarily high levels of consensus that more should be spent on retirement security to a contemporary phase in which majorities, but not extraordinary majorities, favor increased spending.

As noted in chapter 1, these differences in the *distribution* of public opinion should be expected to shape the character of policymaking for various issues. In particular, consensual issues are presumed to be more likely to yield responsiveness to public opinion than are highly divisive issues (Strickland and Whicker, 1992); hence, consensual issues would be more likely to yield the preferred policymaking sequences that feature a responsiveness connection between opinion and policy.

Still other work suggests that issue *salience* is at least if not more important in shaping the prospects for responsiveness than is the directional distribution of public opinion. John Geer (1996), in particular, offers a powerful argument in which issue salience plays a key role in determining the prospects for either issue followership (i.e., responsiveness) or leadership (i.e., opinion manipulation). Based upon a standard set of assumptions concerning political leaders' need for popular approval (both for re-election purposes and in order to successfully enact policy), Geer deduces that rational politicians will always be responsive to public opinion on issues that are highly salient; only for issues that are low in salience are there prospects for the rational politician to attempt to shape and direct an otherwise poorly-formed public opinion rather than responding to it.

In order to assess the relative salience of the various policy topics covered in this volume,[1] the analysis that follows uses a measure of the magnitude of coverage of the issue in popular magazines—i.e., the number of columns' worth of magazine articles on each topic in the *Readers' Guide to Periodical Literature*.[2] As Figure 8-1 shows, for most of the six issues[3] treated in this volume, salience is usually not very high. One or two columns'-worth of magazine articles is a typical level of salience. However, two of the issues—abortion and imprisonment—are above this level throughout the three eras under consideration. Another issue—welfare—is at heightened levels of salience in the early 1970s and in the early 1990s, but drops into the more typical, lower-level of salience in the

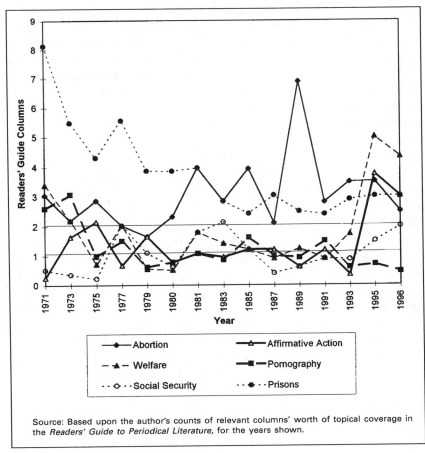

Source: Based upon the author's counts of relevant columns' worth of topical coverage in the *Readers' Guide to Periodical Literature,* for the years shown.

Figure 8-1. Salience of the Six Topics

intervening years. Affirmative action has been a typical, low-salience issue throughout most of the time series under consideration. Only in the most recent period has it vaulted into the high salience category. By contrast, pornography, which was briefly a relatively high salience issue in the early 1970s, drops to a very low level of salience for the remainder of the time series.

But do these differences in issue salience and the differences in level of issue consensus that were described above have a bearing on the likelihood of policy responsiveness and, therefore, the character of the opinion-policymaking sequence that develops? Table 8-2 suggests that *the structure of public opinion does make a difference; but it is the salience dimension rather than the consension dimension that is more important.* In Table 8-2, issues shown in bold-face italics are ones that, for the period in question, exhibited responsiveness that is part of a preferred policymaking sequence.[4] A visual inspection of the table suggests that responsiveness as part of a preferred policymaking sequence is more common among high salience than among low salience issues, but the pattern is not as striking when consensual issues are contrasted with non-consensual issues.

To add a quantitative summary to this visual inspection, we can total the results across the time periods, treating each issue-time period combination as a distinct case (e.g., early 1970s affirmative action, mid-1970s-late 1980s affirmative action, and early 1990s affirmative action yield three cases for analysis). Because it is such a borderline case with respect to the consensual versus non-consensual distinction, the pornography issue is initially excluded from this quantitative summary. When summarized this way, Table 8-2 reveals that there is policy responsiveness in 10 out of 17 (59%) cases involving consensual issues and 4 out of 7 (57%) of cases involving non-consensual issues. By contrast, policy responsiveness is exhibited in 11 out of 16 (69%) cases involving high salience issues, and only 3 out of 8 (37%) cases involving low salience issues. Note however, that if pornography is included in its most appropriate categorization—as a non-consensual issue—the results are that 10 out of 17 (59%) consensual issues and 4 out of 10 (40%) non-consensual issues exhibit policy responsiveness. In short, level of consensus cannot be ruled out as a potentially important contingency in shaping the prospects for policy responsiveness and hence

Table 8-2. Findings on Opinion-Policy Linkage, by Structure of Public Opinion and Era

Early 1970s

	High Salience Issues	Typical Salience Issues
Consensual Issues	Imprisonment *Abortion* [1] *Welfare* [1] Welfare[3]	Social Security Affirmative Action
	Pornography	
Non-Consensual Issues	Abortion[2] *Welfare* [2]	

Mid-1970s—Late 1980s

	High Salience Issues	Typical Salience Issues
Consensual Issues	Imprisonment *Abortion* [1]	Social Security Affirmative Action *Welfare* [1] *Welfare* [3] Pornography
Non-Consensual Issues	Abortion[2]	*Welfare* [2]

Early 1990s

	High Salience Issues	Typical Salience Issues
Consensual Issues	Imprisonment *Abortion* [1] *Affirmative Action* *Welfare* [1] *Welfare* [3] *Welfare* [2]	Pornography
Non-Consensual Issues	*Abortion* [2]	Social Security

Abortion[1] = therapeutic abortion
Abortion[2] = abortion for non-medical reasons
Welfare[1] = work requirements
Welfare[2] = generosity dimension
Welfare[3] = moral regulation aspect

for preferred policymaking sequences; but issue salience is more clearly and dramatically important.

It is not simply the borderline character of the pornography issue that limits the impact of issue consensus. In contrast with many discussions that focus only on whether or not policy is responsive to public opinion, the analysis here treats responsiveness within the context of the opinion-policy *sequences* that have been diagnosed in earlier chapters. From this perspective, a period of responsiveness that occurs within an otherwise flawed policymaking sequence is not the same as a period of responsiveness that occurs within a preferred policymaking sequence. In several of the cases in Table 8-2 where consensual public opinion does *not* yield preferred versions of policy responsiveness, it is because mobilization of mass public opinion has set off broken thermostatic sequences (see Social Security and imprisonment). This reminds us of the important fact that consensual public opinion can be manufactured, and manufactured on the basis of potent symbols that evoke deep-seated fears (i.e., of criminal victimization and lawlessness; of being old and helpless) and offer symbolic reassurances (i.e., of prison bars that can fully insulate society from the criminal element, or of a personal insurance account where the Social Security Administration keeps savings for one's old-age pension). From this perspective, consensual public opinion provides the raw material for *either* flawed or preferred sequences. And both outcomes are evident in American social policy.

Policymaking Venue as a Contingency

The preceding discussion shows that opinion-policy sequences in social policy are in part contingent upon the type of public policy at issue. Is it possible, however, that the venue in which public policy is made is also a significant contingency?

As noted in Chapter 1, the conventional view is that policy is less likely to be responsive to public opinion if it is developed in venues like courts and bureaucracies which are less visible to the mass public and more institutionally insulated from popular pressures. The research in this volume suggests that this is too simplistic. It is true that bureaucratic agencies have been instrumental at the critical phases that have sent policy off onto undesirable, un-responsive sequences. In particular, both bureaucratic and Court venues were critical to the establishment of the Downsian sequence by which affirmative action policy came untethered from the broader national consensus about equality of economic opportunity for racial minorities. The shift toward statistical evidence and preference-based remedies by the Office of Federal Contract Compliance and the Equal Employment Opportunity Commission moved policy away from the race-neutral, anti-discrimination approach that is most consistent with majority views and the Supreme Court's 1971 decision in *Griggs v. Duke Power* legitimated a disparate impact theory of discrimination that provided important support for that new approach to affirmative action; ensuing bureaucratic actions and court decisions sustained that preference-based approach for two-and-a-half decades. Although the court has not been a key player with respect to the development of policy for retirement security, bureaucratic insiders were instrumental in sustaining the broken thermostat pattern that has characterized Social Security. The flawed public understandings and unrealistic expectations of Social Security that have made that retirement security system so politically volatile and difficult to reform were substantially and strategically shaped from the start by bureau leaders with an expansionist vision for the program.

But characterizing the courts and bureaucratic venues as the key to the development of flawed sequences is mistaken on two grounds. First, other policy-making venues have been just as important in the establishment and maintenance of those flawed sequences; and second, the policy histories presented in this volume also yield ample evidence of the role that the court and bureaucratic venues can and do play in the unfolding of preferred sequences. With respect to the first of these points, it is important to note that Congress and the White House were at least as important as bureaucratic agencies in the opinion manipulation that created and sustained a broken thermostatic sequence of Social Security policy development. Furthermore, Congress and the White House, along with state legislatures and governors' offices, have been very important venues in the unfolding of the other broken thermostat sequence observed in this volume—i.e., that involving the arms race for more corrections. The adoption of determinate sentencing policy and the drive for more mandatory minimum sentences and "three-strikes" laws has not occurred in the low visibility context of administrative policy-making nor through the action of courts that are insulated from public opinion. Indeed, some of the strongest criticism of this policy direction has come from judges whose discretion is reduced by determinate sentencing. Finally, while the Supreme Court and bureaucratic agencies were key venues for setting affirmative action policy off in a non-responsive direction, there were occasions when congressional and presidential action might have steered policy back within the zone of popular acceptability, thus yielding something like a thermostatic sequence rather than a sustained Downsian sequence. Indeed, elevated attention to the issue during the Reagan administration suggested that the kind of serial shift described by Jones (1994) might be in the making. But as documented in Chapter 3, the value of affirmative action as a wedge issue, coupled with the difficulties of challenging the civil rights lobby without strong business support, meant that rhetorical attacks rather than substantive change were all that were forthcoming.

With regard to the second point, the courts and bureaucratic venues are also mis-characterized as inherently linked to flawed sequences because they have been important venues in policy-making sequences dominated by responsiveness. On abortion, the courts have played this unexpected role, perhaps veering toward the edge with *Roe v Wade* but sustaining policy for a long period on the side of this divisive issue that encompasses the moderate majority middle, and ultimately empowering states to tone it back even closer to public opinion. On welfare, bureaucratic agencies have had the even more challenging role of finding ways to mesh the realities of program operation with popular concerns about the size and cost of the welfare program and public expectations about work requirements and moral regulation. During much of the history of the AFDC program, this has meant that welfare policy has been in the hands of program administrators who have used their discretionary powers at some times to constrain welfare spending and at other times to mount at least symbolically responsive versions of work programs even if resources were unavailable for meaningful full-blown implementation of such programs.

If the findings in this volume lead us to reject any simplistic view of the Court and bureaucratic agencies as incubators of flawed policy-making sequences, they also suggest a much more positive view of the states than is sometimes held. This is evident when we ask what it is that abortion and welfare have in common that might help us to understand why only these two policy topics generate cases of preferred policy-making sequencing. The key commonality may well be that state governments were important policy-making venues for both.

That state government should emerge as a key to responsiveness-dominated sequences is not necessarily what one would expect. In fact, Page and Shapiro (1983: 176) suggest that, "In contemporary American politics...one might expect the president and Congress to be more responsive to public opinion than are state governments or the courts." Similarly, Erikson, Wright, and McIver (1993: 5) note that the "prevailing scholarly viewpoint" is that "because state politics is beyond the attention of most citizens most of the time, there is little reason to expect state policies to reflect public preferences." In their view, this is a key reason for the lack of scholarly attention to public opinion in state policy studies. But the analyses in this volume, using a longitudinal approach based on policy histories, corroborate what Erikson, Wright, and McIver (1993) and others have found in cross-sectional analyses relying upon aggregate indicators of policy liberalism or conservatism—i.e., that as an institutional venue, state government is an impressive translator of public opinion into policy.

This is not to say that preferred policy sequences are always evidenced whenever state government is involved. State governors and legislators have been heavily implicated in the move to determinate sentencing, mandatory minimum sentences, and the other policy elements that have led to a spiraling pattern of incarcerations and a flawed thermostatic sequence of policy development concerning corrections. But as Table 8-3 shows, in all but one of the cases in which state governments are important venues, policy-making exhibits preferred sequences, while preferred sequences are evident in *none* of the cases in which state governments are *not* important venues.

Furthermore, the difference between state government's role in the cases of abortion and welfare on the one hand and incarceration policy on the other hand suggests a possible refinement in our conclusion. Corrections is a central function for state government

Table 8-3. Key Policy Venues

	Courts	Congress, Presidency	Bureaucratic Agencies	States
Policies Exhibiting Preferred Policy Sequences:				
Welfare-Work Nexus		X	X	X
Welfare-Moral Regulation	X	X	X	X
Welfare-Generosity		X	X	X
Abortion	X	X		X
Policies Not Exhibiting Preferred Policy Sequences:				
Social Security		X	X	
Incarceration		X		X
Pornography	X	X	X	
Affirmative Action	X	X	X	

and a policy domain in which the states are far from subservient to the federal government. Though there are interdependencies, state governments have a degree of autonomous authority in this policy domain that is continuous and distinct from state interrelationships with the federal government over abortion and welfare policy. In the latter two policy domains, state governments do serve as policy venues, but in a state-federal partnership that, at key points in history, has been dominated by the Supreme Court, Congress, and the national executive branch. At other points, policy-making leadership has shifted to the states, as in the period of waiver demonstrations that brought a reassertion of moral regulatory elements to welfare policy and in the post-*Webster v. Reproductive Health Services* era of abortion policy. The results in this volume suggest that states are most likely to be instrumental in preferred policy sequences whenever they are *episodically* rather than *continuously* important venues—i.e., when policy-making leadership shifts to the states after a period of federal dominance. This may mean that state governments serve as a sort of repository for alternative policy values and an important institutional setting for the kind of serial shift that Jones (1994) describes—a shift that can prevent policy from drifting too far from the zone of popular acceptability.

On the Crucial Role of Manipulation
in Policymaking Sequences

The notably missing sequence in all of our findings, of course, is the policy learning sequence. In none of the cases examined did this appear. This is in part because the policy learning sequence, by definition, begins with a scenario of non-attitudes on an issue, non-attitudes which are then transformed through manipulation of public opinion by political elites. And since evidence of a non-attitudes scenario was evident in only one case—that of pornography—the potential for a policy learning sequence is limited in the cases examined here.

In the case of pornography, those non-attitudes have not been transformed. Despite concerted efforts at opinion manipulation by a variety of policy experts and political officials on both sides of the ideological spectrum, the public's views on pornography appear to be mired in non-attitudes. Zaller (1992: 8–9) has argued that the kind of opinion leadership that is at issue here is possible only when political elites proffer a consensus view of a desirable policy direction; when elites are divided on an issue along ideological lines, the result is a corresponding division in the mass public. The case of pornography suggests that the ideologically divided character of mobilization efforts has yielded something more than an ideologically polarized mass public on the issue. It has yielded a mass public that does not know much about the harms that pornography might or might not cause, public opinion that is impervious to high profile debates on the issue, and a mass public that holds superficial and inconsistent beliefs about the subject. The ideological undercurrents in the pornography debate may well have de-legitimized the scientific expertise that both sides have attempted to bring to bear on the issue, leaving an unimpressed public with little motivation to heed the cues from those attempting to lead public opinion either on the basis of values or objective evidence.

The policy learning sequence calls for opinion manipulation in its most constructive sense—i.e., the use of political rhetoric and arguments to educate and inform the public about important public issues. Cynical observers would argue instead that efforts to mobilize the public through opinion manipulation are geared more toward simplistic appeals that have very little to do with any meaningful role in educating the public. From this point of view, opinion manipulation in American politics constitutes demagoguery more than policy learning. And the power of such demagoguery is such that any political leader that abandons it in favor of a straightforward effort to educate the public about the complexities of policy issues is naïve and unlikely to be successful.

But recent experimental research suggests that this is not necessarily the case. Cobb and Kuklinski (1997) distinguish political arguments on the basis of whether they are "pro" (in favor of a policy change) or "con" (against a policy change) and on the basis of whether they are "hard" or "easy." Hard arguments are based on fact, "contain little to which an individual can viscerally react," and involve longer, more complex lines of logic that trace reasoning behind a policy option (Cobb and Kuklinski, 1997: 93). Hard arguments thus entail the kind of content that is implied by the policy learning sequence: ". . . hard arguments include more information than easy ones. The very act of thinking through the antecedents and conclusion of a hard argument can serve as a learning process that brings about true attitude change" (Cobb and Kuklinski, 1997: 96). Easy arguments, on the other hand, would seem to be the raw material for demagoguery. "Short, simple, and symbolic, they conjure up readily accessible images" and they rely on affective appeals rather than "explanations of why something will happen" (Cobb and Kuklinski, 1997: 93). Cobb and Kuklinski find that con arguments are consistently more effective in changing people's views than are pro arguments—an unsurprising finding given the theoretical work in social psychology on risk aversion and the negativity bias. More important for our purposes, they find that hard arguments are more persuasive than easy arguments, at least with respect to the North American Free Trade (NAFTA) issue. And, in contrast with the other issue examined in their research—health care—the NAFTA issue epitomizes the non-attitudes problem. People do not personally relate to matters of foreign trade as easily as they do to health care. The NAFTA proposal was relatively "unfamiliar and inaccessible to the mass public" and respondents had little confidence in the initial opinions that they offered about NAFTA (Cobb and Kuklinski, 1997: 97 and 100). This experimental research thus suggests that, at least where non-attitudes are involved, political leaders can actually be more effective and persuasive with the hard arguments that build policy learning than with the easy arguments that are all too often the stuff of demagoguery.

But if there is genuine potential for opinion manipulation in the constructive sense of a policy learning sequence, is there also potential for a constructive, educative form of opinion leadership when the target is something other than non-attitudes? That is, can we expect to find political leaders taking unpopular stands and using their leadership resources to re-direct public opinion? When considering this question, it may be useful to compare the results in this volume with Geer's (1996) analysis, which assesses the prospects for a concept that contrasts in interesting ways with the notion of policy learning—Wilsonian leadership. Wilsonian leadership does not necessarily entail a full sequence in which opinion is first transformed into something meaningful enough to shape public policy, followed by a stage of actual responsiveness. It entails only the opinion transformation stage. Furthermore, it is not necessarily a transformation of non-attitudes that is at work in Wilsonian leadership, but a successful shifting of public opinion on a low salience issue toward the politician's preferred policy direction. Wilsonian leadership involves opinion manipulation when opinions are poorly developed, but Geer does not go so far as to equate this unsettled opinion with non-attitudes. In short, Geer's conceptualization of Wilsonian leadership is less restrictive than the conceptualization of a policy learning sequence that is advanced in this volume. But it does involve a developmental form of opinion leadership that has at least the potential to anchor a policy learning sequence.

Geer theorizes that politicians are better informed about public opinion now that sophisticated polling is such an institutionalized part of elections and governance. This, he argues, enhances the prospects for Wilsonian leadership because political leaders are better able to identify those low-salience issues that are appropriate for their opinion manipulation efforts, and they are better able to avoid lost opportunities for Wilsonian leadership that stem from mistakenly diagnosing an issue as salient to the public (and hence responding to opinion) when in fact the issue is not a particularly pressing concern. Unfortunately, there is little evidence in the preceding chapters that political leaders have targeted low-salience issues, let alone successfully moved public opinion on those issues. The earliest period of Social Security may constitute the closest thing to such an instance, though ironically this occurred before modern polling methods made politicians more informed about public opinion. But there is little evidence in the policy histories presented in this volume of politicians attempting to undo the public's nascent hostility to affirmative action in the periods when the issue had relatively low salience (see Table 8-2). Instead, politicians chose either to politicize the issue in simplistic and divisive ways *that evoked existing sentiments against affirmative action* or to develop policy in venues that do not allow for effective opinion leadership. Hence, the direction of public opinion has not changed, and policy and opinion have remained at odds. This is hardly the stuff of Wilsonian leadership in its purest sense.

To the extent that political leaders do exhibit efforts at Wilsonian leadership, it is a variant of it that Geer calls "easy" Wilsonian leadership (1997: 114). In this variant, politicians target issues for which aggregate public opinion, while unsettled, nevertheless exhibits a potential for consensus in a direction that the politician favors. In short, politicians use the polls to determine issues on which there is already the core of mass popular attitude trending in a direction that is consistent with the politicians' own.

For high salience issues, the evidence in this volume is quite consistent with Geer's diagnosis that Wilsonian leadership is unlikely to even be attempted. When emotional issues such as crime and punishment are involved, we observe a short-circuiting of the kind of opinion leadership role that we might wish to see. Instead, simplistic appeals, symbolic rhetoric that hides the realities of policy costs and consequences, the "selective introduction of rights-based arguments" (Landy, 1993: 28), and reliance upon social constructions that send subtle messages about the target populations for policy (Ingram and Schneider, 1993) all serve to obfuscate rather than to educate. In short, the research in this volume suggests that if we are expecting public officials to play a leadership role in "framing questions so that the public debate can be made intelligible" and thus empowering citizens to "exercise their capacities for judgment and deliberation" (Landy, 1993: 25), we are likely to be disappointed.

Conclusion

So does the public get what it wants in the social policy realm? This volume suggests that they do, sometimes. This is not to say that the policy responsiveness that we observe is responsiveness to public opinion that is itself unaffected by other forces. The public's responses to questions in opinion polls "do not come from a separate autonomous public but are affected by many of the processes of politics and policy that they may, in turn, influence" (Verba, 1996: 6). And policy that is responsive to public opinion may at the same time be responsive to social movements, organized interests, and political elites, thus making it foolhardy to attribute policy change exclusively to the pressures of prevailing public opinion (Costain and Majstorovic, 1994). Nevertheless, there is more than a little evidence in this volume that the direction and timing of policy change is, at a minimum, constrained by mass preferences and that sequences of policy development that are far removed from popular preferences are unusual.

But does the public get what it *should* want? That is a more difficult question to answer, because it depends upon normative assessment of the content of public opinion. At a minimum, we might acknowledge that responsiveness is not always the appropriate role for government. Presumably, few would applaud the resistance to civil rights that marked a considerable period of Southern states' histories, even though that policy orientation was clearly consistent with majority preferences. From this same perspective, the key failure of affirmative action's Downsian sequence is not simply the disjunction between policy and opinion, but the absence of the kind of leadership that might have made this a less corrosive element in American domestic policy. Furthermore, implicit in the flawed thermostat sequence is the notion that sometimes the public's wants are immoderate and unrealistic and, unfortunately, made so by the opinion manipulation of governing elites.

Notes

Chapter 1

1. While the terminology of the thermostatic model is clearly that of Wlezien and Goggin, much of the spirit of the thermostatic model is reflected in Stimson's (1991) *Public Opinion in America: Moods, Cycles, and Swings*.

2. The problem with any historical perspective, whether of a path dependency sort or a policy learning sort, is that "For those who know the outcome, the unfolding of events seems much more logical and inevitable than for those who had no foreknowledge" Bovens and 't Hart (1996: 8). Bovens and 't Hart (1996: 9) make this observation to caution that the study of policy fiascoes should be based on acknowledgment that such fiascoes were not inevitable, and that "When interpreted in terms of a slightly different historical, institutional, and political perspective, many policy 'fiascoes' could easily have turned out quite differently." In the context of this analysis, their observation points to the need to consider several different possible sequences—some of which involve path dependence and lock-in to less than desirable states of opinion-policy connection (i.e., sustained non-responsiveness, sustained irrelevance of policy to opinion) and some of which involve policy learning or other sequences.

3. Historical sociologists have pointed to the importance of a number of temporal concepts that are relevant to this discussion of sequences (Aminzade, 1992). For example, duration, or the time it takes for a given event or sequence to elapse, may affect the outcome of a process. With respect to the Downsian sequence, this suggests that the longer a sequence of non-responsiveness endures, the more difficult it may be to break out of it and the more explosive will be the event that brings the Downsian sequence to a close.

Chapter 2

1. Such studies appear to have been either off the mark or based on states which were at least temporarily out of synch with national trends. Gottfredson and Taylor (1987) based their analysis on questions asking people to rank the correctional goals of incapacitation, punishment, deterrence, and rehabilitation. Their mismatch conclusions are based on findings showing, for example, that policymakers ranked incapacitation as the goal the public would put the highest while respondents in the general public sample on average ranked incapacitation the lowest.

2. This generalization must be modified somewhat, however, when the death penalty per se is at issue. Public opinion data on the death penalty are available for a longer period of time than the other two indicators, and they exhibit a pattern suggesting that punitiveness, at least with respect to the death penalty, was on the decline in the 1950s and early 1960s. Hence, when the states and the Supreme Court abolished the death penalty, they were responsive to this trend in public opinion.

3. During the Johnson administration, the liberal approach to crime and corrections was evident with respect to street crime issues. The Narcotic Addict Rehabilitation Act of 1966 established a treatment-oriented option of civil commitment for addicts as an alternative to imprisonment. In 1968, the Juvenile Delinquency Prevention and Control Act was enacted, providing grants to the states for the innovative programs to prevent juvenile delinquency and for rehabilitative programs. The President's Commission on Law Enforcement and Administration of Justice, reporting in 1967, "traced the causes of crime to poverty and advocated a treatment approach more than law enforcement" although it "included elements that could be supported by members of both political parties" (Marion, 1994: 53). In 1966, a bail reform act was passed, with liberalizing provisions for bail such as release on personal recognizance. In the corrections area, there was also a focus on rehabilitation rather than punitiveness, as embodied in legislation to promote rehabilitation by providing for "halfway houses" to transition prisoners back into society (Marion, 1994: 53).

4. Once in office, Nixon pursued policies that were a mixture of conservative, get-tough initiatives and surprisingly liberal initiatives. With respect to the former, Nixon called for "more attention on the punishment of people convicted of criminal behavior" (Marion, 1994: 69), including proposals for mandatory minimum sentences, heavier penalties and appointment of judges harder on criminals. In addition, funding for law enforcement via the Law Enforcement Assistance Administration (LEAA)

was dramatically increased and new agencies to fight drug trafficking were created. However, the primary emphasis in the drug area was actually treatment rather than a criminal justice approach (Sharp, 1994b). And while Nixon announced a 10-year plan to expand prison capacity so that punishment could be swift and certain, the only corrections-related legislation actually passed involved expanded use of furloughs (Marion, 1994: 85–6).

5. I am indebted to an anonymous reviewer for this perspective.

6. Again, I am indebted to an anonymous reviewer for this observation. Note however that Wlezien (1995) has found a pattern quite the opposite to that suggested here. Using a very rough indicator of the apparent threat from the Soviet Union, Wlezien (1995: 988; 992) demonstrates that the strong version of the thermostatic model *does* hold for defense spending. That is, preferred levels of defense spending respond to both actual changes in defense appropriations and changing relations between the U.S. and the Soviet Union. But the same cannot be said for a highly aggregated measure of social policy that he examines, at least if economic conditions are treated as relevant, objective conditions.

Chapter 3

1. There are, of course, major differences in the reactions of blacks and whites to the subject of affirmative action. Similarly there are differences across localities, as evidenced by Houston voters' rejection of a 1997 ballot proposition to end affirmative action while voters in California and other settings were apparently much more favorable to anti-affirmative action appeals. This chapter focuses on aggregate, national public opinion concerning affirmative action rather than geographically or racially specific manifestations of public opinion on the topic for several reasons. The most obvious is the lack of comparable, local data on public opinion concerning affirmative action. Second, despite some state and local initiatives, affirmative action policy is largely dictated by federal programs and court rulings. Hence, the relevant "public" for investigating the connection between public opinion and policy is the national aggregate.

2. While it is often argued that affirmative action is politically workable only during periods of an "expanding pie," recent work by Sniderman and Carmines (1997) offers convincing evidence to the contrary, albeit evidence that does not allow for a contrast between the contemporary period and the earliest years of affirmative action. Using the National Election Study's biennial survey data for the period 1986 (when the

affirmative action item was first asked) to 1994, Sniderman and Carmines (1997: 28–30) show that opposition to affirmative action is no higher in the "economically competitive 1990s" than "at the height of the prosperity of the 1980s."

3. There are substantial differences when poll results are broken down by race, with black support for preferential treatment in jobs (Gallup poll item) registering in the range of 21% to 32% in the various years in which it was administered while white support for preferential treatment ranged from 7% to 9%. On the CBS/*New York Times* poll question, more than two-thirds of black respondents typically support employment preferences for blacks while less than one-third of white respondents typically support such preferences. This racial polarization means that there is no unitary "public opinion" on affirmative action. However, this chapter focuses on overall, aggregate public opinion on the issue because, even though there are obvious group differences in reaction to the issue (as there would be other forms of polarization on other social policy issues), the focus of the book is on the linkage between the majority public's sentiments and policy developments.

4. Sniderman and Piazza's experiment also included a question relating to race and employment, but that question is worded to evoke the "fair treatment" theme that Sniderman and Piazza characterize as being part of a "social welfare" agenda on racial issues rather than the "race conscious" agenda that they identify and associate with affirmative action. Hence, the experimental results with respect to that item are actually less relevant than are those with respect to the item on special preferences in college admissions.

Chapter 4

1. The poll results on this item (as compiled by Smith, 1990: 427) are as follows:

	Strongly Agree	Partially Agree	Disagree
1974	42%	32	26
1975	45	19	36
1976	47	22	32
1977	56	20	23
1981	51	18	31
1982	50	22	28
1986	45	27	27

Chapter 6

1. The other programs that carry the connotation of being on the dole are General Assistance programs that most states have had for income support for individuals without dependent children, food stamps, and perhaps Medicaid.

2. In contrast with Teles' interpretation, which includes Piven and Cloward among a set of "consensus" theorists who see that "public values determine public policy" (p. 8), I would interpret Piven and Cloward's interpretation as relegating public opinion to an irrelevant position. Though the dominant values of capitalist society may well be such that mass opinion would be in accord with policy, what matters is that welfare policy regulates the labor market in ways that are functional for the capitalist system—i.e., it responds to the needs of the capitalist class, not to the masses. Other theorists, such as Mead, portray welfare policy change as responsive to both popular values and changing ideas of intellectual elites.

3. Teles (1996: 44) includes poll data from two earlier time points, 1961 and 1969, that illustrate even more dramatically the growth in concern about welfare spending that culminates in this figure. In 1961, less than 10% of those polled said that we were spending too much on welfare, a figure that had grown to roughly 30% by 1969.

Chapter 7

1. On the other hand, Brain's (1991: 140) review of the same poll data suggests that "public knowledge of the program is greater than it initially appears." The discrepancy between Brain and Schiltz appears to be largely a matter of interpreting whether a given level of public awareness means a glass half full or half empty. For example, one of the specific poll results at issue is a 1941 survey item which asked employed respondents who were subject to a social security deduction from wages to indicate its purpose. The results, as classified by Schiltz (1970: 86), have only a little over half (53%) of respondents giving an answer that is even partially accurate (i.e., "social security in old age", "old-age insurance", "retirement fund", "fund for old-age benefits.") In addition to the 17% who said "don't know" or "no opinion," another 30% gave responses that were deemed "clearly inaccurate" by Schiltz, such as the 10% who said the deduction was for unemployment insurance. But another 16% said that the deduction was for "old-age benefits, social security, and unemployment"—a response that Brain (1991: 140) argues

should be classified as partially accurate (i.e., only the unemployment portion of this compound response is inaccurate). With that classification, 69% of respondents would have given partially accurate responses—surely a quite high level of knowledge about a program that was only in its sixth year and which had so far paid out such negligible amounts in benefits that little personal experience of the program could exist. Likewise, Schiltz bases his conclusion about low levels of information on another 1941 survey item in which social security participants and nonparticipants were asked whether they would be entitled to social security benefits. Fifty-five percent of participants "correctly" said yes and 55% of nonparticipants "correctly" said no. Schiltz interprets this as an appallingly low level of information about a basic element of the social security program (Schiltz, 1970: 82), while Brain (1991: 143) is reassured that a majority of both participants and nonparticipants were accurate in their prediction. So the matter of the level of public knowledge is quite contentious.

Chapter 8

1. I am indebted to an anonymous reviewer for pointing out the potential relevance of Geer's work to this analysis.

2. The primary alternative for assessing the salience of issues over time is the Gallup poll's open-ended question about the "most important problem facing the country." While this poll question has the virtue of having been asked consistently over a long period of time, it's open-ended character makes it less than useful for assessing the relative importance of particular issues. In most years, most issues are not explicitly mentioned by enough respondents to be reported individually. Instead, the results of this poll question are reduced into a fairly small number of quite broad categories. Hence, the item does not have the precision necessary to assess the relative importance of issues such as those considered in this volume.

3. For this portion of the analysis, it will not be possible to distinguish among the various aspects of the welfare issue (i.e., generosity, work requirements, and moral regulation) or to distinguish between the two faces of the abortion issue. Instead, the salience of the welfare issue overall is rated, and the corresponding value is assigned equally to each aspect of that issue; similarly, the abortion issue is treated, for salience purposes, as a unitary issue.

4. Thus, even though Social Security policy was responsive to public opinion in the first period shown, this issue is not highlighted in the table because that episode of responsiveness was part of a flawed sequence—i.e., the broken thermostat.

References

Achen, Christopher H. 1975. "Mass Political Attitudes and the Survey Response." *American Political Science Review* 69: 1218–31.

Adamek, Raymond J. 1994. "Public Opinion and *Roe v. Wade*: Measurement Difficulties." *Public Opinion Quarterly* 58: 409–18.

Adams, Greg D. 1997. "Abortion: Evidence of Issue Evolution." *American Journal of Political Science* 41 (July): 718–737.

"After Years of Debate, Welfare Reform Clears." 1989. *CQ 1988 Almanac*. Washington, DC: Congressional Quarterly, Inc., pp. 349–364.

Alvarez, R. Michael and John Brehm. 1995. "American Ambivalence Toward Abortion Policy: Development of a Heteroskedastic Probit Model of Competing Values." *American Journal of Political Science* 39 (November): 1055–1082.

Amenta, Edwin, Bruce Carruthers, and Yvonne Zylan. 1992. "A Hero for the Aged? The Townsend Movement, the Political Mediation Model, and U.S. Old-Age Policy, 1934–1950." *American Journal of Sociology* 98 (No. 2, September): 308–39.

Aminzade, Ronald. 1992. "Historical Sociology and Time." *Sociological Methods & Research* 20 (May): 456–80.

Apple, R. W. Jr. 1995. "Poll Shows Disenchantment with Politicians and Politics." *New York Times*, Saturday, August 12, 1995, pp. A1 and A8(N).

Baggette, Jennifer, Robert Y. Shapiro, and Lawrence R. Jacobs. 1995. "Social Security—an Update." *Public Opinion Quarterly* 59: 420–442.

Ball, Robert M. 1988. "The Original Understanding on Social Security: Implications for Later Developments." In Theodore R. Marmor and Jerry L. Mashaw, eds., *Social Security: Beyond the Rhetoric of Crisis*. Princeton: Princeton University Press, pp. 17–40.

Baron, Larry and Murray A. Straus. 1989. *Four Theories of Rape in American Society: A State-Level Analysis*. New Haven, CT: Yale University Press.

Baumgartner, Frank R. and Bryan D. Jones. 1993. *Agendas and Instability in American Politics*. Chicago: University of Chicago Press.

Bellah, Robert N., Richard Madsen, William M. Sullivan, Ann Swidler, and Steven M. Tipton. 1985. *Habits of the Heart*. Berkeley: University of California Press.

Belz, Herman. 1991. *Equality Transformed: A Quarter-Century of Affirmative Action*. New Brunswick: Transaction.

Benekos, Peter J. 1992. "Public Policy and Sentencing Reform: The Politics of Corrections." *Federal Probation* 56 (March): 4–10.

Berger, Ronald J., Patricia Searles, and Charles E. Cottle. 1991. *Feminism and Pornography*. Westport, CT: Praeger.

Berkowitz, Dan. 1992. "Who Sets the Media Agenda? The Ability of Policymakers to Determine News Decisions." In J. David Kennamer, ed., *Public Opinion, the Press, and Public Policy*. Westport, CT: Greenwood, pp. 81–102.

Berkowitz, Edward D. 1991. *America's Welfare State: From Roosevelt to Reagan*. Baltimore: Johns Hopkins University Press.

Bernstein, Merton and Joan Brodshaug Bernstein. 1988. *Social Security: The System That Works*. New York: Basic Books.

Best, Sam. 1995. "Exposing the National Mood: A Note on Stimson's Policy Mood." Paper presented at the annual meeting of the Midwest Political Science Association, Chicago, Illinois, April 1995.

"Bills Seek to Ensure Abortion Clinic Access." 1994. *1993 CQ Almanac*. Washington, DC: Congressional Quarterly, pp. 354–356.

Blumstein, Alfred. 1983. "Prisons: Population, Capacity and Alternatives." In James Q. Wilson, ed., *Crime and Public Policy*. San Francisco: ICS Press: 229–250.

Board of Trustees, Social Security. 1995. Status of the Social Security and Medicare Programs: A Summary of the 1995 Annual Reports. WWW.SSA.GOV/POLICY/TRUSTEES.

Board of Trustees, Social Security. 1996. Status of the Social Security and Medicare Programs: A Summary of the 1996 Annual Reports. WWW.SSA.GOV/OACT/TRSUM/trsummary.html.

Borden, Karl. 1995. *Dismantling the Pyramid: The Why and How of Privatizing Social Security*. Available from http://www.cato.org/main/ss_pyrmd.html.

Bovens, Mark and Paul 't Hart. 1996. *Understanding Policy Fiascoes*. New Brunswick: Transaction Publishers.

Brain, Charles M. 1991. *Social Security at the Crossroads: Public Opinion and Public Policy*. New York: Garland Publishing.

Brodkin, Evelyn Z. 1995. "The War Against Welfare." *Dissent* (Spring): 211–220.

Buchanan, James M. 1990. "The Budgetary Politics of Social Security." In Carolyn L. Weaver, ed., *Social Security's Looming Surpluses: Prospects and Implications*. Washington, DC: AEI Press, pp. 45–56.

Burstein, Paul. 1985. *Discrimination, Jobs, and Politics: The Struggle for Equal Employment Opportunity in the United States Since the New Deal*. Chicago: University of Chicago Press.

Butterfield, Fox. 1996. " 'Three Strikes' Rare Invoked in Courtrooms." *New York Times*, September 10, 1996, pp. A1 and A15(N).

Butterfield, Fox. 1995. "Political Gains by Prison Guards." *New York Times*, November 7, 1995, pp. a and 13(N).

Byrnes, Timothy. 1995. "Conclusion: The Future of Abortion Politics in American States." In Mary C. Segers and Timothy A. Byrnes, eds., *Abortion Politics in American States*. Armonk, NY: M.E. Sharpe, pp. 246–264.

Canon, Bradley C. 1992. "The Supreme Court as a Cheerleader in Politico-Moral Disputes." *Journal of Politics* 54 (August): 637–653.

Carmines, Edward G. and James A. Stimson. 1989. *Issue Evolution: Race and the Transformation of American Politics*. Princeton: Princeton University Press.

Carmines, Edward G. and James H. Kuklinski. 1990. "Incentives, Opportunities, and the Logic of Public Opinion in American Political Representation." In John A. Ferejohn and James H. Kuklinski, eds., *Information and Democratic Processes*. Urbana: University of Illinois Press, pp. 240–268.

Casey, Robert P. and Montgomery, David B. 1992. "New Act Clarifies Disparate-Impact Law." *The National Law Journal* 14, No. 27: 19.

"Child Pornography Bill." 1984. *CQ Almanac*, 98th Cong., 2nd sess, 1984. Washington, DC: CQ Inc, p. 225.

Church, George J. and Richard Lacayo. 1995. "Social Security." *Time*, March 20, 1995: 24–32.

Clark, Charles S. 1991. "The Obscenity Debate." *CQ Researcher*, December 20, 1991, pp. 971–989.

Clark, Charles S. 1995. "Regulating the Internet." *CQ Researcher*, June 30, 1995, pp. 563–581.

Cobb, Michael D. and James H. Kuklinski. 1997. "Changing Minds: Political Arguments and Political Persuasion." *American Journal of Political Science* 41 (January): 88–121.

Cockburn, Alexander. 1994. "Social Cleansing." *New Statesman & Society*. August 5, pp. 16–18.

Cohen, Bernard C. 1973. *The Public's Impact on Foreign Policy*. Boston: Little Brown.

Cohen, Jeffrey E. 1995. "Presidential Rhetoric and the Public Agenda." *American Journal of Political Science* 39 (February): 87–107.

———. 1997. *Presidential Responsiveness and Public Policymaking*. Ann Arbor: University of Michigan Press.

Cohen, Jeffrey E. and Charles Barrilleaux. 1993. "Public Opinion, Interest Groups, and Public Policy Making: Abortion Policy in the American States." In Malcolm L. Goggin, ed., *Understanding the New Politics of Abortion*. Newbury Park, CA: Sage, pp. 203–221.

Combs, James E. and Dan Nimmo. 1993. *The New Propaganda*. White Plains, NY: Longman Publishing.

"Compromise Civil Rights Bill Passed." 1992. *CQ Almanac 1991*. Washington, DC: Congressional Quarterly Inc.

Converse, Philip. 1964. "The Nature of Belief Systems in Mass Publics." In David Apter, ed., *Ideology and Discontent*. New York: Free Press, pp. 206–261.

Converse, Philip E. 1970. "Attitudes and Nonattitudes: Continuation of a Dialog." In Edward R. Tufte, ed., *The Quantitative Analysis of Social Problems*. Reading, MA: Addison-Wesley, pp. 168–189.

Cook, Elizabeth Adell, Ted G. Jelen, and Clyde Wilcox. 1992. *Between Two Absolutes: Public Opinion and the Politics of Abortion*. Boulder: Westview Press.

Cook, Fay Lomax, Victor W. Marshall, Joanne Gard Marshall, and Julie E. Kaufman. 1994. "The Salience of Intergenerational Equity in Canada and the United States." In Theodore R. Marmor, Timothy M. Smeeding and Vernon L. Greene, eds., *Economic Security and Intergenerational Justice: A Look at North America*. Washington, DC: Urban Institute Press, pp. 91–129.

Cook, Fay Lomax and Edith J. Barrett. 1992. *Support for the American Welfare State*. New York: Columbia University Press.

Corbett, Thomas J. 1995. "Welfare Reform in Wisconsin: The Rhetoric and the Reality." In Donald F. Norris and Lyke Thompson, eds., *The Politics of Welfare Reform*. Thousand Oaks, CA: Sage, pp. 19–55.

Costain, Anne N. and Steven Majstorovic. 1994. "Congress, Social Movements and Public Opinion: Multiple Origins of Women's Rights Legislation." *Political Research Quarterly* (March): 111–132.

Craig, Barbara Hinkson and David M. O'Brien. 1993. *Abortion and American Politics*. Chatham, NJ: Chatham House.

Cronin, Thomas E., Tania Z. Cronin and Michael E. Milakovich. 1981. *U.S. v. Crime in the Streets*. Bloomington: Indiana University Press.

David, Paul. 1985. "Clio and the Economics of QWERTY." *American Economic Review* 75: 332–337.

Day, Christine L. 1993. "Public Opinion Toward Costs and Benefits of Social Security and Medicare." *Research on Aging* 15 (September): 279–98.

Delli Carpini, Michael X. and Scott Keeter. 1996. *What Americans Know About Politics and Why It Matters*. New Haven: Yale University Press.

Derthick, Martha. 1979. *Policymaking for Social Security*. Washington, DC: Brookings.

"Dial-A-Porn Restrictions." 1989. *CQ Almanac*. Washington, DC: CQ Incorporated, p. 382.

Dickenson, Rachel and Paula Mergenhagen. 1996. "The Prison Population Bomb." *American Demographics* 18 (February): 36–43.

Donziger, Steven R. 1996. *The Real War on Crime: The Report of the National Criminal Justice Commission*. New York: HarperCollins.

Dority, Barbara. 1992. "The Justice Department's Morality Brigade." *The Humanist* 52 (July–August): 39–43.

Downs, Anthony. 1972. "Up and Down with Ecology: The Issue Attention Cycle. *Public Interest* 28: 38–50.

Downs, Donald Alexander. 1989. *The New Politics of Pornography*. Chicago: University of Chicago Press.

Dumas, Kitty. 1992. "Future Unclear for Pornography Bill." *Congressional Quarterly Weekly Report* 50, No. 26 (June 27): 1887.

Dworkin, Andrea and Catharine MacKinnon. 1988. *Pornography & Civil Rights: A New Day for Women's Equality*. Minneapolis: Organizing Against Pornography.

Easton, Susan M. 1994. *The Problem of Pornography*. New York: Routledge.

Eckle, Corina. 1994. "Legislators and the Public Demand Stiff Penalties for Criminals, But the Costs May Mean the Taxpayer Strikes Out." *State Legislatures* (September): 14–19.

Ellis, Richard J. 1994. *Presidential Lightning Rods*. Lawrence, KS: University Press of Kansas.

Erikson, Robert S., Gerald C. Wright and John P. McIver. 1993. *Statehouse Democracy: Public Opinion and Policy in the American States*. Cambridge: Cambridge University Press.

Erikson, Robert S. and Kent L. Tedin. 1995. *American Public Opinion: Its Origins, Content, and Impact*. 5th Edition. Boston: Allyn and Bacon.

Fan, David, Robert Y. Shapiro, Lawrence R. Jacobs, and Mark D. Watts. 1995. "The Media's Persuasive Influence on Public Opinion: The Case of Social Security." Paper prepared for presentation at the 1995 Annual Meetings of the American Political Science Association, August 31–September 3, Chicago, Illinois.

Finkel, Norman J., Stephen T. Maloney, Monique Z. Valbuena, and Jennifer Groscup. 1996. "Recidivism, Proportionalism, and Individualized Punishment." *American Behavioral Scientist* 39, No. 4: 474–87.

Franklin, Charles H. and Liane C. Kosaki. 1989. "Republican Schoolmaster: The U.S. Supreme Court, Public Opinion, and Abortion." *American Political Science Review* 83 (September): 751–771.

Freeman, Gary P. 1988. "Voters, Bureaucrats, and the State: On the Autonomy of Social Security Policymaking." In Gerald D. Nash, Noel H. Pugach, and Richard F. Tomasson, eds., *Social Security: The First Half-Century*. Albuquerque: University of New Mexico Press, pp. 145–180.

Gallup, George H. 1972. *The Gallup Poll: Public Opinion 1935–1971*. New York: Random House.

Gebotys, R.J., Roberts, J.V. and DasGupta, B. 1988. "News Media Use and Public Perceptions of Crime Seriousness." *Canadian Journal of Criminology* 30(1): 3–16.

Geer, John G. 1996. *From Tea Leaves to Opinion Polls: A Theory of Democratic Leadership*. New York: Columbia University Press.

Gilens, Martin. 1996. "'Race Coding' and White Opposition to Welfare." *American Journal of Political Science* 90 (September): 593–604.

Ginsberg, Benjamin. 1986. *The Captive Public: How Mass Opinion Promotes State Power*. New York: Basic Books.

Goertzel, Ted George and John Hart. 1995. "New Jersey's $64 Question: Legislative Entrepreneurship and the Family Cap." In Donald F. Norris and Lyke Thompson, eds., *The Politics of Welfare Reform*. Thousand Oaks, CA: Sage, pp. 109–145.

Goggin, Malcolm and Christopher Wlezien. 1993. "Abortion Opinion and Policy in the American States." In M. Goggin, ed., *Understanding the New Politics of Abortion*. Newbury Park: Sage, 1993, pp. 190–202.

Gottfredson, Stephen D. and Ralph B. Taylor. 1987. "Attitudes of Correctional Policymakers and the Public." In S. Gottfredson and S. McConville, eds. *America's Correctional Crisis: Prison Populations and Public Policy*. New York: Greenwood Press, pp. 57–75.

Graham, Hugh Davis. 1990. *The Civil Rights Era: Origins and Development of National Policy 1960–1972*. New York: Oxford University Press.

Greenhouse, Linda. 1982. "Justices Uphold Barring Children in Pornography." *New York Times*, Saturday, July 3, 1982, p. 1 and p. 36.

———. 1995. "By 5-4, Justices Cast Doubts on U.S. Programs That Give Preferences Based on Race." *New York Times*, Tuesday, June 13, 1995, p. 1 and p. 9(N).

———. 1996a. "Court Says It Will Not Hear Appeal on Affirmative Action." *New York Times*, Tuesday, July 2, 1996, p. 1 and p. 9(N).

———. 1996b. "Curb on Smut Is Allowed." *New York Times*, Tuesday, January 9, 1996, p. A5(N).

Griset, Pamala L. 1991. *Determinate Sentencing: The Promise and the Reality of Retributive Justice*. Albany: State University of New York Press.

Griset, Pamala L. 1996. "Determinate Sentencing and Administrative Discretion Over Time Served in Prison: A Case Study of Florida." *Crime & Delinquency* 42 (January): 127–143.

Grossback, Lawrence J. 1996. "On the Relationship between Public Opinion and Supreme Court Decisionmaking." Paper presented at the 1996 Annual Meeting of the Midwest Political Science Association, Chicago, Illinois.

Gunther, Albert C. 1995. "Overrating the X-Rating: The Third-Person Perception and Support for Censorship of Pornography." *Journal of Communication* 45 (Winter): 27–38.

Handler, Joel. 1995. *The Poverty of Welfare Reform.* New Haven: Yale University Press.

Handler, Joel F. and Yeheskel Hasenfeld. 1991. *The Moral Construction of Poverty.* Newbury Park, CA: Sage.

Handler, Joel and Hollingsworth, Ellen. 1971. *The "Deserving Poor."* New York: Academic Press.

Hawkins, Gordon and Franklin E. Zimring. 1988. *Pornography in a Free Society.* Cambridge: Cambridge University Press.

Heath, Linda and Kevin Gilbert. 1996. "Mass Media and Fear of Crime." *American Behavioral Scientist* 39 (February): 379–386.

Hense, Richard and Christian Wright. 1992. "The Development of the Attitudes toward Censorship Questionnaire." *Journal of Applied Social Psychology* 22, 1: 1666–1675.

Hill, Kim Quaile and Angela Hinton-Andersson. 1995. "Pathways of Representation: A Causal Analysis of Public Opinion-Public Policy Linkages." *American Journal of Political Science* 39 (November): 924–935.

Holmes, Steven A. 1996. "White House to Suspend a Program for Minorities." *New York Times* Friday, March 8, 1996, p. A1 and A10(N).

Howell, Susan E. and Robert T. Sims. 1993. "Abortion Attitudes and the Louisiana Governor's Election." In Malcolm Goggin, ed., *Understanding the New Politics of Abortion.* Newbury Park: Sage: 154–161.

Idelson, Holly. 1994. " 'Buffer Zone' Ruling Bodes Well for Abortion Access Law." *Congressional Quarterly Weekly Report* 52 (July 2): 1810.

Ingram, Helen and Anne Schneider. 1993. "Constructing Citizenship: The Subtle Messages of Policy Design." In Helen Ingram and Steven Rathgeb Smith, eds., *Public Policy for Democracy.* Washington, DC: Brookings, pp. 68–98.

Innes, Christopher A. 1993. "Recent Public Opinion in the United States Toward Punishment and Corrections." *The Prison Journal* 73 (June): 221–236.

"Interior Provisions." 1991. *CQ Almanac*. Washington, DC: CQ Inc., pp. 559–568.

Irwin, John and James Austin. 1994. *It's About Time: America's Imprisonment Binge*. Belmont, CA: Wadsworth Publishing.

Iyengar, Shanto. 1996. "Framing Responsibility for Political Issues." *Annals of the American Academy of Political and Social Science* 546 (July): 59–70.

Iyengar, Shanto and Donald R. Kinder. 1987. *News That Matters: Television and American Opinion*. Chicago: Univ. of Chicago Press.

Jackson, Jesse Sr. 1996. "Race-Baiting and the 1996 Presidential Campaign." In George E. Curry, editor, *The Affirmative Action Debate*. Reading, Mass: Addison-Wesley, pp. 288–298.

Jacobs, Lawrence R. 1993. *The Health of Nations: Public Opinion and the Making of American and British Health Policy*. Ithaca: Cornell University Press.

Jacobs, Lawrence R. and Robert Y. Shapiro. 1994. "Issues, Candidate Image, and Priming: The Use of Private Polls in Kennedy's 1960 Presidential Campaign." *American Political Science Review* 88 (September): 527–540.

———. 1995. "The Rise of Presidential Polling: The Nixon White House in Historical Perspective." *Public Opinion Quarterly* 59: 163–195.

Jamieson, Kathleen Hall. 1992. *Dirty Politics*. New York: Oxford University Press.

Jencks, Christopher. 1992. *Rethinking Social Policy: Race, Poverty, and the Underclass*. Cambridge: Harvard University Press.

Johnston, David, and Tim Weiner. 1996. "Seizing the Crime Issue, Clinton Blurs Party Lines." *New York Times*, August 1, 1996, pp. 1 and 12(N).

Jones, Bryan D. 1994. *Reconceiving Decision-Making in Democratic Politics: Attention, Choice, and Public Policy*. Chicago: University of Chicago Press.

Kass, David. 1995. Testimony before the hearing on AFDC Waiver Demonstration Programs: Necessary Flexibility or AD Hoc Decisionmaking? U.S. House of Representatives, Committee on Government Operations, Human Resources and Intergovernmental Relations Subcommittee, 103 Congress, 2nd Session, September 29, 1994. Washington, DC: U.S. Government Printing Office.

Kennamer, J. David. 1992. "Public Opinion, the Press, and Public Policy: An Introduction." In J. D. Kennamer, ed., *Public Opinion, The Press, and Public Policy*. Westport: Praeger, pp. 1–18.

Kernell, Samuel. 1986. *Going Public: New Strategies of Presidential Leadership*. Washington, DC: Congressional Quarterly, Inc.

Kilborn, Peter T. and Sam Howe Verhovek. 1996. "Clinton's Welfare Shift Reflects New Democrat." *New York Times*, Friday, August 2, 1996, pp. A1 and A8(N).

Kilborn, Peter T. 1996. "Welfare Mothers Losing Bonus They Got to Help Track Fathers." *New York Times*, November 12, 1996, p. A1 and A9(N).

Kingdon, John W. 1995. *Agendas, Alternatives, and Public Policies*. 2nd Edition. New York: HarperCollins.

Kellough, J. Edward. 1989. *Federal Equal Employment Opportunity Policy and Numerical Goals and Timetables*. New York: Praeger.

Kluegel, James R. and Eliot R. Smith. 1986. *Beliefs About Inequality*. New York: Aldine de Gruyter.

Kobylka, Joseph F. 1991. *The Politics of Obscenity: Group Litigation in a Time of Legal Change*. New York: Greenwood Press.

Kuklinski, James H. and Norman L. Hurley. 1994. "On Hearing and Interpreting Political Messages: A Cautionary Tale of Citizen Cue-Taking." *Journal of Politics* 56 (No. 3): 729–751.

Kuklinski, James H. and Norman L. Hurley. 1996. "It's a Matter of Interpretation." In Diana C. Mutz, Paul M. Sniderman, and Richard A. Brody, eds., *Political Persuasion and Attitude Change*. Ann Arbor: University of Michigan Press, pp. 125–144.

Landy, Marc. 1993. "Public Policy and Citizenship." In Helen Ingram and Steven Rathgeb Smith, eds., *Public Policy for Democracy*. Washington, DC: Brookings, 19–44.

"Language on Obscene Art Hangs Up Interior Bill." 1989. *CQ Almanac*, Washington, DC: CQ Incorporated, pp. 731–5.

LaNoue, George R. 1992. "Split Visions: Minority Business Set-Asides." *The Annals of the American Academy of Political and Social Science* 523 (September): 104 (13): 104–116.

Lemert, James B. 1992. "Effective Public Opinion." In J. David Kennamer, *Public Opinion, The Press and Public Policy*. Westport, CT: Praeger, pp. 41–62.

Leonard, Herman B. 1990. "In God We Trust—The Political Economy of the Social Security Reserves." In Carolyn L. Weaver, ed., *Social Security's Looming Surpluses: Prospects and Implications*: Washington, DC: AEI Press., pp. 57–73.

Lewis, Peter H. 1996. "Judges Turn Back Law to Regulate Internet Decency." *New York Times,* Thursday, June 13, 1996, p. 1 and p. 18 (N).

Linz, Daniel and Neil Malamuth. 1993. *Pornography*. Newbury Park: Sage.

Light, Paul. 1995. *Still Artful Work: The Politics of Social Security Reform*. 2nd Edition. New York: McGraw-Hill.

Lilly, J. Robert and Mathieu Deflem. 1996. "Profit and Penalty: An Analysis of the Corrections-Commercial Complex." *Crime & Delinquency* 42 (January): 3–20.

Lowery, David, Virginia Gray and Gregory Hager. 1989. "Public Opinion and Policy Change in the American States." *American Politics Quarterly* 17 (Jan.) 3–31.

Lowi, Theodore. 1964. "American Business, Public Policy, Case Studies, and Political Theory." *World Politics* 16: 677–715.

———. 1972. "Four Systems of Policy, Politics and Choice." *Public Administration Review* 11: 298–310.

MacKuen, Michael Bruce and Steven Lane Coombs. 1981. *More Than News.* Beverly Hills: Sage.

Maltese, John Anthony. 1994. *Spin Control: The White House Office of Communications and the Management of Presidential News.* 2nd Edition. Chapel Hill: University of North Carolina Press.

Marion, Nancy E. 1994. *A History of Federal Crime Control Initiatives, 1960–1993.* Westport, CT: Praeger.

Marmor, Theodore, Jerry L. Mashaw and Philip L. Harvey. 1990. *America's Misunderstood Welfare State.* New York: Basic Books.

Marvell, Thomas B. and Carlisle E. Moody. 1996. "Determinate Sentencing and Abolishing Parole: The Long-Term Impacts on Prisons and Crime." *Criminology* 34, No. 1: 107–129.

Mayer, William G. 1992. *The Changing American Mind.* Ann Arbor: University of Michigan Press.

McClosky, Herbert and Alida Brill. 1983. *Dimensions of Political Tolerance.* New York: Russell Sage.

McGarrell, Edmund F. 1991. "Differential Effects of Juvenile Justice Reform on Incarceration Rates of the States." *Crime & Delinquency* 37 (April): 262–277.

McGarrell, Edmund F. and Marla Sandys. 1996. "The Misperception of Public Opinion Toward Capital Punishment." *American Behavioral Scientist* 39, No. 4: 500–513.

McGraw, Kathleen M., Samuel Best and Richard Timpone. 1995. "'What They Say or What They Do?' The Impact of Elite Explanation and Policy Outcomes on Public Opinion." *American Journal of Political Science* 39 (February): 53–74.

McGraw, Kathleen M. and Clark Hubbard. 1996. "Some of the People Some of the Time: Individual Differences in Acceptance of Political Accounts." In Diana C. Mutz, Paul M. Sniderman, and Richard A. Brody, eds., *Political Persuasion and Attitude Change.* Ann Arbor: University of Michigan Press, pp. 145–170.

Mead, Lawrence M. 1992. *The New Politics of Poverty: The Nonworking Poor in America.* New York: Basic Books.

Mishler, William and Reginald S. Sheehan. 1993. "The Supreme Court As a Counter-majoritarian Institution? The Impact of Public Opinion on Supreme Court Decisions." *American Political Science Review* 87: 87–101.

Mitchell, Alison. 1997. "Clinton Seems to Keep Running Though the Race Is Run and Won." *New York Times*, February 12, 1997, p. A1 and A12(N).

Mooney, Christopher Z. and Mei-Hsien Lee. 1995. "Legislating Morality in the American States: The Case of Pre-*Roe* Abortion Regulation Reform." *American Journal of Political Science* 39 (August): 599–627.

Nemko, Amy N. 1996. "Saving FACE: Clinic Access under a New Commerce Clause." *Yale Law Journal* 106, no. 2 (November): 525–530.

Nie, Norman, Sidney Verba and John R. Petrocik. 1976. *The Changing American Voter*. Cambridge: Harvard University Press.

Niemi, Richard G., John Mueller and Tom W. Smith. 1989. *Trends in Public Opinion: A Compendium of Survey Data*. New York: Greenwood Press.

Neuman, W. Russell. 1986. *The Paradox of Mass Politics: Knowledge and Opinion in the American Electorate*. Cambridge: Harvard University Press.

Page, Benjamin I. 1994. "Democratic Responsiveness? Untangling the Links between Public Opinion and Policy." *PS: Political Science & Politics* XXVII (March): 25–29.

Page, Benjamin I. and Robert Y. Shapiro. 1983. "Effects of Public Opinion on Public Policy." *American Political Science Review* 77 (March): 175–90.

Page, Benjamin and Robert Shapiro. 1992. *The Rational Public*. Chicago: University of Chicago Press

Pear, Robert. 1996a. "House Approves Shift on Welfare." *New York Times*, July 19, 1996, pp. A1 and A10(N).

Pear, Robert. 1996b. "Panel in Discord on the Financing of Social Security." *New York Times*, Sunday, December 1, 1996, pp. A1 and A26(N).

Piven, Frances Fox and Richard A. Cloward. 1993. *Regulating the Poor: The Functions of Public Welfare*. 2nd Edition. New York: Vintage Books.

Polsby, Nelson W. 1984. *Political Innovation in America: The Politics of Policy Initiation*. New Haven: Yale University Press.

"Prisons Go Private." 1995. *State Legislatures* 21 (No. 10, December): 27.

Randolph, Jennifer G. 1995. "RICO—The Rejection of an Economic Motive Requirement." *Journal of Criminal Law and Criminology* 85 (Spring): 1189–1222.

Rhodebeck, Laurie A. 1993. "The Politics of Greed? Political Preferences among the Elderly." *Journal of Politics* 55 (May): 342–64.

Riley, P.J. and McN. Rose. 1980. "Public Opinion vs. Elite Opinion on Correctional Reform." *Journal of Criminal Justice* 8: 345–56.

Roberts, Julian. 1996. "Public Opinion, Criminal Record, and the Sentencing Process." *American Behavioral Scientist* 39, No. 4 (February): 488–499.

Rosch, Joel. 1985. "Crime as an Issue in American Politics." In Erika S. Fairchild and Vincent J. Webb, eds., *The Politics of Crime and Criminal Justice*. Beverly Hills: Sage, pp. 19–36.

Rosenberg, Gerald N. 1991. *The Hollow Hope*. Chicago: University of Chicago Press.

Rosenbloom, David H. 1977. *Federal Equal Employment Opportunity: Politics and Public Personnel Administration*. New York: Praeger.

Ross, Julia C. 1992. "New Civil Rights Act: Law Reverses Several Recent High Court Decisions." *ABA Journal* 78 (January): 85 (1).

Rothman, David J. 1995. "More of the Same: American Criminal Justice Policies in the 1990s." In Thomas G. Blomberg and Stanley Cohen, eds., *Punishment and Social Control*. New York: Aldine de Gruyter, pp. 29–44.

Rubin, Eva R. 1994. "Epilogue: 1993 and After." In Eva R. Rubin, ed., *The Abortion Controversy: A Documentary History*. Westport, CT: Greenwood Press, pp. 285–289.

Russell, Diana E. 1993. "The Experts Cop Out." In Diana E. Russell, ed., *Making Violence Sexy: Feminist Views on Pornography*. New York: Teachers College Press, pp. 151–166.

Sabatier, Paul A. and Hank C. Jenkins-Smith. 1993. *Policy Change and Learning: An Advocacy Coalition Approach*. Boulder: Westview Press.

Sackett, Victoria A. 1985. "Between Pro-Life and Pro-Choice." *Public Opinion* 8: 53–55.

Sanders, Arthur. 1988. "Rationality, Self-Interest, and Public Attitudes on Public Spending." *Social Science Quarterly* 69 (June): 311–324.

Schiltz, Michael. 1970. *Public Attitudes toward Social Security, 1935–1965*. Washington, DC: U.S. Department of Health, Education and Welfare, Social Security Administration, Research Report No. 33.

Schneider, Anne and Helen Ingram. 1993. "Social Construction of Target Populations: Implications for Politics and Policy." *American Political Science Review* 87: 334–47.

Scott, Joseph E. and Loretta A. Schwalm. 1988. "Pornography and Rape: An Examination of Adult Theatre Rates by State." In J. Scott and T. Hirschi, eds., *Controversial Issues in Crime and Justice*. Newbury Park, CA: Sage, pp. 40–53.

Sears, David O. and Jack Citrin. 1982. *Tax Revolt: Something for Nothing in California*. Cambridge: Harvard University Press.

Selke, William L. 1993. *Prisons in Crisis*. Bloomington: Indiana University Press

Shapiro, Robert Y. and Tom W. Smith. 1985. "The Polls: Social Security." *Public Opinion Quarterly* 49 (Winter): 561–572.

Shapiro, Joseph P. 1994. *No Pity: People with Disabilities Forging a New Civil Rights Movement*. New York: Random House.

Sharp, Elaine B. 1994a. "The Dynamics of Issue Expansion: Cases from Disability Rights and Fetal Research Controversy." *Journal of Politics* 56 (November): 919–939.

Sharp, Elaine B. 1994b. *The Dilemma of Drug Policy in the United States*. New York: HarperCollins.

Skocpol, Theda. 1994. "From Social Security to Health Security? Opinion and Rhetoric. In U.S. Social Policy Making." *PS: Political Science & Politics* 27 (March):21–25.

Skocpol, Theda and John Ikenberry. 1983. "The Political Formation of the American Welfare State in Historical and Comparative Perspective." *Comparative Social Research* 6: 87–148.

Skrentny, John David. 1996. *The Ironies of Affirmative Action*. Chicago: University of Chicago Press.

Sloan, Allan. 1997. "Retirement Roulette." *Newsweek* 129 (January 20): 25–28.

Smith, Eric R.A.N. 1989. *The Unchanging American Voter*. Berkeley: University of California Press.

Smith, Tom W. 1990. "The Polls—A Report: The Sexual Revolution?" *Public Opinion Quarterly* 54 (Fall): 415–435.

Sniderman, Paul M., Philip E. Tetlock, and Anthony Tyler. 1993. "The Dynamics of Public Opinion in Political Behavior." Paper presented at the Political Psychology Conference, University of Illinois, Champaign-Urbana.

Sniderman, Paul M. and Thomas Piazza. 1993. *The Scar of Race*. Cambridge: Harvard University Press.

Sniderman, Paul M. and Edward G. Carmines. 1997. *Reaching Beyond Race*. Cambridge: Harvard University Press.

"Social Insecurity." 1993. *American Demographics*, February 1993, p. 6.

Social Security Administration. 1996. *Curent Operating Statistics on the World Wide Web*. "Old Age and Survivors Insurance Trust Fund: Status, 1940–1994, unpaginated.

Spitzer, Robert J. 1995. *The Politics of Gun Control*. Chatham, NJ: Chatham House.

"Statistical Guessing Game." 1996. *The Economist* 341 (December 7): 25–27.

Steeh, Charlotte and Maria Krysan. 1996. "The Polls—Trends: Affirmative Action and the Public, 1970–1995." *Public Opinion Quarterly* 60 (Spring): 128–158.

Stimson, James A. 1991. *Public Opinion in America: Moods, Cycles and Swings*. Boulder, CO: Westview.

Stimson, James A., Michael B. MacKuen and Robert Erikson. 1995. "Dynamic Representation." *American Political Science Review* 89 (September): 543–565.

Strickland, Ruth Ann and Marcia Lynn Whicker. 1992. "Political and Socioeconomic Indicators of State Restrictiveness Toward Abortion." *Policy Studies Journal* 20 (Winter): 598–620.

Sullivan, John L., James E. Piereson, and George E. Marcus. 1982. *Political Tolerance and American Democracy*. Chicago: University of Chicago Press.

Tatalovich, Raymond and Byron Daynes. 1988. "Introduction: What Is Social Regulatory Policy?" In *Social Regulatory Policy: Moral Controversies in American Politics*. Westview: Boulder.

Tatalovich, Raymond and Byron W. Daynes. 1981. *The Politics of Abortion*. New York: Praeger.

Tatalovich, Raymond and Byron W. Daynes. 1988. *Social Regulatory Policy: Moral Controversies in American Politics*. Boulder: Westview.

Tatalovich, Raymond and David Schier. 1993. "The Persistence of Ideological Cleavage in Voting on Abortion Legislation in the House of Representatives, 1973–1988." In Malcolm Goggin, ed., *Understanding the New Politics of Abortion*. Newbury Park: Sage, pp. 109–122.

Teles, Steven M. 1996. *Whose Welfare? AFDC and Elite Politics*. Lawrence, KS: University Press of Kansas.

"The Civil Rights Act of 1991: The Business Necessity Standard." 1993. *Harvard Law Review* 106 (no. 4): 896–913.

Thompson, Lyke and Donald F. Norris. 1995. "Introduction: The Politics of Welfare Reform." In D. Norris and L. Thompson, eds., *The Politics of Welfare Reform*. Thousand Oaks, CA: Sage, pp. 1–18.

Thompson, Margaret E., Steven H. Chaffee, and Hayg H. Oshagan. 1990. "Regulating Pornography: A Public Dilemma." *Journal of Communication* 40(3), Summer: 73–83.

Tonry, Michael. 1991. "The Politics and Processes of Sentencing Commissions." *Crime & Delinquency* 37, no. 3: 307–329.

Tonry, Michael. 1993. "The Failure of the U.S. Sentencing Commission's Guidelines." *Crime & Delinquency* 39, No. 2: 131–149.

Twight, Charlotte. 1993. "Channeling Ideological Change: The Political Economy of Dependence on Government." *Kyklos* 46: 497–527.

Uchitelle, Louis. 1997. "The Negotiators Forgo a Cut in Inflation Index." *New York Times* 146 (May 3): 8(N).

U.S. Bureau of the Census. 1996. *Statistical Abstract of the United States: 1996* (116th Edition). Washington, DC: U.S. Government Printing Office.

U.S. Department of Justice. 1986. *Attorney General's Commission on Pornography Final Report*. Washington, DC: U.S. Government Printing Office.

U.S. House of Representatives. Committee on Ways and Means (104th Congress, 2nd Session). 1996. *1996 Green Book*. Washington, DC: U.S. Government Printing Office.

Uslaner, Eric M. and Ronald E. Weber. 1980. "Public Support for Pro-Choice Abortion Policies in the Nation and the States: Changes and Stability after the *Roe* and *Doe* Decisions." In Carl E. Schneider and Maris A. Vinovskis, eds. *The Law and Politics of Abortion*. Lexington, MA: Lexington.

Verba, Sidney. 1996. "The Citizen as Respondent: Sample Surveys and American Democracy (Presidential Address, American Political Science Association, 1995). *American Political Science Review* 90 (March): 1–7.

Wald, Kenneth D., James W. Button and Barbara A. Rienzo. 1995. "The Politics of Gay Rights in American Communities: Explaining Antidiscrimination Ordinances and Policies." Paper prepared for delivery at the 1995 Annual Meeting of the American Political Science Association, Chicago, Illinois.

Wallace, Henry Scott. 1993. "Mandatory Minimums and the Betrayal of Sentencing Reform: A Legislative Dr. Jekyll and Mr. Hyde." *Federal Probation* 57 (September): 9–19.

Waste, Robert J. 1995. "From Workfare for the Poor to Warfare on the Poor in California." In Donald F. Norris and Lyke Thompson, eds., *The Politics of Welfare Reform*. Thousand Oaks, CA: Sage, pp. 55–78.

Weaver, Carolyn. 1982. *The Crisis in Social Security: Economic and Political Origins*. Durham, NC: Duke University Press.

Weaver, Carolyn. 1990. "Introduction." In C. Weaver, ed., *Social Security's Looming Surpluses: Prospects and Implications*. Washington, DC: AEI Press, pp. 1–13.

Weaver, R. Kent. 1986. "The Politics of Blame Avoidance." *Journal of Public Policy* October–December: 371–98.

Weidlich, Thom. 1995. "Pro-Choice Forces Score Wins in State Courts; Activists Rely on State Constitutions to Secure Medicaid Abortion Money." *The National Law Journal* 17 (August 7), p. A11.

Weir, Margaret. 1992. *Politics and Jobs: The Boundaries of Employment Policy in the United States*. Princeton: Princeton University Press.

"Welfare by Waiver." 1995. *Public Welfare* (Winter, 1995): 4–5.

Welsh, Wayne N. 1993. "Ideologies and Incarceration: Legislator Attitudes toward Jail Overcrowding." *The Prison Journal* 73 (March): 46–71.

Wetstein, Matthew E. and Robert B. Albritton. 1995. "Effects of Public Opinion on Abortion Policies and Use in the American States." *Publius* 25 (Fall): 91–105.

Wetstein, Matthew E. 1996. *Abortion Rates in the United States: The Influence of Opinion and Policy*. Albany: State University of New York Press.

White House. 1995a. Report on the Review of Federal Affirmative Action Programs. Available from http://www.whitehouse.gov/White_House/EOP/OP/html/aa/aa/aa01.html.

White House. Office of the Press Secretary. 1995b. *Remarks by the President on Affirmative Action. The Rotunda National Archives.* Availablle from gopher://info.tamu.edu: 70/00/.data/politics/1995/affirmative.0719.

Williams, Linda Faye. 1996. "Tracing the Politics of Affirmative Action." In George E. Curry, ed., *The Affirmative Action Debate*. Reading, MA: Addison-Wesley, ap. 241–257.

Wilsford, David. 1994. "Path Dependency, or Why History Makes It Difficult But Not Impossible to Reform Health Care Systems in a Big Way." *Journal of Public Policy* 14 (July–December): 251–283.

Wilson, James Q. 1975. "Violence, Pornography and Social Science." In Ray C. Rist, ed., *The Pornography Controversy*. New Brunswick: Transaction Books: 225–243.

———. 1989. *Bureaucracy*. New York: Basic Books.

Wilson, Le Von E. 1992. "Temporary Measures or Permanent Solution: Affirmative Action and the Future of Race-Based Preferences in Hiring." *Urban League Review* (Summer): 35–44.

Wiseman, Michael. 1995. Testimony before the hearing on AFDC Waiver Demonstration Programs: Necessary Flexibility or AD Hoc Decisionmaking? U.S. House of Representatives, Comm. on Government Operations, Human Resources and Intergovernmental Relations Subcommittee, 103rd Congress, 2nd Session, September 29, 1994. Washington, DC: U.S. Government Printing Office.

Wlezien, Christopher. 1995. "The Public As Thermostat: Dynamics of Preferences for Spending." *American Journal of Political Science* 39 (November): 981–1000.

———. 1996. "Dynamics of Representation: The Case of U.S. Spending on Defence." *British Journal of Political Science* 26 (January): 81–103.

Wood, B. Dan and Richard W. Waterman. 1991. "The Dynamics of Political Control of the Bureaucracy." *American Political Science Review* 85 (September): 801–828.

Yale, Marilyn A. 1993. "Abortion, Elections and the Media." In Malcolm Goggin, ed., *Understanding the New Politics of Abortion*. Newbury Park: Sage, pp. 134–153.

Zaller, John and Stanley Feldman. 1992. "A Simple Theory of the Survey Response: Answering Questions versus Revealing Preferences." *American Journal of Political Science* 36 (August): 579–616.

Zaller, John R. 1996. "The Myth of Massive Media Impact Revived: New Support for a Discredited Idea." In Diana C. Mutz, Paul Sniderman, and Richard A. Brody, eds., *Political Persuasion and Attitude Change*. Ann Arbor: University of Michigan Press, pp. 125–144.

Zaller, John R. 1992. *The Nature and Origins of Mass Opinion*. New York: Cambridge University Press.

Zimring, Franklin E. and Gordon Hawkins. 1995. *Incapacitation: Penal Confinement and the Restraint of Crime*. New York: Oxford University Press.

Zimring, Franklin E. and Gordon Hawkins. 1991. *The Scale of Imprisonment*. Chicago: University of Chicago Press.

Index